FOCUS ON

ORSON WELLES

❖❖

edited by

RONALD GOTTESMAN

A SPECTRUM BOOK

Prentice-Hall, Inc.
Englewood Cliffs, N.J.

Library of Congress Cataloging in Publication Data

Main entry under title:
Focus on Orson Welles.

   (A Spectrum Book)
   Bibliography:p.
   1. Welles, Orson, 1915–   I. Gottesman, Ronald.
PN2287.W456F6   791.43'0233'0924 [B]   75-26932
ISBN 0-13-949214-3
ISBN 0-13-949206-2 pbk.

FILM FOCUS

Ronald Gottesman and Harry M. Geduld
General Editors

RONALD GOTTESMAN *is Director of the Center for the Humanities and Professor of English at the University of Southern California.*

For HARRY M. GEDULD:
colleague, collaborator, mentor, and friend

A SPECTRUM BOOK

10   9   8   7   6   5   4   3   2   1

Printed in the United States of America

Prentice-Hall International, Inc., *London*
Prentice-Hall of Australia Pty. Limited, *Sydney*
Prentice-Hall of Canada, Ltd., *Toronto*
Prentice-Hall of India Private Limited, *New Delhi*
Prentice-Hall of Japan, Inc., *Tokyo*
Prentice-Hall of South-East Asia Private Limited, *Singapore*

CONTENTS

ACKNOWLEDGMENTS

My chief pleasure in preparing this book has been in calling on old friends who helped out of interest and loyalty, and in making new friends who initially offered assistance out of a shared concern for the subject. The following list does not distinguish between old and new friends; all have my deepest appreciation for the various timely services performed. My special debt to Harry M. Geduld, however, is only partially indicated by the dedication of this volume to him. I am also indebted to: Robert Carringer, Mary Corliss, Kathy Goff, Alice Hammond, Judy Hamilton, Bruce Hoffman, Richard T. Jameson, Jack Jorgens, Eric Krueger, Mary Jo Morris, Joe McBride, Jimmy Naremore, Gloria Prochaska, Diane Rosenfeldt, Darlene Safransky, Maureen Shucard, Michael Silverman, Sandi Thomason, Walt Ulbricht, Louise Woitishek, and the students in a Bergman-Welles course I offered with much pleasure in 1973–74. To many others, including my wife Val and our children Lann and Grant, who listened patiently and asked the right questions, I am also grateful. Like those listed above—and those many whose help I have forgotten—they are not responsible for my failure to listen to their advice or to be more accurate.

ACKNOWLEDGMENTS

Introduction
Orson Welles: Obedient Servant
and Disobedient Master

by RONALD GOTTESMAN

The Public hates you if it thinks you wrote,
directed and produced the entire film yourself.
It's the quickest way to make enemies.

D.W. GRIFFITH

When I make a film,
I simply make a film.

ORSON WELLES

Homage best describes the motive for this collection. For I firmly believe that the "Welles Phenomenon" is based on a demonstrably brilliant directorial achievement destined to grow in esteem as our knowledge of the facts and our critical resources for dealing with rich and difficult films develop. As George Sadoul rightly insists, Welles has been a major force in film history. His influence on Kubrick, Malle, Preminger, Aldrich, Polanski, and Bogdanovich, as Peter Cowie also rightly insists, is plain to see (and hear). More to the point, he has so far given world cinema at least four major works: *Citizen Kane*, *The Magnificent Ambersons*, *Touch of Evil*, and *Chimes at Midnight*. Has any director given us more? And even Welles' harshest critics (most of them American) would agree, moreover, that any one of his films has several scenes and sequences that would be the making of a lesser artist.

Welles is a curiously composite figure. He is, as his published interviews suggest, an avant-garde artist with relatively uncomplicated (if unconventional) views on the nature and destiny of man. Fascinated like other modernists by the problematic nature of reality and identity, he is also absorbed by the enduring—perhaps

1

old-fashioned—problem of good and evil. He has an astonishing command of the technical and expressive resources of the medium and the compulsion to put them to use in the service of subjects and themes rooted in Western culture. Although his signature is unmistakably inscribed in virtually every frame, in distinctive editing patterns and recurrent imagery, perhaps the most remarkable quality of each of his films is its freshness. For thirty-five years he has done what every artist—what all who would make of life an art—fear they will not be equal to: he has renewed himself in fresh creation. The necessities of his art derive from his originality and inventiveness in response to the demands of specific film projects, not from the expectations of an audience or from habit. Although he has favorite techniques, devices, strategies, even "objects" (canes, snow, fire), Welles never merely repeats himself. His techniques are the stuff of his craft, not mannerisms. Had he worked regularly in Hollywood, with its incomparable financial and technical resources and personnel, he might well have dominated American filmmaking in the way Samuel Johnson dominated English intellectual life in the last half of the eighteenth century. Even as it stands, his accomplishment should be cherished and celebrated, not tut-tutted over as if it were some betrayal or retreat or failure of character and talent. The dominant view that since *Citizen Kane* Welles' career has been a steady decline and fall seems to me as wrong-headed as it is mean-spirited.

We should also be grateful for Welles' profound humanism, for his enactment and assertion of individualism in the face of an increasingly bureaucratized and dehumanizing world. Sensitive to the point of morbidity about mortality, the tenuousness of human relations, and the potential autocracy of powerful individuals, Welles has also celebrated the autonomy of the single self and recalled us to the power of human love and loyalties. Welles understands deeply the unresolved struggle between the human capacity to murder and to create. Neither cynical nor sentimental, Welles has been a humanist in the best sense. No American intellectual of his generation has been more faithful to the best human causes while refusing the easy acceptations of simple position taking. Perhaps, beyond his technical skills, this aesthetic, moral, and intellectual integrity has been the source of his extraordinary success as a director of actors and actresses.

Having thus declared myself, I hasten to insist that the most distressing aspect of the generally sad history of Welles criticism is the discrepancy between broad generalizations—positive or negative—about his stature as a filmmaker and the careful, detailed examination of individual films or specific features of his style and moral vision. For three decades Welles has been both news and cause, but we know, in fact, very little authoritatively about his life, even less about the intellectual, imaginative, political, economic, and technical sources and circumstances that have conditioned the form and content of his films. Paradoxically, even though several books and scores of critical pieces devoted to Welles have been published, we have only begun to view and listen to his films with the kind of attention they deserve.

We all know what it takes to be a great artist: a powerful, fresh imagination, complete mastery of the resources of a medium, a penetrating sense of life, and the capacity to marshal energies, to see things through. We also know that, in particular, a film director must have the eyes and compositional gifts of a painter, the spatial grasp of a sculptor and architect, the ears and rhythmic acuity of a composer, the kinetic feel of a choreographer, the linguistic powers of a poet, the dramatic timing of a playwright, the analytic penetration of a philosopher, the inspirational aura of a military or religious leader, and the financial acumen of a banker. With the possible exception of the last of these attributes, there is not much argument that Welles has the requisite equipment.[1] The central question Welles criticism should address, then, is what has Welles as a film director done with these extraordinary gifts? How well, that is, has he integrated his revolutionary technical perspective with his radically humanist outlook?

To a large extent, this question has been my guide in selecting the pieces included in this volume. I wanted, of course, to be sure that each of the major films received extended treatment. In this respect as in others, space constraints made this goal difficult to realize, though for a number of the films there was surprisingly little to choose from. In particular, I regret that there was not more first-rate material available on *The Magnificent Ambersons* and *The Trial*. And even though considerable space is devoted to *Touch of Evil*, much remains to be said about this provocative and disturbing

---

[1] But see the exchange in *The New York Times* between Charles Higham and Peter Bogdanovich listed in the bibliography to this volume.

film. For instance, though the film is very plainly (among other things) a study of the confused sexual identity and impotence that result from the loss of innocence—what Welles has characterized as "the central theme in Western culture"—none of the criticism of *Touch of Evil* confronts this important topic.[2] Indeed, the question of sexuality in the modern world—a central concern in all of Welles' films—is virtually untouched by the director's critics.

Several items were commissioned for this volume. Richard Jameson's overview clearly emerges from a profound engagement with Welles' entire oeuvre. In its own way I believe it is as useful an orientation to Welles as William Johnson's "Orson Welles: Of Time and Loss," reprinted in my *Focus on "Citizen Kane"* in this series. James Naremore's speculation on the question of unauthorized changes—both omissions and additions—in an obviously flawed film like *The Lady From Shanghai* confronts directly one of the questions that must be dealt with in all of Welles' (or any director's) films:[3] To what extent does the finished film represent Welles' intentions? When and how, that is, do the economics of the industry impinge on the aesthetic effect of the product? At the same time, he doesn't lose sight of the film's distinctively Wellesian density, its "seven-layer cake profusion," and its thrust toward surrealism. Similarly, both Mullin's and Jorgens' commissioned essays offer fresh analyses of two of the troubled Shakespeare adaptations. Although sensitive to the films' deficiencies, both properly call attention to Welles' characteristic willingness to take risks, to place the demands of his vision before the obligations of Shakespeare's text and world-view. Almost alone among film adapters of Shakespeare, Welles has shared Shakespeare's understanding of sources: they are materials to the artist's shaping imagination, not totemic objects of worship. If the artist holds his mirror up to art, he will reflect someone else's face.

Apart from their intrinsic interest and merit, the reprinted pieces serve various purposes important in any attempt to "cover" Welles.

[2] In one of those frantic sentences that futilely tries to keep pace with a mind that works like a string of large lady-finger firecrackers, Manny Farber characterizes *Touch of Evil* as "a sexual allegory" but then drops the matter. See Manny Farber, *Negative Space* (New York: 1971), p. 7.

[3] *Variety* for June 25, 1975, pp. 2 and 78, carries a story about the prospective release of a version of *Touch of Evil* fifteen minutes longer than the release print and "apparently corresponding closely to original cut made by Welles himself. . . ."

Tynan's biographical essay provides both essential facts and a nice sense of Welles' character and personality. Joseph McBride's piece on *The Hearts of Age* fills in the fascinating pre-history to Welles' public career as a film director. David Bordwell's resonant essay on *Citizen Kane* (and *Chimes at Midnight*) sets a standard for all Welles scholars. Since Pauline Kael published her long, polemical, controversial (and easily available) introduction to *The Citizen Kane Book*, there has been no way to avoid a confrontation with her claims about Welles' character, his "shallow masterpiece," and his role in the preparation of the screenplay for *Citizen Kane*. Apart from supplying a defense of Welles, Bogdanovich's piece, by quoting Welles' liberally, offers privileged glimpses into at least some aspects of his shrewd, introspective, and self-critical friend. (I also thought it should be as easily accessible as Kael's introductory essay.) Joseph McBride's chapter on *Chimes at Midnight* is that rare phenomenon—the perfect matching of critical tone and heft to creative mood and substance. No one can claim to understand Welles and his films until he has studied this essay. Though much shorter and slighter contributions, the pieces by Silver and Taylor are valuable reflections on relatively little-known films. Charles Champlin's interview both returns us to *Citizen Kane* and provides a tantalizing glimpse of the film Welles previewed for us when he received the American Film Institute's Life Award in the spring of 1975. Finally, because I believe that Welles' contributions to sound—that exponentially complicating and opportunity-making element—have been neglected (despite the drone of vague praise), I wanted to include at least one essay that made a very clear case for the nature and large significance of that contribution. Beyond its pertinence to Welles, Goldfarb's essay suggests how astonishingly dumb most film criticism has been in being so deaf.

As I said earlier in this introduction, Welles criticism is only now beginning. I hope this volume will give impetus to that development and soon make this collection obsolete. Even more, I hope that Welles will continue to make the films that call forth and justify our admiration and our best criticism.

THE MAN

Orson Welles

by KENNETH TYNAN

Some eighteen years ago, in the pages of an English school magazine, there appeared a brief and sickeningly lush essay, entitled "The New Playboy of the Western World." It read, in part:

> There is a man flourishing now and being mighty on the other side of the Atlantic. He has a lovely wife and twenty-odd years of flamboyant youth, but his accomplishments do not end here. He has burst on the American scene with a heavy gesture of ineffable superiority; he is the artistic saviour of a broad land, and he knows it. For Orson Welles is a self-made man, and how he loves his maker. . . . He moulds art out of radio, the scourge of art; he is a wit as only Americans can be wits; and he is a dandy among impromptu speakers. He is a director of plays in kingly fashion, independent as a signpost in all he does; and he has carved out of a face of massy granite the subtle lineaments of a great actor. He is a gross and glorious director of motion pictures, the like of which we have not seen since the great days of the German cinema; he reproduces life as it is sometimes seen in winged dreams.
>
> He is all these things, vastly exaggerated and blown up into a balloon of bold promise and brash achievement. Yet with all his many-sidedness he has no dignity. "I have," he once said, "the dignity of a nude at high noon on Fifth Avenue." One requisite of greatness he lacks: artistic integrity. Perhaps he has burgeoned too soon and too wildly; but it will come with praise and age, and then we shall behold a gorgeous, patriarchal figure, worthy of the Old Testament. Until then, watch him, watch him well, for he is

First published in Show, *October–November, 1961. Reprinted by permission of the author.*

8

a major prophet, with the hopes of a generation clinging to his heels.

I was sixteen when I wrote that. I wince today at its alliterations, its borrowed sonorities, and its tone of midget exhortation. Even more, I wince at the calmness of my assertion that Welles was deficient in "artistic integrity," since that is one kind of integrity he has seldom been accused of wanting; perhaps I meant "integration," which would make a little more sense.

I quote from the piece not out of vainglory but merely to establish my credentials. In 1943 I was committed to Welles as to nobody else then active in the performing arts; and I am sure there were thousands like me, young people in their teens and twenties for whom Welles was Renaissance man reborn. He seemed to have shortened, almost to vanishing point, the distance between ambition and achievement; no sooner did he approach an art than it surrendered to him. Theatre was the first to fall. We had read of the Negro *Macbeth* he directed in Harlem, and of his two audacious seasons at the helm of the Mercury Theatre. In his spare time he had conquered radio, unhinging America in 1938 with his adaptation of H. G. Wells's *The War of the Worlds*. Then he had gone to Hollywood and subjected the film industry to its first major upheaval since the advent of sound.

Nobody who saw *Citizen Kane* at an impressionable age will ever forget the experience; overnight, the American cinema had acquired an adult vocabulary, a dictionary instead of a phrase book for semiliterates. I first saw it on a Monday afternoon in the English provinces, and was lastingly dazzled by its narrative virtuosity, its shocking but always relevant cuts (do you remember that screeching cockatoo?), its brilliantly orchestrated dialogue, and its use of deep focus in sound as well as in vision. About a dozen other people, scattered throughout the theatre, shared the revelation with me. By the end of the week I had seen the film five times, once with my eyes shut in order to prove to myself that the sound track was expressive enough to be listened to in its own right. That was in 1941; and when *The Magnificent Ambersons* came along, a year or so later, my capitulation was complete. Sceptics had told me that Welles was a technical maestro, incapable of feeling; to confound them, I had only to point to his handling of Booth Tarkington's family saga, in which there were scenes of a naked emotional intimacy rarely matched in the history of Hollywood. Agnes Moorehead's portrait of Aunt Fanny, eaten up with frustrated love for her nephew, seemed to me then (and seems to me still) the best performance of its kind in the English-speaking cinema. At the end of the film came the credit titles, after which a microphone suspended from a boom swung into view. "I wrote the picture and directed it," said a serene bass voice. "My name is Orson Welles." If my prayer at that moment had been answered, Welles would have written and directed the whole subsequent output of the American film industry. Thus infatuated, I sat down and penned my eulogy.

Time, I am told by many of my friends, has proved me mistaken; if the "hopes of a generation" ever clung to Welles's heels, they have long since been trampled underfoot. What, I am asked, has the man accomplished in the past eighteen years? A handful of stylish thrillers, a couple of bombastic Shakespeare films, a few hit-or-miss stage productions, a number of self-exploiting television appearances, and several tongue-in-cheek performances in other people's bad epics—what, beyond these, has Welles to show for himself? For one thing, I sometimes reply, he has scars, inflicted by a society which demands that the making of art and the making of money should be yokefellows. For another, he shares with people like Chaplin, Cocteau, Picasso, Ellington, and Hemingway a fixed international reputation that can never wholly be tarnished. Even in eclipse, he remains among the elite, to be judged on their level; the quickest ears prick up and the keenest eyes brighten at the advent of a new Orson Welles production—or rather, manifestation, since one can never predict the form in which his talent will choose to reveal itself. Apart from writing and directing films and plays, and apart from acting in both, he has tried his hand as a novelist, a painter, a ballet scenarist, a public orator, a magician, a columnist, and a bullfighter.

To understand why he carries with him this permanent aura of expectation, it is perhaps necessary to know him. Last spring [1960] I spent a week in Spain at his elbow, listening while he talked about his life and times. In Welles' company, on this occasion as on all previous ones, I automatically assumed the role of stooge. What follow are my memories of what he said, and my comments thereon, which I hope may provide some explanation of why, whenever I find myself bored and wondering whom I would most like to see coming in at the door, the answer is always Orson.

First, a sketch of his physical presence, which is overwhelming. He has the sauntering bulk of a fastidious yet insatiable glutton. Welles is perilously fat, having taken none but the slightest exercise since the time, thirty years ago, when he leapt in to challenge the bulls at every village *corrida* within striking distance of Seville. Jean Cocteau rightly called him "a giant with the face of a child," adding that he was also "an active loafer, a wise madman, a solitude surrounded by humanity." Watch him in repose at a bullfight, lonely in the crowd, his brow contracted above the vast tanned jowls and his eyes bulging with reproach; into such a frame, one feels, the soul of the last American bison might easily migrate. From the pursed lips a tremendous cigar protrudes, and the chin is grimly outthrust; yet in all this dignity there is somehow an element of dimpled mischief. Beneath the swelling forehead a schoolboy winks, and can readily be coaxed into chuckling. Orson amused is an engulfing spectacle, as irresistible as Niagara. The remark (frequently his) is made; a moment of silence ensues, during which his forehead retracts, causing his eyes to pop and his cheeks to sag, turning his face into a tragic mask. For an instant he looks appalled; and then there breaks through the thunderous cachinnation of his laughter. "A wonderful laugh," said Tennessee Williams, having listened to it, "forced and defensive, like mine." But I think he was wrong: Orson laughs to goad others out of awe into participation. "I like people to talk to me," he says, "What I can't stand is when they talk to Orson Welles."

Lunch in the garden of the Ritz in Madrid: Orson, surging across the terrace in white shirt and white tie, arouses thoughts of Moby Dick. Spanish decorum has overcome his habitual tielessness. He is in Spain for three reasons: to shoot a documentary for Italian television, to finish off his movie adaptation of *Don Quixote* (with Akim Tamiroff as Sancho Panza and an unknown Mexican as the Don), and to go to the bullfights. The first two projects are tending to overlap, as Orson intended they should. Last year, dwindling funds forced him to abandon his own picture, with two weeks' shooting still to be done, and when an Italian TV network invited him to direct a series of documentaries, he agreed on condition that the first should deal with Spain. As a title, he suggested *The Land of Don Quixote*. Thus he manages to work for himself while working for somebody else; Orson has spent much of his life in this kind of double harness. As for the bulls, they are his passion; he is one of the very few Anglo-Saxons whose opinions are valued by the Spanish taurine initiates. Among contemporary matadors his favourite is Antonio Ordóñez, the graceful young maestro from Ronda, who achieves with the bulls he fights an intimacy so profound, so devoid of arrogance, that it once moved Orson to observe: "With Antonio, each pass asserts not 'how great *I am!*' but 'how great *we are!*' " The remark may stand as a definition of good bullfighting. Though addicted to the bulls, Orson is bored by all other competitive sports; he has no interest in skills he has never practised.

As we eat, he talks about his childhood, and Madrid society pretends not to listen—an effort that must be made by all those who find themselves in public places where Orson is conducting a private conversation. It is not that he shouts, merely that he cannot help resounding. Except in solitude, a state rare with him, Orson has no private personality; everything about him is public, and he is open daily. This has been true as long as he can remember. "Orson at twenty-six," it was wickedly said at the height of his Hollywood success "is still overshadowed by the glorious memory of Orson at six." He was born in Kenosha, Wisconsin, forty-six years ago last May, and claims to be more English than the English, springing as he does from generations of unmixed colonial stock. "You can find eighteenth-century Englishmen in the Middle West," he says, "just as you can find sixteenth-century Spaniards in Peru." I begin to see in him an extravagant Whig on the model of Charles James Fox, tinged with more than a hint of Byron, the first of the great romantic expatriates. But I remember that Orson hates to be called an expatriate; since the term applies only to people who exile themselves from the country in which they were raised, how can it apply to him, who was not brought up in America? And he has a point: until he was eighteen years old, Orson spent most of his time abroad.

Both his parents were travellers. His father, Richard Welles, was a Virginian who moved to Wisconsin because he owned two factories there. He was an accomplished gambler, a sedulous globe-trotter, and an unpredictable inventor. One of his inventions was a carbide bicycle lamp that made him a great deal of money; others turned out less encouragingly. "He tried very hard to invent the airplane," Orson says. "He thought the Wright brothers were working on the wrong principles, so he designed a steam-driven car with a kind of glider attached to it. He put a Negro servant into the glider and started out, but the steam got into the Negro's eyes and he crashed into a tree. He and my father were photographed afterward, smiling across the wreckage." Orson's mother was Beatrice Ives of Springfield, Illinois, a gifted pianist, radical in her view of politics and art, and ravishing in her beauty. To this union of playboy and aesthete, at a time when both partners were approaching middle age, George Orson Welles was born, owing his first name to George Ade, the humourist, and his second to a Chicago businessman called Orson Wells. He says he had two remote cousins who later became politically eminent: Sumner Welles and Adlai Stevenson. He also had a brother, Richard, Jr., some ten years his senior, of whose subsequent history little is known; a dreamer and roamer, he was last heard of in Seattle, upholding the family tradition of intelligent dilettantism.

One dwells on Orson's parents because so much about them helped to shape him. He got on splendidly with them both, rather better than they did with each other; where mother had her salon, father favoured the saloon. The child's precociousness was Mozartean. At the age of two he spoke fluent and considered English, and was familiar with the plays of Shakespeare from his mother's readings. The first great wrench came when he was six. He parents separated, and Orson went to live with his mother for two halcyon years, during which he adoringly absorbed her passion for music, poetry, and painting. He hated, however, to practise scales on the piano, and once, at the age of seven, stationed himself on a high window ledge of the Ritz Hotel in Paris, threatening to jump unless his mother told his music teacher to stop badgering him. As always, she complied. The idyll ended when he was eight. Beatrice Welles died, and Orson, already an adult in feeling, was whisked off to share his father's way of life, which revolved round late nights, stage doors, and constant changes of country. "He was a wandering *bon viveur*," Orson says, "and he revelled in theatre people. Before my mother died, painting and music were what interested me most. I'd never thought seriously about the theatre."

Through his mother he had met Ravel and Stravinsky; through his father he met John Barrymore, together with innumerable circus performers and magicians. He acquired a showman's eye (which later enabled him to act as an unpaid scout for John Ringling North) and an illusionist's dexterity. "My father loved magic," he says. "That's what bound us together." Such masters as

Harry Houdini and Long Tack Sam, the Chinese conjurer who revolutionised card manipulation, were called in to teach him their mysteries. If anything, he improved on what he learned; today Orson is one of the best paid magicians alive. In 1960, at a London hotel, he received more than $1,500 for one performance of a single trick: seizing an axe, he splintered a block of ice within which there was frozen a strongbox, inside which there was locked a scrap of paper, upon which there was inscribed the official registration number of a taxi-driver whom an unbribed guest had brought in from the street just before the axe was lifted. Some years ago Orson agreed to lend his arcane skills to a Hollywood celebration in honour of Louis B. Mayer. So many stars preceded him that by the time his turn came the rabbit concealed in the lining of his suit had urinated "roughly twenty-seven times." He has been wary of unpaid performances ever since.

Above all, Orson learned from his father the art of travelling. Who else of his age can declare nowadays, with eyewitness authority, that "the two great artistic centres of the twenties were Budapest and Peking"? He explored Europe in the care of various tutors, one of whom took him when he was nine to an uncommonly noisy dinner party at Innsbruck, of which he remembers little except the name of the man at the head of the table, one Adolf Hitler. Life with father was more restless and uncertain than it had been with mother. "How is it," I suddenly ask Orson, "that the heroes of your films have no fathers?" I am thinking not so much of Macbeth and Othello as of George in *The Magnificent Ambersons*, who ruins the life of his widowed mother; and especially of Charles Foster Kane, whose father never appears [*sic*] and who is taken away from his mother as a child and transported into an alien world of men and money, rather like George Orson Welles. In answer to my question, Orson says that there is no reason, that he adored his father; and no doubt he did. All the same, the parallel with Kane is curiously haunting. One recalls the sled named Rosebud, Kane's symbol of maternal affection, the loss of which deprives him irrecoverably of the power to love or be loved. (Mr Bernstein [Kane's loyal business manager] is admittedly based on Dr. Maurice Bernstein, the family physician who acted as Welles's unofficial guardian after his father died in 1928.) It is not inconceivable, as a perceptive American director once suggested to me, that Orson reached a state of perfect self-fulfilment just before his mother's death, and that he has been trying ever since to recapture it.

At ten, under heavy persuasion from his father and Dr. Bernstein, Orson joined the progressive Todd School for Boys in Woodstock, Illinois, where he flourished for five years, admiringly encouraged by the school director, Roger Hill, with whom, while still in his teens, he wrote a fledgling play and edited a popular textbook called *Everybody's Shakespeare.* On principle, however, he disapproves of conventional education in any form, and will have none of it for Beatrice, his five-year-old daughter: "What does it teach you except to show up at the same hour every morning—and still learn nothing?" In his fourteenth year the death of his father cast him upon a world from which security, as his parents had known it, was about to be banished by the Wall Street crash. An orphaned prodigy, he grew up hoarding nostalgia; in particular, a nostalgia for old-fashioned melodrama, for stock companies, for turn-of-the-century Americana, which he had imbibed from his father. It persisted into later life, as many of his stage productions bear witness: *The Drunkard,* William Gillette's *Too Much Johnson, The Green Goddess, Around the World in Eighty Days,* and *Moby Dick,* which Orson directed in London as it might have been presented by a touring company in the nineties. Again and again he has gone back to the flamboyant era of the actor-manager in the astrakhan collar, the era of Tarkington's Ambersons and Citizen Kane's infancy. Orson has always secretly thought of himself as a vagabond rogue.

Just before he graduated from Todd, at the age of fifteen, an ad appeared in *The Billboard.* It read, in part:

ORSON WELLES—Stock, Characters, Heavies, Juveniles or as cast . . . Lots of pep, experience and ability. Close in Chicago early in June and want place in good stock company for remainder of season.

He was on his own. It is not fanciful to see Orson's life as an unfinished picaresque novel, each chapter of which is a bizarre adventure strung like a bead on the thread of the hero's personality; the raw material, in fact, for a new *Citizen Kane,* different from the old in that the central character would be a maker of art, not merely a collector.

The lunch is over. Orson insists on paying, and summons his

Italian henchman, a minor but authentic prince, to look after the
bill. The prince sportively doubts whether he has enough cash.
"Very well," says the ventripotent Orson, beaming broadly. "My
signature against the world!"

I never cease to be fascinated by the spectacle of a talent so huge
yet so homeless, so vast yet so vagrant. Other people sink roots; but
Orson perpetually wanders, a citizen of no fixed territory save that
of art. I had already heard him on the subject of his upbringing; I
wanted now to discuss his adult life, during which he had spanned
the globe in an effort to recapture the creative security of his
childhood.

The next day I lunched with him again, this time at Horcher's,
his favourite among the city's great restaurants. Spain has always
been one of his chosen countries. Although he is no believer in
formal education, he is having his daughter, Beatrice, taught to
dance flamenco; when I asked her what she thought about while
stamping her feet and flashing her eyes in such precocious frenzy,
she pondered and replied, "I think that I *hate* the *floor*."

Talking to Orson can be a disquieting experience; one feels one is
boring him, wasting his time, especially if the purpose of the
meeting is professional. He has so often suffered at the hands of
journalists. "The French are the worst," he says. "They ask long
questions that *are* the answers. I nod, and the question is printed
without the question mark, as my idea." Having ordered caviare,
blintzes, and venison, he tells me that his greatest burden has
always been his grandiose physical appearance. "My trouble is that
I exude affluence," he says. "I look successful. Whenever the critics
see me, they say to themselves: 'It's time he was knocked—he's had
it too good for too long.' But I *haven't* had it so good; I just look that
way. I need jobs like anyone else." He splutters with baritone
laughter. "Every time I bring out a new movie," he goes on,
"nobody bothers to review it—at least, not until the last paragraph.
Instead, they write a long essay on 'the Welles Phenomenon and
what has become of it.' They don't review my work; they review
me!"

He left school in 1930, an orphan aged fifteen, and at once set
about the task, which proved to be lifelong, of inventing himself.
His first parentless years were favoured ones. Thanks to his father's
legacy, he never felt the pinch of the Depression. Intended for
Harvard, he embarked instead on a painting trip to Ireland, where

he gate-crashed the Dublin Gate Theatre and became a professional actor. "You handle your voice like a singer," said the
director, Hilton Edwards, "and there isn't a note of sincerity in it."
He was then sixteen. We next hear of him sketching in Morocco,
fighting bulls around Seville, and returning unsung to the States in
1933, when Thornton Wilder gave him a letter to Alexander
Woollcott, who in turn introduced him to Katharine Cornell. The
last lady of the American theatre (as I sometimes think of her) hired
him to join her company in a tour of *Romeo and Juliet* and *Candida*.
Already, at seventeen, he thought of himself as past the age when he
could convincingly play juveniles, and he turned up at the first
rehearsal of the Shaw comedy assuming that he had been cast as
Morell, Candida's husband. He was surprised to see that Basil
Rathbone was also present: "I took Miss Cornell to one side and
told her that I didn't want to interfere, but didn't she think
Rathbone was a little elderly to be playing Marchbanks, the
adolescent poet?" It had to be carefully explained to him that that
was *his* role; Mr. Rathbone had been engaged as Morell.

One of the dates the company played was Atlantic City, where
Orson dabbled for the first time in professional magic. He practised
palmistry in a booth on the boardwalk, so successfully that he
almost unnerved himself. To begin with, he confined himself to
simple exercises in applied psychology: "I would look into the
crystal ball and then say to the customer: 'You have a scar on your
knee'—because in fact most people have. If that didn't work, I
would say: 'You had a profound emotional experience between the
ages of eleven and thirteen.' I don't think I ever failed with that
one." But he soon discovered that he was less of a charlatan than he
had imagined; too many of his intuitions turned out to be correct.
"I began," he says, "to think of myself as Ming the Merciless." That
Orson is capable of insights amounting to prophecy is borne out of a
number of stories, the best known of which concerns the occasion
when he escorted Eugene O'Neill's daughter Oona to a Hollywood
night club and offered, on the strength of two hours' acquaintance,
to read her hand. "Within a very short time," he declared, "you
will meet and marry Charles Chaplin." Like so many of her father's
heroines, Miss O'Neill obeyed the voice of destiny.

Orson made his Broadway debut in December 1934, playing the
Chorus and Tybalt in *Romeo and Juliet*. There ensues the first
familiar period of his legend—the four-year battle with the

American theatre. "Paris is the playwright's city," he says, "London is the actor's city, and New York is the director's city." Or if New York wasn't, Orson did much to make it so. In the late thirties, more than at any other time in American history, the development of the theatre seemed intimately bound up with the development of the country as a whole; a radical adventure was under way, and the nation's culture was among the spearheads of the nation's hopes. In 1935 the New Deal sired the Federal Theatre Project, devised not only to alleviate unemployment in the theatre but to bring good drama within the reach of the unemployed audiences. By subsidising the Project, Washington accepted the principle that the fostering of culture was a matter for public as well as private concern. Progressive artists, in a period when nearly all artists were progressives, embraced the scheme; and no one who hopes to understand Orson should forget that his career as a director was launched under its liberal auspices.

The Project set up a Negro branch at the old Lafayette Theatre in Harlem, and it was here, in the spring of 1936, that Orson and John Houseman staged their shattering Negro production of *Macbeth.* "On opening night," Orson recalls, "the curtain never fell. The audience swarmed up onto the stage, cheering." He afterwards went on tour with the show: "We had a temperamental Macbeth, and in Indianapolis we lost him. I blacked myself up about three shades darker than anyone else in the cast and played the part for two weeks. Nobody in the audience noticed anything unusual." Back at the Lafayette, he directed a fiercely anti-segregationist piece called *Turpentine,* and remembers his horror when Noble Sissle's pit orchestra played the first-night audience out to the reactionary strains of "Is it true what they say about Dixie?"

On Broadway, still for the Federal Theatre, he staged and starred in Marlowe's *Doctor Faustus,* which ran for six months; but the cultural euphoria in Washington was being blown away by hot winds from the right, whose breath Orson felt in the summer of 1937, when government sponsorship was abruptly withdrawn from his production of Marc Blitzstein's leftist opera *The Cradle Will Rock* on the eve of its première. Locked out of the Maxine Elliot Theatre, he found another (the Venice, later renamed the Century) and led the first-nighters thither on a triumphal march up Sixth Avenue. Confronted by an Actors' Equity ruling that forbade the actors to appear on the stage, he seated them among the audience and had

them sing their parts from there. It was a great cı
Tom Paine would have enjoyed it; and there is no oı
history (I have his word for this) Orson would raı
than Tom Paine.

In 1939 the Federal Theatre Project was voted c
By then Orson and John Houseman had spent
private enterprise, running the Mercury Theatre on 41st Street,
getting simultaneously into debt and the history books with a string
of productions that included *Danton's Death*, *Heartbreak House*, and
the startling modern-dress version of *Julius Caesar*. They regarded
the Mercury Theatre's broadcasts simply as money-making ad-
juncts to its theatrical activities; nobody was more astonished than
Orson when, taking a stroll during a break in the dress rehearsal of
Danton's Death, he saw his name travelling in lights around the
Times Building, followed by an announcement that he had
panicked America with his radio adaptation of H. G. Wells' *War of
the Worlds*. He had intended the programme as a Halloween joke;
not for the first time, and certainly not the last, he had over-esti-
mated the intelligence of his audience. Such errors are healthy:
what kills art is the assumption that people are stupid. "About three
years after the Martian broadcast," Orson says, "I was reading a
Whitman poem on a patriotic Sunday programme, when someone
ran into the studio and shouted into the mike that Pearl Harbour
had been attacked. Nobody paid any attention. They just shrugged
and said, 'There he goes again.' " The Mercury Theatre survived
on Broadway until the spring of 1939 having demonstrated that a
repertory company needs more than critical applause and intermit-
tently filled houses to keep it alive; it needs the continuity and
security that only steady subsidies can provide.

Lunch, the long Spanish lunch, has come to an end. It is time for
the bullfight; and I ask Orson what would have happened if, twenty
years ago, he had been given a theatre of his own and enough
money to hold a permanent company together. "No question about
it," he says at once; "I'd be running it today." Orson's kind of
theatre belongs in a tradition that looks beyond the next flop or the
next season's deficit; its affinities are with the great non-commercial
institutions—the Comédie Française, the Moscow Art Theatre, the
Berliner Ensemble. Even as I say that, I shush myself, realising how
much harm it may do to Orson's Broadway reputation.

His relationship with money requires a brief rubric. The legend that Orson overspends; the truth is that he is a delayed *ner. Citizen Kane* was a flop in 1941, but over the years it has returned its investment many times over, and the same applies to *The Magnificent Ambersons*. Orson's pictures are long-distance runners in a system dedicated to sprinters. True, *The Lady from Shanghai* was disproportionately expensive, but against that one must balance *The Stranger* and *Macbeth,* both of which he brought in on schedule and under budget. Orson's first large debt was to the United States government, which refused to allow him tax deductions on personal losses (amounting to $350,000) that were incurred by his 1946 Broadway production of *Around the World in Eighty Days*. He moved to Europe, leaving the argument to his lawyers; and since then his financial problems have affected none but his own productions. They have sometimes lost money and left behind them a trail of unpaid bills; but this, in our society, is precisely what one would expect of a man who rates his responsibility to the cause of art above his responsibility to private investment. More subsidy from the state, not less extravagance on Orson's part, is the answer to the perennial Welles predicament. He regards art as a social right, not as an accidental privilege; as a matter for public endowment, not as incentive to private speculation. That his work should occasionally lose money is not only inevitable but honourable.

We meet in the bar of the Palace Hotel after the bullfight; it has been a bad one, but Orson is not depressed, for to the true *aficionado* there are no dull bullfights. He watches them with the analytical scrutiny of an initiate, which means that he is never bored and rarely transported. He watches films in the same way: "I'm like a vivisectionist. I dissect them shot by shot. I'd give half my kingdom to be able to see a movie and forget what I know about movie technique." He responds politely to the group that gathers around him in the bar; perhaps too politely, making me wish he would squander less of his energy in a form as perishable as talk. Tennessee Williams, one of the circle, extracts from his mouth a cigarette holder full of cancer-repelling crystals and murmurs to me that no one should ever attack Orson—"a man so vulnerable, and of such magnitude." Everyone is vulnerable who is at once gifted and gregarious. Orson is fully aware that for him, as for all great talkers, conversation is what Cyril Connolly once called it, "a ceremony of self-wastage." I record a few overheard snatches. Of Antonioni, the director of the wildly praised Italian film *L'Avventura,* he says: "The critics tell me he's a stylist of the cinema. But how can you be a stylist if you don't understand grammar?" Of a famous American actor, generally renowned for his modesty offscreen: "There is nothing more frightening than quiet vanity." Of Oscar Wilde's comedies: "Why don't people realise that they were written to be acted by tweedy, red-faced Victorian squires, not by attractive faggots?" He flies these conversational kites because they are expected of him, and then subsides into heavy, abstracted brooding. The circle disperses, and he generously wastes himself on me.

We talk about his Hollywood epoch, which lasted on and off for roughly seven years. Leaving Broadway in 1939, he brought the Mercury actors—among them Joseph Cotten and Agnes Moorehead—out to work with him for RKO. The trip produced *Citizen Kane*, which stands in no need of eulogy from me. It revolutionised Hollywood rather as the aeroplane revolutionised warfare; it drove William Randolph Hearst, on whom Kane was putatively modelled, to declare war on Orson in his newspapers; and it cost less than $750,000, which seems a reasonable price to pay for a landmark in cinema history. In 1941 Orson started to shoot *The Magnificent Ambersons*, based on Booth Tarkington's story about the decline of a prosperous Southern [*sic*] family. "I'd finished the rough cut," Orson says, "and I needed about two weeks more work to get the picture ready, when Jock Whitney and Nelson Rockefeller, who were both RKO shareholders, asked me to go down to South America and make a film about Latin-American solidarity." By then the United States had entered the war, and Orson patriotically agreed. The course of shooting was not uneventful; headlines were made in Rio de Janeiro when Orson and the Mexican Ambassador to Brazil protested against an exorbitant hotel bill by carefully throwing a great deal of furniture out of a window of His Excellency's suite.

Meanwhile, in Orson's words: "RKO had shown *The Ambersons* at a sneak preview, probably in Pomona. The audience laughed at it, so they cut it to pieces, shot a new ending, and released it before I could do anything about it. They called me in Brazil to say they'd broken my contract." Among the cuts were Agnes Moorehead's finest moments, many of them improvised during the six-week rehearsal period on which Orson had insisted; and the whole epilogue was lopped off, in which Joseph Cotten visited Miss Moorehead in a shabby rooming house and learned from her how and why the magnificence of the Ambersons had faded. "Nowa-days," Orson says, "everybody makes pictures three hours long—it's almost obligatory. There are times when I feel a little bit jealous." He likes the efficiency of Hollywood studios ("where there's no difference between you and the workers except that they're earning more") and admits that his veneration for the cinema derives from his period at RKO. "The cinema has no boundaries," he says. "It's a ribbon of dream." He sounds genuinely awed.

His later Hollywood pictures, such as *Journey into Fear, The Stranger,* and *The Lady from Shanghai,* are as different from *Kane* and *The Ambersons* as Graham Greene's "entertainments" are different from his serious novels; in fact, it may even be that Welles influenced Greene's thrillers by his use of shock cutting, bizarre settings, and eccentric characterisation. The last shot of *The Lady from Shanghai,* completed in 1946, symbolises the end of a phase in Orson's life. The film is socially quite outspoken; Orson plays an ingenuous Irish sailor, once a fighter for the Spanish Republic, who gets involved in what he describes as the "bright, guilty world" of the rich. He falls for, and is cold-bloodedly deceived by, the wife of a millionaire lawyer. After a horrendous showdown in a deserted fun fair, she is shot by her husband, and appeals to Orson for help. Her injury is mortal; but his decision is moral. He rejects her plea; he has compromised too often, and leaves her, walking out of the fun fair into the grey dawn of a new morning. (The riddled victim was played by his second wife, Rita Hayworth; they were divorced in 1947 after four years together. His first marriage, to a Chicago actress named Virginia Nicholson, had broken up in 1939.)

One tends to forget that his Hollywood days coincide with the Second World War. Orson himself has not forgotten. Flat feet kept him out of the armed forces: "I'm still suffering," he says, "from the traumatic effect of being forbidden to do what all my friends were doing." He who had addressed innumerable anti-Nazi rallies, who had rabidly supported the fight against Fascism in Spain, now found himself condemned to inactivity when the crucial battle was joined. He pulled what political strings he could, and from time to time he was bundled out of the country under a false name to examine captured Nazi newsreels and other filmic trivia. But his missions were few, and seldom very secret: "I was flown into Lisbon as Harrison Carstairs, the ball-bearings manufacturer, and there were twenty people waiting at the airport for my autograph." (On one such errand he met and briefly beguiled himself with an Argentinian radio actress named Eva, who later emerged from obscurity as the wife of Juan Peron.) Meanwhile, the Hearst press regularly printed snide items inquiring why the playboy Welles was lounging around swimming pools when democracy was in danger; and after each new gibe, Orson usually received a draft notice. One of his periodic medical examinations took place when he had just returned from a mission to Latin America, for the purposes of which he had been created a temporary brigadier general. "Any of you men ever hold rank above a private?" asked the sergeant at the recruiting depot. Orson shuffled forward. "State the rank you held." Orson told him. "O.K., Brigadier General," said the sergeant enticingly, "get down on your hands and knees and clean up those cigarette butts."

Orson has always had a passion for politics. At one time he thought seriously of running for the Senate on the Democratic ticket; had he done so, it would have made a provocative contest, because the Republican candidate in the state of Wisconsin was the late Joseph McCarthy. "Basically," Orson says, "I'm a public orator (as was Charles Foster Kane) and that isn't the same as a television orator, which is what a lot of TV producers keep asking me to be. Television is talking to two or three people through a box, instead of talking to two thousand people and making them *feel* like two or three people." If Orson were ever to join a party, he would be its first member, and its label would be Liberal Hedonist, or Collective Individualist. Its sympathies would be leftish but it would remain, like its founder, an unaffiliated maverick.

The streets of Madrid have darkened, and drinks have faded into dinner. Orson continues, unfading. After Broadway and Hollywood came his wandering period, which is not yet, and may never be, over. His career since 1946 is a kaleidoscope that baffles chronology. He bids farewell to Broadway with *Around the World in Eighty Days*, the most opulent of his many tributes to the free-wheeling, actor-managing days of the late Victorian era. He departs for Europe, leaving a wake of tax problems behind him, but not before filming a sombre truncation of *Macbeth*—around the Bard in twenty-one shooting days. Later, after numerous halts and hazards due to inadequate finances, he directs and stars in a massively picturesque film of *Othello*, to be described in some quarters as the movie version of Ruskin's *Stones of Venice*. The echoing voices and footsteps, and the sudden cuts from long-shot silence to close-up animation, stamp it as unmistakably Wellesian; so, alas, does the scrambled text, not to mention Orson's own resonantly impassive performance. "He never acts," says Eric Bentley; "he is photographed." With peerless skill, he plays the mischievously corrupt Harry Lime in *The Third Man*, and improvises a memorable exchange with its producer, the late Alexander Korda.

Orson: I wish the Pope would make you a cardinal, Alex.

Korda: Why a cardinal?

Orson: Because then we'd only have to kiss your ring.

He is also alleged to have improvised Harry Lime's famous observation that after centuries of democracy the Swiss have produced nothing more inspiring than the cuckoo clock; falsely attributed to Orson, the line was actually written by Graham Greene.

In Paris, Orson presents a double bill of his own composition, consisting of a play about Hollywood called *The Unthinking Lobster* and a modern revamping of the Faust legend, with music by Duke Ellington. Between whiles he plays fiends and frauds in other people's films. He flies to New York to appear, outrageously bewhiskered, in Peter Brook's TV production of *King Lear*. For a day's work as Father Mapple in John Huston's film of *Moby Dick* he is paid $20,000, whereafter he makes his own dramatization of the novel and stages it in London, transforming the gilded Duke of York's Theatre into a storm-tossed whaling ship, without benefit of scenery. By now he has remarried, his new wife being Paola Mori, a shrewd, lissome Italian actress of noble birth. In 1956 he returns to Broadway in a production of *Lear*. It flops. During the previews, Orson sprains one ankle and breaks the other, and plays the opening performance from a wheelchair, thereby supplying further fuel for those who think him congenitally self-destructive. His acting ability comes up for reappraisal; Walter Kerr contributes a damaging analysis: "As an emotional actor, Welles is without insight, accuracy, power, or grace. In short, without talent. The only parts he could ever play were parts that were cold, intellectual, emotionally dead."

In 1958 Orson is summoned back to Hollywood to play a venal

cop in a thriller called *Touch of Evil*. While he is considering the offer in the producer's office, the telephone rings; it is Charlton Heston, who has been approached to play the lead but wants to know who else has been signed. "Well, we've got Orson Welles—" the producer begins. "Great!" says Heston, cutting in. "I'll appear in anything he directs." "Hold on a minute," says the producer, feeling that events are slipping out of his hands. Hastily he asks Orson whether he will direct, to which Orson agrees, on condition that he have full control of script and casting. After a pause: "Sure," the producer tells Heston, "sure Welles is directing." The result is a picture of enormous virtuosity. Orson demands two weeks of private rehearsal before shooting begins, and gets from his actors performances of fantastic, unguarded intimacy. They are shamelessly themselves, and seem imbued with his own conviction that in show business being inhibited gets you nowhere. Meanwhile, the camera swoops and hovers like a kingfisher, inscribing Orson's autograph on every sequence. Charlton Heston, as a Mexican lawyer, gives the best performance of his life. The film wins prizes in Europe, but is shunned in America. Soon afterwards we find Orson directing Olivier in the London production of *Rhinoceros*.

No one is more fertile than Orson in ideas that, for one reason or another, never get carried out. There was *Monsieur Verdoux*, for which he supplied the original script; and which he was to direct, until Chaplin decided to direct it himself. There was the satire, drawn from the love affair of D'Annunzio and Duse, which he planned for Chaplin and Garbo. There was Homer's *Odyssey*, for which he hired a writer whom he was tardy in paying, and to whose repeated pleas for advice about how to make ends meet he finally replied with a single cable: DEAR ———, LIVE SIMPLY, AFFECTIONATE REGARDS, ORSON WELLES. There were also projects involving Conrad, Dickens, Dostoevski, Rostand, and Tolstoy, of which nothing tangible came.[1]

At dinner we are joined by the Earl of Harewood, who runs the Edinburgh Festival and wonders whether Orson would like to bring a production to it in 1962. In principle, Orson would be delighted. In the course of conversation, Harewood remarks that he was lately

[1] See Peter Cowie, *A Ribbon of Dreams* (New York and London: 1973), Appendix 4, for a list of "Welles' Unrealised Film Projects." [Editor's note.]

in Japan, where he saw the Kabuki Theatre and didn't tremendously like it. Orson rounds on him, mountainously glowering, and observes that anyone who doesn't appreciate Kabuki must be an ignoramus. Harewood nods, adding that he must have seen them on a bad night. Even on a bad night, Orson insists, they are far superior to anything the Western theatre can produce. A firework display, marking the end of the Madrid *feria,* explodes in the park outside the restaurant. Hoping to pacify Orson, Harewood explains that he immensely enjoyed the Kabuki performers Sol Hurok brought to New York. He hopes wrong. "That," Orson thunders, "was a contemptible travesty. If you liked that, you don't like Kabuki." Yet within minutes he has charmed us out of embarrassment into laughter; and next day I hear from Harewood that the Edinburgh offer still stands, and that Orson and Maria Callas are the only genuine *monstres sacrés* he has ever met.

At times Orson is prey to depressions, onslaughts of gloom, spleen, and sulks that the Middle Ages would probably have ascribed to the cardinal sin of accidie, which induces a sense of futility and a temporary paralysis of the will. "From *accidie,*" Aldous Huxley once wrote, "comes dread to begin to work any good deeds, and finally wanhope, or despair. On its way to ultimate wanhope, *accidie* produces a whole crop of minor sins, such as idleness, tardiness, *lâchesse. . . .*" It also means *ennui,* the French brand of philosophic boredom. When *accidie* grips him, you feel that Orson has given up people; that he has already seen everything on earth he will ever want to see, and met everyone he will ever want to meet. Faced with that suggestion, however, he will suddenly revive and deny it; Isak Dinesen, Chou En-lai, and Robert Graves are three people he venerates and would adore to meet, if only he felt less intimidated by the prospect. Soon his spirits are soaring, and he is telling you that the only hope for American drama lies (as well it may) in theatres outside New York, municipally supported so that every year they can present their best productions for a short season on Broadway. You feel kindled by his presence, by his mastery of rhetoric, by his uncalculating generosity. "A superb bravura director," I once called him, "a fair bravura actor, and a limited bravura writer; but an incomparable bravura personality." Orson is a genius without portfolio. When he leaves a room, something irreplaceable and life-enhancing goes with him; something that may eventually install him, given luck and our help, in the special pantheon whose other occupants are Stanislavsky, Gordon Craig, Max Reinhardt, Jacques Copeau, and Bertolt Brecht.

The Kane Mutiny

by PETER BOGDANOVICH

In an international poll taken in 1962 by the leading film quarterly, *Sight and Sound*, Orson Welles' *Citizen Kane* was ranked above such masterpieces as *Greed* and *Potemkin*, the vote placing it first among all the great films ever made. The same magazine took a similar poll ten years later and though other films on the list had changed, *Kane* once again came first. In fact, this year another Welles film, *The Magnificent Ambersons*, was also included in the top ten of all time, and Welles was voted the greatest director in movie history. Back in 1963, Jean-Luc Godard succinctly expressed the sentiment of most contemporary directors: "All of us will always owe him everything."

Personally I don't think *Citizen Kane* is the greatest movie ever made. Orson Welles himself has made better films. Of course, this is a matter of opinion, but that *Kane* represents an important landmark in film history is not really open to dispute. When the shooting script was finally published last year (by Little, Brown) as a lavishly illustrated $15.00 volume, the task of writing the 50,000-word introduction in what must surely remain a standard book in its field was given to Miss Pauline Kael. This might have been considered as an exciting and difficult challenge to be met with respect, if not for the subject, at least for the facts pertaining to it. Miss Kael made peculiar uses of her opportunity. What she produced (it was first printed some months before in *The New Yorker*) is so loaded with error and faulty supposition presented as fact that it would require at least as many words as were at her disposal to correct, disprove, and properly refute it. Very little has been done about that.

Reprinted by permission of Esquire *Magazine.* © *1972 by Esquire, Inc. Slightly revised by the author.*

In film magazines there have been one or two short pieces. Andrew Sarris disagreed angrily in *The Village Voice*, and, in London's, *The Observer*, Kenneth Tynan wrote, uneasily, "The Kael version leaves too many queries unanswered." This is putting it mildly. Ken Russell (in *Books and Bookmen*) was more forthright: "All directors are the same, she screams, they always steal the poor screenwriter's credit. . . ." It has not escaped Russell that, over the years, Miss Kael has been writing against those of her fellow critics, like Sarris (and he is now in the majority), who believe that when a film aspires to the level of art, the man in charge of its making, the director, must be held responsible for the result and praised or blamed accordingly. Miss Kael would have it otherwise. By taking a great director (Welles) and seeking to prove that a great film of his (*Kane*) was actually the creation of an "old-time" screenwriter (Herman J. Mankiewicz), a member and product of the old Hollywood system, she clearly hopes to demolish this idea forever.

Welles was a shrewd choice. He's somebody people love to attack, anyway. Whether he deserves all that kicking around is another matter of opinion. It may easily be argued that he brings it on himself, and just as easily that it's not only in Hollywood that the price of real stature in a man is the eager venom with which others try to cut him down. For over three years now I've been working on a book about Welles, not so much straining for new aesthetic evaluations, but quite simply, trying to pin down what can be documented as the truth about his career to date as a filmmaker. Not an easy job, but, nearing the end of it, I think I can state with some authority that Ken Russell does not exaggerate when he calls Miss Kael's article "Hedda Hopperish and Louella Parsonish." Strong words, but, unfortunately, Miss Kael does indeed manage to reach the level of the old gossipmongers when she claims that Mankiewicz, the credited co-author of the *Kane* script, "was blackmailed into sharing credit with Welles." Equally strong words, and the bitter fact is that in the published version of his own film Welles stands accused of being, in effect, a liar and a thief. Well, either he is or he isn't.

Miss Kael passes on a particularly scabrous anecdote from screenwriter Nunnally Johnson, who, she says, told her Mankiewicz had once told him that Welles had offered a $10,000 bribe to Mankiewicz to leave his name off the screen. To speculate that Johnson, an able scenarist, may feel (as so many others do) justifiably bitter about the degree of credit directors are often given at the writers' expense, would probably be playing Miss Kael's guessing game. But Johnson's reply to her when she asked him if he actually believed this piece of gossip speaks for itself. Said Johnson: *"I like to believe he did"* (italics mine). Charles Lederer, another screenwriter, one of the best and wittiest, and an intimate friend of Mankiewicz's, told me *he* didn't believe this story for a minute. But Miss Kael, like Johnson, *would* "like to believe it," and leaves this ugly little rumor unresearched but on the record.

As far as books are concerned, this has been a bad year for Orson Welles. His ex-partner, John Houseman, has published *Run-Through: A Memoir* (Simon and Schuster). Written with great urbanity, it presents a portrait of Welles calculated to impress you as a fair and friendly view of an unstable egomaniac, a sympathetic picture of an unsympathetic subject. This is accomplished with the highest skill. Only careful reading, backed up, in my own case, by not a little research, reveals what I believe to be the truth, not only about Welles, but about Houseman.

But we'll get back to Houseman later, since he is most certainly involved in Pauline Kael's righteous indignation with Welles for supposedly not giving other writers their due. Incidentally, she would seem to have no compunction about doing the same thing herself. The Chairman of the Critical Studies Program at U.C.L.A., Dr. Howard Suber, who conducted a seminar on *Citizen Kane* in 1968, did very thorough research on the film and its various extant drafts. Because, at one point, they were to collaborate in writing the prefatory material to the published screenplay, Miss Kael had full access to this material. She takes full credit for whatever use she made of it, and gives none at all to Dr. Suber.

What upsets Suber, however, are Miss Kael's conclusions: "After months of investigation," he told me, "I regard the authorship of *Kane* as a very open question. Unfortunately, both sides would have to be consulted, and Miss Kael never spoke to Mr. Welles, which, as I see it, violates all the principles of historical research." True enough. In preparing a lengthy introduction to *Citizen Kane*, which was less a critical assessment than a purported history of the making of the film, Miss Kael did not trouble to obtain even a brief statement from the director-producer-co-author-star of the picture. She quotes Welles only from other (unspecified) sources, laying special emphasis on his general denigration of Mankiewicz's importance to the picture.

OW: Mankiewicz's contribution? It was enormous.

That comes from the tape of an interview I had with Welles in 1968. The following quotes were all tape-recorded well *before* the Kael articles were published. Welles had agreed to talk to me for a book after I managed to persuade him that because so much of what has been written about his working life is based on empty legend, it was time to try to get it right at last. Many of my early questions had to do with remarks of his quoted in newspapers and magazines. Some, he said, were misquotes, others sheer invention. I have only his word for this, but having been through my own share of interviews lately, I must say that there is often a very sizable gap between what is said and what is printed. (Welles once told me that since the advent of the talk shows, there isn't much point in giving print interviews any longer because on TV you can at least be sure what you say is what reaches the public.)

PB: You want to talk about him [Mankiewicz]?

OW: I'd love to. I loved *him.* People did. He was much admired, you know.

PB: Except for his part in the writing of the *Kane* script. . . . Well, I've read the list of his other credits. . . . *[Even Miss Kael has to admit that most of this list is, in her own words, "embarrassing."]*

OW: Oh, the hell with lists—a lot of bad writers have wonderful credits.

PB: Can you explain that?

OW: Luck. The lucky bad writers got good directors who could write. Some of these, like Hawks and McCarey, wrote very well indeed. Screenwriters didn't like that at all. Think of those old pros in the film factories. They had to punch in every morning, and sit all day in front of their typewriters in those terrible "writers' buildings." The way they saw it, the director was even worse than the producer, because in the end, what really mattered in moving pictures, of course, was the man actually making the pictures. The big studio system often made writers feel like second-class citizens— no matter how good the money was. They laughed it off, of course, and provided a good deal of the best fun—when Hollywood, you understand, was still a funny place. But basically, you know, a lot of them were pretty bitter and miserable. And nobody was *more* miserable, *more* bitter and *funnier* than Mank. . . . A perfect monument of self-destruction. But, you know, when the bitterness wasn't focused straight onto you—he was the best company in the world.

This is a fair sample of Welles' feeling about Mankiewicz as expressed in many interviews we did, taped in various parts of the world in 1968, 1969, and 1970. During one session we got to talking about the scene in *Kane* between Bernstein (played by Everett Sloane) and the reporter (Bill Alland):

OW: That was *all* Mank—it's my favorite scene.

PB: And the story about the girl: "One day, back in 1896, I was crossing over to Jersey on a ferry . . . there was another ferry . . . and a girl waiting to get off. A white dress she had on. . . . I only saw her for a second, but I'll bet a month hasn't gone by since that I haven't thought of that girl. . . ."

OW: It goes longer than that.

PB: Yes, but who wrote it?

OW: Mankiewicz, and it's the best thing in the movie. "A month hasn't gone by that I haven't thought of that girl." That's Mankiewicz. I *wish* it was me.

PB: Great scene.

OW: If I were in hell and they gave me a day off and said what part of any movie you ever made do you want to see, I'd say that scene of Mank's about Bernstein. All the rest could have been better, but that was just right.

Of course, since Mankiewicz is dead, it is impossible to ascertain his definitive opinion of the movie, but it's interesting to compare Welles' affectionate gratitude for the Bernstein-reporter scene with Mankiewicz's own reaction to this sequence (and to some others) during the shooting of the film. A memo, dated August 26, 1940, from Herbert Drake, Mercury Productions' Press Agent:

RE: . . . TELEPHONE CONVERSATION WITH HERMAN J. MANKIEWICZ RE CUT STUFF HE SAW . . .

1. In Bernstein's office with Bill Alland: Everett Sloane is an unsympathetic looking man, and anyway you shouldn't have two Jews in one scene.
2. Dorothy Comingore [as Susan Alexander Kane] looks much better now so Mr. M. suggests you re-shoot the Atlantic City cabaret scene. [Miss Comingore had been carefully made up to look as badly as possible.]
3. There are not enough standard movie conventions being observed, including too few close-ups and very little evidence of action. *It is too much like a play,* says Mr. M. [italics mine].

Contrary to what Miss Kael would have us believe, Mankiewicz was more than a little concerned about the Welles version of the screenplay. Charles Lederer described it to me: "Manky was always complaining and sighing about Orson's changes. And I heard from Benny [Hecht] too, that Manky was terribly upset. But, you see, Manky was a great *paragrapher*—he wasn't really a picture writer. I read *his* script of the film—the long one called *America*—before Orson really got to changing it and making his version of it—and I thought it was pretty dull."

Miss Kael turns this incident into a key event: the direct cause of the fracas that very nearly led to the film's being suppressed. Hearst's mistress was the actress Marion Davies (a good portion of Miss Kael's attacks on the film are aimed at those places where it departs from the real Hearst-Davies story) and Mankiewicz asked Lederer, who was Miss Davies' nephew, to read his script and tell him if he thought the principals, particularly his aunt, would be angry with him about it.

Miss Kael writes that after reading it, Lederer was extremely concerned, as a result of which the Hearst lawyers were finally called in. "That," Lederer told me, "is 100 percent, whole cloth lying." He did not, as Miss Kael claims (she never bothered to check with him), give the script to Miss Davies: "I gave it *back* to *him*. He asked me if I thought Marion would be offended and I said I didn't think so. The script I read didn't have any flavor of Marion and Hearst—Robert McCormick was the man it was about." McCormick, the Chicago press lord, divorced his first wife, Edith Rockefeller, and married Gauma Walska, whom he tried to push into prominence as an opera star. Kane divorces his first wife (the daughter of an American president) and tries to make Susan Alexander an opera star. Miss Kael barely mentions this obvious parallel, and the weight of her piece plays it down. It should be clear that the story of the Chicago press lord and his fairly untalented mistress contributed even more to Kane's personal story than did Hearst's backing of the delightful screen comedienne Marion Davies often was.

Lederer went on: "Also, I knew Marion would never read it. As I said, it [Mankiewicz's script] was pretty dull—which is not to say that I thought the picture was dull. Orson vivified the material, changed it a lot, and I believe transcended it with his direction. There *were* things in it that were based on Hearst and Marion—the jigsaw puzzles, Marion's drinking—though this was played up more in the movie than in the script I read, probably because it was a convenient peg for the girl's characterization. You see, Manky had just been out to the ranch [San Simeon, which became Xanadu in the movie], and was a great admirer of Hearst—he thought Hearst was marvelous, and certainly didn't want to forfeit his entree there. . . . Then, later, when those people currying Hearst's favor got into the act—Louella Parsons, Bill Hearst, Jr.—and caused a fuss (I really don't believe W.R. ever gave a damn) I think Orson began to *encourage* the Hearst reference. He's a showman, after all. Instead of being annoyed, he was delighted that Hearst might be offended, and went along with the bad joke."

Welles gives a similar impression:

PB: Can we talk a little about Hearst's intervention in *Kane*. . . .

OW: He didn't really intervene—they intervened in his behalf. It began badly because Louella Parsons had been on the set and had written a wonderful article about this lovely picture I was making. . . . And it was Hedda Hopper, her old enemy, who blew the whistle. Think of the weapon that gave to the competition! After that it was the Hearst hatchetmen who were after me—more than the old man himself. Hollywood was scared to death; they were ready to burn the film—anything.

PB: But wasn't Hedda Hopper supposedly your friend?

OW: Sure—but what a break for her as a newspaper woman. Couldn't blame her. Imagine what that did to Louella!

PB: After *Kane*, you once said, "Some day, if Mr. Hearst isn't frightfully careful, I'm going to make a film that's really based on his life."

OW: Well, you know, the real story of Hearst is quite different from Kane's. And Hearst, himself—as a *man,* I mean—he was *very* different. There's all that stuff about McCormick and the opera. I drew a lot from that—from my Chicago days. . . . And Samuel Insull. . . . As for Marion, she was an extraordinary woman—nothing like the character Dorothy Comingore played in the movie. I always felt he had the right to be upset about that.

PB: Davies was actually quite a good actress.

OW: And a fine woman. She pawned all her jewels for the old man when he was broke. Or broke enough to need a lot of cash. She gave him everything. Stayed by him. Just the opposite to Susan. *That* was the libel. In other words, Kane was better than Hearst, and Marion was much better than Susan—whom people wrongly equated with her.

PB: You said once that Kane would have enjoyed seeing a film based on his life, but not Hearst.

OW: Well, that's what I said to Hearst.

PB: When!?

OW: I found myself alone with him in an elevator in the Fairmont Hotel on the night *Kane* was opening in San Francisco. He and my father had been chums, so I introduced myself and asked him if he'd like to come to the opening of the picture. He didn't answer. And as he was getting off at his floor, I said, "Charles Foster Kane would have *accepted.*" No reply. . . . And Kane *would* have, you know. That was his style—just as he finished Jed Leland's bad review of Susan as an opera singer. . . .

This next is from a later interview in the same year (1969):

PB: Isn't Bernstein named after your guardian, *Doctor* Bernstein?

OW: That was a family joke. I sketched out the character in our preliminary sessions—Mank did all the best writing for Bernstein. I'd call that *the* most valuable thing he gave us. . . .

PB: And Jed Leland [the character played by Joseph Cotten]?

OW: Well, Jed was really based on a close childhood friend of mine—George Stevens' uncle, Ashton Stevens. He was practically my uncle, too.

Miss Kael makes much of the fact that Hearst drama critic Ashton Stevens knew Mankiewicz, claiming that he supplied the writer with many great Hearst stories. She mentions, but only in passing, that Welles knew Stevens, too. The following, from Stevens' newspaper column, was written in 1930, when Orson was fifteen years old. It appeared in Hearst's Chicago paper, *The Daily American*: ". . . Orson Welles is as likely as not to become my favorite actor. . . . I am going to put a clipping of this paragraph in my betting book. If Orson is not at least a leading man by the time it has yellowed, I'll never make another prophecy."

PB: Did you tell Stevens the character was based on him?

OW: Oh, God, he could see it—I didn't have to *tell* him. I sent him the script before we began, of course, and while he was visiting me on the coast I brought him on the set during shooting. Later he saw the movie and thought the old man would be thrilled by it. As it turned out, after *Kane* was released, Ashton was forbidden by his Hearst editors to even mention my name. . . . What I knew about Hearst came even more from him than from my father—though my father did know him well. There was a long story about putting a chamber pot on a flag pole, things like that. . . . But I didn't get too much from *that* source. My father and Hearst were only close as young swingers. But Ashton had taught Hearst to play the banjo, which is how he first got to be a drama critic, and, you know, Ashton really was one of the great ones. The last of the dandies—he worked for Hearst for some fifty years or so—and adored him. . . . A gentleman . . . very much like Jed.

PB: Jed Leland is really not all that endearing a character—I mean, you like him but finally one's sympathies somehow are with Kane in the scene where he attacks Kane so strongly.

OW: Well, you know—when a man takes a stand on some question of principle at the expense of a personal friendship, the sympathy has to go to the victim of the righteousness, now doesn't it?

In taking Welles and Mankiewicz to task for presuming to make changes in the real Hearst story to suit their own purposes in *Kane*, Miss Kael's reasoning is pretty difficult to follow. What they were setting out to write was not a biographical movie, so what possible obligation could there be for sticking to facts? They were writing fiction; it is Miss Kael who is supposed to be writing history.

Taking a sample almost at random, from this Kael version of history, we have her statement that the opera sequence in *Kane* actually derived from the Marx Brothers. (Mankiewicz, she points out meaningfully, had been taking off *A Night at the Opera*.) Susan was supposed to have been singing *Thaïs*, but this was changed, she says, to save the composer's fee, and *another* composer, Bernard Herrmann, was commissioned to write a new opera, which was ultimately called *Salammbo* in the film.

Herrmann was interviewed in the Spring '72 issue of *Sight and Sound*, along with George Coulouris (who played Thatcher in *Kane*), about their reactions to Miss Kael's piece. Coulouris characterized a good part of it as "twaddle," Herrmann as "rubbish," but specifically concerning the opera sequences, Herrmann said, "Pauline Kael was never in touch with me while her book was being written. . . . If the rest of her opinions are as accurate as her statements about the music, none of it is to be taken very seriously. . . . It had nothing to do with the Brothers Marx."

If Miss Kael had consulted the Mercury files, she might have found the following rather revealing telegram from Welles, dated July 18, 1940, just a few days before shooting began on *Kane*:

To: Mr. Benny Herrmann
    Columbia Broadcasting System
    New York City, New York
. . . Opera sequence is early in shooting, so must have fully orchestrated recorded track before shooting. Susie sings as curtain goes up in first act, and I believe there is no opera of importance where soprano leads with chin like this. Therefore suggest it be original . . . by you—parody on typical Mary Garden vehicle. . . . Suggest *Salambo* which gives us phony production scene of Ancient Rome and Carthage, and Susie can dress like Grand Opera neoclassic courtesan. . . . Here is chance for you to do something witty and amusing—and now is the time for you to do it. I love you dearly.

                                        Orson

Film directors are taken to task in the Kael article for claiming in interviews to have taken some part in writing their films when they did not receive screenplay credit. She quotes a story of Howard Hawks', which, by the way, she got (without giving the source) from an interview I did with him. Hawks had told me he was reading with a girl friend the Hecht-MacArthur play, *The Front Page*, and that he'd asked her to read the reporter's part, which was written originally for a man, while he read the editor. He said, "Hell, it's better between a girl and a man, than between two men," so he decided to do the film that way—it became *His Girl Friday*. Miss Kael doesn't really want to believe this anecdote: "Nothing but a charming and superficial story." Hawks told me when I checked recently, "It happened all right—I wouldn't make up as lousy a story as that." Which brings us back to Charles Lederer, who, as it happened, did the script for *His Girl Friday*, and says that Hawks' story is absolutely true. "Howard *sold* the project on the basis of that," he told me. In this context, Miss Kael makes a declaration which is, to say the least, ironic: "Young interviewers," she writes, ". . . don't bother to check the statements of their subjects—they seem to regard that as outside their province. . . ."

The following was recorded in 1969:

PB: I'm sorry—*Kane* again. . . .

OW: O.K., O.K.

PB: How did the story begin?

OW: I'd been nursing an old notion—the idea of telling the same thing several times—and showing exactly the same scene from wholly different points of view. Basically, the idea *Rashomon* used later on. . . . Mank liked it, so we started searching for the man it was going to be about. Some big American figure—couldn't be a politician, because you'd have to pinpoint him. . . . Howard Hughes was the first idea. But we got pretty quickly to the press lords.

PB: The first drafts were in separate versions, so when was the whole construction of the script—the intricate flashback pattern—worked out between you?

OW: The actual writing came only after lots of talk, naturally. . . . Just the two of us, yelling at each other—not too angrily.

PB: What about the *Rashomon* idea? It's still there to a degree.

OW: It withered away from what was originally intended. I wanted the man to seem a very different person depending on who was talking about him. Rosebud was Mank's and the many-sided gimmick was mine. Rosebud remained, because it was the only way we could find to get off, as they used to say in vaudeville. It manages to work, but I'm still not too keen about it, and I don't think that he was, either. The whole schtick is the sort of thing that can finally date in some funny way.

PB: Toward the close you have the reporter say that it doesn't matter what it means?

OW: We did everything we could to take the mickey out of it.

PB: The reporter says at the end: ". . . Charles Foster Kane was a man who got everything he wanted, and then lost it. Maybe Rosebud was something he couldn't get or something he lost, but it wouldn't have explained anything. . . ."

OW: I guess you might call that a disclaimer—a bit corny, too. . . . More than a bit. And it's mine, I'm afraid.

PB: I read the script that went into production . . . there were so many things you changed on the set, or anyway, after you'd started shooting. . . . From the point of view of Kane's character, one of the most interesting is the scene where you're remaking the front page for about the twentieth time. In the script, Kane is arrogant and rather nasty to the typesetter. In the movie he's very nice, even rather sweet. How did that evolve?

OW: Well, all he *had* was charm—besides the money. He was one of those amiable, rather likable monsters who was able to command people's allegiance for a time without giving too much in return. Certainly not love; he was raised by a bank, remember. He uses charm the way such people often do. So when he changes the front page, of course—it's done on the basis of a sort of charm, rather than real conviction. He didn't have any. . . . Charley Kane was a maneater.

PB: Well, why was it in the script the other way?

OW: I found out more about the character as I went along.

PB: And what were the reactions of Mankiewicz to these changes?

OW: Well, he only came once to the set for a visit. Or, just maybe, it was twice. . . .

[Sometime after this conversation I turned up the memo quoted earlier, in which Mankiewicz comments on the rushes.]

PB: Before shooting began, how were differences about the script worked out between you?

OW: That's why I left him on his own finally, because we'd started to waste too much time haggling. So, after mutual agreements on storyline and character, Mank went off with Houseman and did his version, while I stayed in Hollywood and wrote mine. At the end, naturally, I was the one who was making the picture, after all—who had to make the decisions. I used what I wanted of Mank's and, rightly or wrongly, kept what I liked of my own.

PB: And that was it?

OW: That was it.

PB: What about Houseman?

OW: Yes, what about Houseman.

We'll get to that later.

"The revisions made by Welles were not limited to mere general suggestions, but included the actual rewriting of words, dialogue, changing of sequences, ideas, and characterizations, and also the elimination and addition of certain scenes." I am quoting the associate producer of *Citizen Kane*, Mr. Richard Barr. (He is now the president of the League of New York Theaters and the producer of all the Edward Albee plays, among many others.)

This (and the preceding) is from an affidavit Barr swore out in May 1941 concerning the writing of *Kane* (the necessity for this document had arisen from trouble—or the threat of it—from the Hearst powers): "Mankiewicz was engaged by Mercury or RKO for the purpose of *assisting* [italics mine] in writing a script. . . ." Miss Kael failed to interview Welles' secretary. Her name is Katherine Trosper and she was with him from the rough-draft beginnings, through the final "mix" of the finished print of the film. Is there a better witness? Not for Miss Kael's purpose. She prefers to take on face value a statement by Mankiewicz's secretary that "Orson Welles never wrote (or dictated) one word of *Citizen Kane*." This secretary was employed by Mankiewicz when he was working quite separately, in another part of California, where he was sent by

Welles to put together his own draft of a shooting script, based on their meetings together. She could have had no knowledge of Welles' script; she was never present during the working meetings between the two, when the conception and basic shape of the story was developed, nor could she have known what happened to the Mankiewicz drafts *after* they were passed on to Welles, changed and rewritten by him, and incorporated in his own screenplay. When I repeated to Miss Trosper recently Miss Kael's assertion that Mankiewicz was the sole author of *Kane*, her answer was not a little derisive: "Then I'd like to know," she said, "what was all that stuff I was always typing for Mr. Welles!"

"It is not possible," says Mr. Barr in his affidavit, "to fix the actual number of complete redrafts [by Welles] as changes were being continuously made on portions that had previously been written." In my own conversations with Mr. Barr, he told me he remembered seeing Orson "fume about the pages that arrived from Mankiewicz. He thought a lot of it was dreadful." Barr says he, himself, was "in the room and *saw* . . ." the writing of various important scenes in the script. Miss Trosper agrees. "Orson was always writing and rewriting. I saw scenes written during production. Even while he was being made up, he'd be dictating dialogue."

Miss Trosper and Mr. Barr are active, in good health, accessible, and both are living, as Miss Kael does, in New York City. Neither received so much as an inquiry about their part in the making of *Citizen Kane*. But then, neither did Welles. In fact, there is nothing to show that Miss Kael interviewed anyone of real importance associated with the actual making of the film.

In 1940, the year before *Kane*, screenplay credit was given to a director or producer on only five pictures out of 590 released in the U.S. In two cases out of these five the producers (Gene Towne and Graham Baker) were script writers who had become producers and always wrote their own screenplays. Yet, Miss Kael maintains that it was not only easy, but common practice, for directors and producers to grab screenwriting credits that they didn't deserve, because at this period the real authors had no power to stop them. "That's one of the main reasons why the Screen Writers' guild was started," says Lederer. "But by the time of *Kane* it was quite effective in preventing that sort of thing. It had to be *proved* by them, as it does now, that the director or producer contributed *more* than

50 percent of the script." The *Kane* case never came before the Guild's Board. "If *Kane* had gone to arbitration," Lederer concludes, "Orson would certainly have won, and Manky must have known that."

Far from trying to bribe his co-author to consent to having his name taken off the screen, Welles, entirely on his own initiative, and not bound by any such contractual requirement, gave Mankiewicz top billing.

Miss Kael on cameraman Gregg Toland: "I think he not only provided the visual style of *Citizen Kane*, but was responsible for affecting the conception, and even for introducing a few elements that are not in the script. . . . I had always been puzzled by the fact that *Kane* seemed to draw not only on the Expressionist theatrical style of Welles' stage productions but on the German Expressionist and Gothic movies of the silent period." (It will be noticed that she mentions the whole body of Welles' theater work only in passing. A glance at photos of those stage productions reveals the same chiaroscuro evident throughout *Kane* and, indeed, in all his subsequent movies.) "I wondered," she continues, "what Welles was talking about when he said he had prepared for *Kane* by running John Ford's *Stagecoach* forty times. Even allowing for the hyperbole of the forty times. . . ." (She won't buy a single thing a director says! In fact, Orson looked at *Stagecoach* every night, and always, according to several whom I have interviewed, with a different member of his staff.) "Why," Miss Kael goes on, "should Orson Welles have studied *Stagecoach* and come up with a film that looked more like *The Cabinet of Dr. Caligari*?" (*Kane* actually resembles *Caligari* in no single image.) But in her role as aesthetic sleuth, she is now hot on the trail of what she calls "a link between Gregg Toland and the German tradition. . . ." She looks up Toland's credits and a little 1935 quickie called *Mad Love*, starring Peter Lorre, and directed by the famous German cameraman Karl Freund, "rings a bell." She looks at the film again, and concludes: ". . . The resemblances to *Citizen Kane* are even greater than my memories of it suggested. Not only is the large room with the fireplace at Xanadu similar to Lorre's domain as a mad doctor, with similar lighting and similar placement of figures, but Kane's appearance and make-up . . . might be a facsimile of Lorre's. . . . And, amusingly, that screeching white cockatoo, which wasn't in the script of *Kane* but appeared out of nowhere in the movie to provide an extra 'touch,' is a regular member of Lorre's household. . . . [Therefore] Toland probably suggested the make-up and the doll-like, jerky use of the body of Kane in his rage and as a lonely old man, and, having enjoyed the flamboyant photographic effect of the cockatoo in *Mad Love*, suggested that, too. . . . Toland . . . had passed on Freund's techniques to Welles."

I ran *Mad Love* the other night. Lorre's head is shaved; Welles, playing the older Kane, is naturally slightly bald—there the resemblance stops dead. Orson had had his greatest successes in the theatre playing old men. His first professional triumph, at the age of sixteen, was as a seventy-year-old duke in *Jew Suss*, and when he made the cover of *Time* (almost three years before *Citizen Kane*) it was in his old-age make-up for Captain Shotover in his own production of Shaw's *Heartbreak House*. Cameramen don't presume to teach actors how to act, and to suggest that Toland would have explained to Welles how to portray old age is malicious nonsense. The sets of *Mad Love*—which, by the way, has got to be one of the worst movies I've ever seen—suggest nothing of *Citizen Kane*, nor is there anything in the photography bearing the remotest similarity to Orson's work *or* Toland's. This is not surprising since Toland, far from being the sole cameraman on *Mad Love*, is listed *second* in the credits, after photographer Chester Lyons, who was responsible for most of the filming. Miss Kael avoids that bit of information.

We come now to the cockatoo—a fairly common exotic prop. In *Mad Love*, the bird is a household pet flapping about throughout the film. In *Kane* it shrieks across the screen for only one startling flash. During a taped interview (in 1969) I asked Orson why it was there.

OW: Wake 'em up.

PB: Literally?

OW: Yeah. Getting late in the evening, you know—time to brighten up anybody who might be nodding off [Laughs].

PB: It has no other purpose?

OW: Theatrical shock effect, if you want to be grand about it—you can say it's placed at a certain *musical* moment when I felt the need for something short and exclamatory. So it has a sort of purpose, but no *meaning*. What's fascinating, though, is that because of some accident in the trick department, you can see right through the bird's eye into the scenery behind.

PB: I always thought that was intentional.

OW: We don't know why it happened. Some accident—I'm very fond of parrots.

PB: There's one in *Mr. Arkadin* [a 1955 Welles film].

OW: Yeah—I have a wonderful one at home in Spain.

Welles never claimed to have prepared for *Kane* by studying *Stagecoach*; he used Ford's film to teach himself about movies in general. This notwithstanding, if Miss Kael had not been so busy sending us off on another wild parrot chase, she would have been better advised to compare the two pictures a few more times. Ford was obviously a greater influence on Welles than she noticed. *Stagecoach* is a surprisingly dark western, there are several quite stylized photographic sequences, and at least one set with a low, claustrophobic ceiling: *Kane* was much praised for bringing ceilings into pictures for the first time. (Something which makes Orson wince when he hears it, because he knows better. He just used more of them and shot them more often.)

PB: Some people have said that the look of *Citizen Kane* is a result of Gregg Toland's photography, but all your pictures have the same visual signature, and you only worked with Toland once. . . .

OW: It's impossible to say how much I owe to Gregg. He was superb.

Miss Kael gives us a different picture of Welles' attitude toward his collaborators. Having interviewed him rather exhaustively—returning many times over the years to the subject of *Kane*—I can report that I have never caught him with a single ungenerous word for all those who helped him in the making of the picture. He gives great credit to his art director, Perry Ferguson, to the composer Bernard Herrmann (an old collaborator), to his make-up man— even to a grip named Red who thought up a funny piece of business—and finally to the then-head of RKO, George Schaefer, who, Orson told me, thought up the title, *Citizen Kane*. He makes much of his luck in having these people at his side, but the fact remains, of course, that the movie is stamped with Welles' personality and obsessions, something that can be seen only through an examination of the movies he made afterward (and which has, in fact, been done in numerous articles and several full-length books).

OW: You know how I happened to get to work with Gregg? He was, just then, the number one cameraman in the world and I found him sitting out in the waiting room of my office. "My name's Toland," he said, "and I want you to use me on your picture." I asked him why, and he said he's seen some of our plays in New York. He asked me who did the lighting. I told him in the theater most directors have a lot to do with it (and they used to, back then), and he said, "Well, fine. I want to work with somebody who never made a movie." Now partly because of that, I somehow assumed that movie lighting was supervised by movie *directors*. And, like a damned fool, for the first few days of *Kane* I "supervised" like crazy. Behind me, of course, Gregg was balancing lights and telling everybody to shut their faces. He was angry when somebody finally came to me and said, "You know, that's really supposed to be Mr. Toland's job."

PB: You mean he was protecting you?

OW: Yes! He was quietly fixing it so as many of my notions as possible would work. Later he told me, "That's the only way to learn anything—from somebody who doesn't know anything." And, by the way, Gregg was also the *fastest* cameraman who ever lived, and used fewer lights. And he had this extraordinary crew—his own men. You never heard a sound on a Toland set, except what came from the actors or the director. There was never a voice raised; only signs given. Almost Germanic—it was so hushed. Everybody wore neckties. Sounds depressing, but we had a jazz combo to keep our spirits up.

PB: Toland didn't mind that?

OW: Not so you could notice. With all his discipline, he was easy-going and quite a swinger off the set.

PB: How did you get along with him after you found out that the lighting was his job?

OW: Wonderfully. I started asking for lots of strange, new things—depth-of-focus and so on. . . .

PB: An elementary question: why did you *want* so much depth-of-focus?

OW: Well, in life you see everything in focus at the same time, so why not in the movies? We used split-screen sometimes, but mostly a wide-angle lens, lots of juice, and stopped way the hell down. We called it 'pan focus' in some idiot interview—just for the fun of it—

PB: Didn't mean anything?

OW: Of course not; but for quite awhile that word kept turning up in books and high-brow articles—as though there really *was* something you could do called 'pan focusing.' . . . Christ, he was the greatest gift any director—young or old—could ever, ever have. And he never tried to impress us that he was doing any miracles. He just went ahead and performed them. *Fast.* I was calling for things only a beginner would have been ignorant enough to think anybody could ever do, and there he was, *doing* them. His whole point was, "There's no mystery to it." He said, "*You* can be a cameraman, too—in a couple of days I can teach you everything that matters." So we spent the next weekend together and he showed me the inside of that bag of tricks, and, like all good magic, the secrets are ridiculously simple. Well, that was Gregg for you—that was how big he was. Can you imagine somebody they now call 'a director of photography' coming right out and admitting you can bone up on the basic technical side of it all in a weekend? Like magic again: the secret of the trick is nothing; what counts is not the mechanics, but how you can make 'em work.

In the Kael version of this, Welles is shown to be arrogantly contemptuous of the whole canon of film technique, boasting that he was smart enough to pick it all up in a couple of days.

PB: You gave Toland credit on the same card with yourself.

OW: Up till then, cameramen were listed with about eight other names. Nobody those days—only the stars, the director, and the producer—got separate cards. Gregg deserved it, didn't he?

"There's the scene of Welles eating in the newspaper office," writes Miss Kael, "which was obviously *caught* by the camera crew" [italics mine] "and which, to be 'a good sport' he had to use." To imagine that a sequence so meticulously timed, involving several players and lasting, without a cut, for a full minute of interaction and movement within a fixed camera frame could possibly have been "caught" without Welles even realizing he was being photographed betrays a terrifying ignorance of the A-B-C's of how movies are made. The scene seems so spontaneous—it couldn't possibly have been *staged* by Welles—it had to be a trick somebody else played on him.

Pushing on with her case against Welles, and giving away as many of the other credits in his career as she can manage, Miss Kael attributes merely a director's clever "touch" to Welles' role in the celebrated 1938 Martian radio broadcast. She accuses him of hogging all the kudos for *The War of the Worlds*, the script for which was written by Howard Koch. Now this was Welles' own show— just as "The Jack Benny Program" or "The Bob Hope Show" belonged to Benny and Hope, and as "The Lux Radio Theatre" belonged to C. B. DeMille. With an hour to fill every week, he worked, as they did, with a staff of writers. When the media descended on him after the broadcast had caused a nationwide furor, it was naturally assumed that, like Benny, Hope or DeMille, he was responsible for his own show. Questions about the broadcast were naturally concerned with its producer and star performer, but the point is that the great majority of voices were raised in *protest, not praise.* If Welles had insisted that a man called Koch had done the radio script, he would not have been sharing the applause but passing on the blame. When excerpts from the show were published, however, Koch was given his full credit, and Welles has always emphasized the importance of his other collaborators, in particular Paul Stewart, who directed rehearsals of all the shows up to the day of the broadcast.

Miss Kael glosses over the following point in an ambiguous parenthetical aside: "He [Koch] says it was, however, Welles' idea that he do the Martian show in the form of radio bulletins." This is a meaningless sentence for those unfamiliar with the broadcast, and easily missed by those why may vaguely remember it now. Listen to it, though—the recording is for sale—and you will see that it is precisely this conception which was the guide for the dialogue, radio effects, the whole organization of the material. It is the heart of the matter. Everyone connected with the show—including John Houseman—has gone on record that it was Welles, and this basic conception of his, which was responsible for making it come off in the way it did. Listen to the show now and try to imagine what it

would have been like done straight—not as a series of news
bulletins, but simply as a radio play—rather old-fashioned science
fiction. Certainly it would never have caused even a backward child
to go running out into the streets in panic, nor to make radio history
as it did.

Miss Kael is nothing if not an entertaining writer, and she clearly
invested a good deal of effort in her piece; the result is lively and
readable fiction. She obviously has high regard for *Kane*—no one
spends 50,000 words on an insignificant work—and there are
several complimentary paragraphs on Welles as a director. Nonetheless, despite everything, the weight of her piece is reportage, not
criticism, and in the latter department I cannot help feeling that
though, as I said earlier, there are greater films than *Kane*, there is
surely something more to be said than that it is "dramatic fun," or
the "culmination (of) Thirties' comedy" (of all things), "comic-strip
tragic," "Pop Gothic," or, the archetypal Kael phrase, "*Kitsch*
redeemed." (The Kitsch in *Kane*, of course, and the Pop Gothic are
no accidents of taste, but a deliberate social comment by Welles.)
She brusquely dismisses the books that have been written about the
picture, and, in particular, the writings of those despised young film
enthusiasts who see something more in movies than what she
characterizes as gimmicks, tricks, and cleverness.

"I found it easy," Orson writes me in a recent letter from Spain,
"to heed your advice about not sending to America for Jack
Houseman's autobiography. My mood is less delicately melancholy
than you seem to fear—I'm too busy, thank Christ—but you do
have a point: a guided tour with Houseman over the same old Kael
country might be depressing."

I'm afraid "Kael country" was Houseman country to begin with;
the debt she owes him as a guide must be incalculable. In putting
forward these conclusions I may seem to be borrowing something
from Miss Kael, who delivers her wildest guesses in the style of some
master sleuth in the last chapter of an old-fashioned mystery story.
But her case against Welles had to have had a beginning
somewhere.

For many years now, Houseman has been actively promoting the
picture of Welles as a credit-thief, and had been in print to that
effect long before Miss Kael took up the cry. It was for this

reason—when I mentioned his recently published autobiography to Orson in a letter of my own—I suggested he avoid it. I knew how the first of the Kael articles in *The New Yorker* (he never read the second) had affected him. He was getting a new picture together in Arizona, and the people there told me what a shock it had been for him.

"Why, then—," he writes, with some justice, "did you send me that piece of Virgil's?" [A review of Houseman's book by Virgil Thomson, in *The New York Review of Books*, which generally confirmed and endorsed the author's view of Welles.] "What useful comment can be expected from me? I'll have to leave Virgil to you, and you'll probably want to leave him alone. After all, we can't take on *everybody*. He's always been formidable, and here I'm sure he thinks he's being quite scrupulously just. And, as Jack's oldest friend, I guess he is.

"By the way, there was another review of Jack's book in one of the magazines—just two paragraphs—of which one was exclusively given over to that currently celebrated scene Houseman must have described in which I'm supposed to have hurled a chafing dish and a whole lot of other firey furniture at my ex-partner. In its time, you can bet the back room at Chasen's [restaurant] saw much better fight scenes than that one. . . . Think of one small can of sterno making it between hard covers in two expensive books thirty years afterwards!" [The affair of the chafing dish is also dramatized by Miss Kael.] "Not that I'm proud of the incident," Orson goes on, "but I ask you to believe that at a range of three yards—if I'd been *aiming* at Houseman—the target would have been hit. What I am rather ashamed of is a certain lurking touch of cold-bloodedness beneath that slightly theatrical fury. The act itself didn't really amount to much. A restaurant service trolley was indeed, very lamentably, tossed over and the heater under the dish landed by a curtain. After a squirt or two from a soda syphon the threat of fire ceased to alarm even Jack. He has many qualities, but courage, and in particular the physical variety, is not the most fully developed. And that, I'm afraid, is what I was banking on. The chafing dish put him onto the next train for New York. The Kael version has me rushing after him and wheedling him into coming back to our aid in California. The truth (which has just got to sound patronizing) is not that we needed him, but that he needed the bread. Or could use it. Or so I thought. As it turned out, he was quite wonderfully helpful with Mank. Not just keeping him dried out, but also making, I'm sure, real contributions to Mank's part in the script-writing. But the business with the canned heat was *not,* as Pauline Kael insists, anybody's inspiration for Kane's busting up Susan's boudoir. I lifted that one from an old play of mine called *Last Stand*—a sort of rough sketch for *Kane* about the boss of a kind of King Ranch who (like Kane) fights a losing battle against the twentieth century, breaks up some furniture, and breaks down himself in the process.

"What did distress me in Virgil's piece was his declaration that he and I didn't much like each other. ['I never liked Welles much, nor he me.'] Then he mentions that I once came to his aid in Paris during rehearsals of his opera, *Four Saints in Three Acts.* That was years after the Mercury; and why does he suppose I did that, if I wasn't fond of him? I was and am. I've spent my life in the blissful assumption that my friendships are mostly requited. Better not peer too closely into that. I'm going to go on clinging to the myth that I'm almost as popular with people as they are with me. So you take on Virgil yourself, if you've got room for him. . . ."

Frankly admitting to a personal antipathy for Welles, Thomson, in his review of Houseman's book, very fairly assigns the functions provided by the two partners in the Mercury Theatre. "Welles," he writes, "was full of striking production ideas, designed the lay-out of his own stage sets, discovered many an unknown actor, and made him famous—Joseph Cotten, for instance, and Hiram Sherman—*directed all the plays* [italics mine] and often acted in them." Houseman, on the other hand, "ran the office. . . ."

Thomson, of course, has more than this to say in behalf of his good friend ("sturdy qualities," for instance, and "practical intelligence"), but of Welles, he uses the word "genius." He then goes on to speak of Orson's having "accepted full credit" for what he calls his and Houseman's "joint work." Having climbed and tunneled through mountains of press material covering those theater years, I can report that such famous productions as *Dr. Faustus, Horse Eats Hat, The Cradle Will Rock,* the anti-Fascist *Julius Caesar,* and the black *Macbeth* are virtually never mentioned anywhere except as the "*Houseman-Welles Caesar*" . . . and so on. Welles does sometimes get first billing, but Houseman is always up there; and since he, not

Welles, was in charge of publicity, it seems a little hard on Welles to accuse him of any effort to cast his partner into the shade. In books on American stage history, Houseman remains so firmly co-starred that it is all but impossible to discover that this "front man with brains" (to use Thomson's phrase), was not himself a full co-author and fellow creator with Welles of every one of those extraordinary theatrical events for which the Mercury was responsible. It would seem fairly natural for Welles to seek to correct this impression, but I have found no record of any effort on his part to do so.

The truth is that when Houseman went to work on Welles' radio program—particularly after the furor over the Mars broadcast—he was working *for* Welles, and, given the new level of show-biz big-time into which Orson's personal success had now taken him, neither the reality nor the fiction that they were equals could be sustained for very much longer. Houseman's contribution to the radio series was, in point of fact, far closer to the creative side of things than it had ever been in the theater, but by then he was no longer a partner, but a salaried employee in Welles' enterprises. As such, he was brought to Hollywood. Orson, I gather, was uncomfortably aware that in acting, to some extent, as Houseman's benefactor, he was inadvertently offering rather the contrary of the favor he intended. "Of course, Houseman hates Orson," Charles Lederer told me. "He owes everything to Orson. It reminds me of a story about Hearst. I told him once that so-and-so hated him, and W.R. said, 'That's funny—I can't recall ever doing him a favor.' "

In Hollywood the ex-partner was well paid, but he was downgraded. It is fairly easy to see how the co-founder of the Mercury Theater could have felt some resentment at finding himself a mere hireling in a film unit calling itself Mercury Productions. He now had no function except as script editor on the radio shows, while Orson was busy writing screenplays and doing very full pre-production work on two films (which RKO subsequently refused to O.K. for budget reasons).

During this period, Thomson states that Houseman "became furiously impatient with Welles's having loafed in Hollywood for upwards of a year." There are voluminous records to show that what Orson was up to at his typewriter was the very opposite of "loafing," but Miss Kael, in one of her more "Parsonish-Hopperish" moments, reports that his time was wholly dedicated to Miss Dolores Del Rio. Having no role to play in Welles' central

occupation, Houseman's furious impatience is understandable. As
script editor, he was working with Mankiewicz, Orson's friend, who
had been virtually black-listed (not for political reasons) from all
the major studios and whom Orson had added to the writing staff of
his radio series. It would be idle to speculate about the precise
nature of the relationship that grew up between these two
intelligent and deeply disappointed men. "Sadly," Welles writes,
"the closer Jack got to Mank, the further Mank moved away from
me."

When his session with Mankiewicz was over, Houseman was no
longer involved (apart from adding a few lines to the opera scene),
even as a witness, in the making of *Citizen Kane.* This does not deter
him from stating in his memoir that Pauline Kael's account is the
best and truest ever written. If you believe, as I do, that he was
himself her principal source of information, this opinion is not very
surprising. He is strongly motivated. His association with Welles is
the one great event in an otherwise not overly distinguished career.
Such feelings are suavely veiled in his book, but he would be less
than human if there was no bitterness in the loss of such a partner.

"I hate to think—" [Orson's letter again] "what my grandchil-
dren, if I ever get any, and if they should ever bother to look into
either of those books, are going to think of their ancestor: something
rather special in the line of megalomaniac lice. Of course, I'd be
grateful for a chance to send some sort of signal to those mythical
descendants— But how? Fight for my honor? And it really is, of
course, an old-fashioned question of personal honor. But the world
was young when I shot my can of sterno at Houseman, and even if
the code of the duello weren't defunct—how the hell do you 'call
out' a lady movie critic at dawn? Besides, who's this character I'd
be defending? I look at those old pictures you're collecting for the
book, and the person who looks back at me is not somebody I could
ever learn now to be fond of. I see an uppish (vaguely poufish!)
smart-ass. . . . But still, not really the moral crook you'll find in
those books.

"Anyway, there's just one of them who could be fought at all.
. . . Forget Houseman. The old sweet-speaker hurts most not as a
gossip himself, but as the cause that gossiping is in other men. And
women. To root out the hostility behind that mandarin benevolence
is a job for the students of his life and career, and these are not

likely to be numerous. . . . Peter! That last didn't seem too bad while I was typing it, but now it's in front of me on the page I'm abashed by my own bitchiness. . . . The cute sneer is catching. A contamination. Bitches ought to have to wear a bell. Makes me think of Molnar's theory: 'Never touch shit,' he used to say, 'even with gloves on. The gloves get shittier; the shit doesn't get glovier.'

"No, if there's anything that could maybe be dealt with in clear terms, it's the greasy smoke coming out of the book version of *Kane*. A dirty trick, worked without a spark of fire, but how to scrape off all that smudge? The job would take more time than you've got, more words than anybody will print, and what's worse—to be totally convincing—it's bound to be unreadable. Cleaning up after Miss Kael is going to take a lot of scrubbing."

Yes, but every filmmaker since 1941 is, to some degree, in debt to Orson Welles, and the very least one of them can do—if he happens to have under his hands some useful facts—is to roll up his sleeves and make a start.

Heston on Welles

An Interview by JAMES DELSON

How did the Touch of Evil *project come to be produced?*

It was submitted to me in December of 1956 by Universal, for whom I had made a successful comedy called *The Private War of Major Benson.* Since its release I had finished *Ten Commandments*, done a play in New York, and I was loafing over the holiday when Universal sent the script.

"It's a good enough script," I said, "but police stories, like westerns and war stories, have been so overdone that it really depends on who's going to direct it." I told them I'd put it down and call them later.

They told me that although they didn't know who was going to direct it, Orson Welles was going to play the heavy. "You know, Orson Welles is a pretty good director," I said. "Did it ever occur to you to have him direct it?" At that time, Orson had not directed a picture in America since *Macbeth.* They were a bit nonplussed, but they got back to me in a couple of days and said "Yeah, well that's a very good idea. A startling idea."

At this time, was Welles considered a cult figure at all?

About *Citizen Kane* he was. There was a rich preoccupation with the idea of Welles as a rebel, I guess, but they brought him in on the picture. He totally re-wrote the script in about seventeen days, which I knew he would, and didn't object to.

He got a solo writing credit for it.

Well he deserved it. He gives you your value. He has a reputation as being an extravagant director, but there are directors who have *wasted* more money on one film than Orson has spent on all the pictures he's directed in his career.

Originally published in Take One *(Vol. 3, No. 6), Box 1778, Station B, Montreal, Canada H3B 3L3.*

Nonetheless, people say "Oh, you can't hire Orson because he's extravagant." Mike Nichols went farther over budget on *Catch-22* than Orson has spent on all the films he has directed, put together. In my experience, in the one film I made for him, Orson is by no means an extravagant director. As I recall, we had something like a forty or forty-two-day shooting schedule and a budget of slightly under a million dollars, and we went a couple of days and about $75,000 over the budget. Now that really is not an outlandish, horrifying situation at all. The difference between that film *with* Welles and that film *without* Welles would be remarkable. His contribution as an actor, of course, was incredible. I would say the only major error that Orson made in the film was his conviction that he had to conceal something: the fact that his part was the best part in the film, as he had re-written the script. In fact, it was evident anyway—I knew it. *Touch of Evil* is about the decline and fall of Captain Quinlan. My part is a kind of witness to this. It would have. . . .

I agree that he wrote the best part for himself, but you're one of the three or four actors who have worked with Welles without being dwarfed by him, physically in terms of screen persona, or dramatically in terms of just plain showmanship. In watching the film recently this is one of its aspects that I noted most carefully, knowing that this point would come up. I was looking to see how you would handle yourself when the famous Wellesian scene-stealing took place. In the scene where Joe Calleia "finds" the sticks of dynamite in the shoebox, Welles is playing it up, but you, through the opposite means, subduing every gesture and restraining yourself, manage to hold your own, which is a feat.

Well, I am happy to subscribe to the thesis that I can stand on equal ground with Orson in a scene, but that doesn't change the fact that Orson is party to that part, and that the film is *about* Captain Quinlan, really. But that's the way it should be. That's the story. I play a man who's looking for his wife, really.

Actually, I have Orson to thank for the fact that the part is as interesting as it was, because it was his idea to make it a Mexican detective. I said "I can't play a Mexican detective!" He said "Sure you can! We'll dye your hair black, and put on some dark makeup and draw a black moustache, sure you can! We'll get a Mexican tailor to cut you a good Mexican suit." And they did, and it's plausible enough I suppose. I play a plausible Mexican. As a matter of fact it doesn't contribute to the stereotype of the sombrero Mexican lazing around in the shade.

Did Universal agree to let Welles act in the film so long as he directed it?

They imposed on him, for budget reasons. They were willing to take a chance on him directing, but only on that budget.

Was casting begun immediately upon the signing of Welles?

No. The first thing was his re-working of the script. He wanted it to be set on the Mexican border, and they wouldn't go for location work at that time. You must remember that this was sixteen years ago. Welles found an entirely acceptable substitute in Venice, California.

It was more than acceptable. Remind me not to visit Venice, California. Welles achieved a new low in ramshackle buildings, locations, and degeneracy, as played most ably by U.S.-for-Mexico shooting. In searching for locations, and other pre-production work, did you play an active part?

Not *nearly* the amount I do now. I was consulted about things, but did not really participate on a serious level. I helped in things like casting. I had approval.

Was there anybody cast who you were either exceedingly pleased or displeased over?

I thought all of the casting was marvelous. There was some uncertainty over the casting of the girl, who was played by Janet Leigh.

I guess she was very big at that time.

The studio wanted to use her very much. This casting was, in fact, almost imposed, and . . . as a matter of fact, it turned out better than I thought it would. I thought she was quite good. I don't think Orson was terribly upset about it. All the other casting I had approval on and, as far as I know, Orson made all the other castings. There were some fine performances, especially Joe Calleia. I think it's one of the very best pieces of work he did in his whole career.

I thought the cameos were a nice touch.

Orson got his cronies to do them. Joe Cotten and Marlene Dietrich were fun, yeah.

Orson Welles as director. That's the dream of many fine actors. What is it that makes him special to work with?

He's exciting. He makes it fun.

Then why is it that he can't get the money to make films? He makes films that are literate, and as close as one can get to pure cinema, both in terms of artistic achievement and entertainment. I'm sorry. That was a rhetorical outburst. We were talking about how Welles works.

Film acting is not often very interesting. Even if you have a fascinating part with four or five major scenes, which is unusual, those scenes don't take up half the running time of the film, or the shooting time of the film, either. The bulk of your day is . . . well a good case in point is a scene from *Skyjacked*, where I came out of the flight deck and went into the john, where I saw the scrawled message saying that the plane was being skyjacked. I didn't say anything. I looked at Yvette (Mimieux), and in the course of that look, what they describe as a "charged look," I had to show "problems, what am I doing here, what are all these carryings on," and also "I'm involved in some kind of complicated relationship with this girl, and I'd really rather not be flying with her. All things considered, but on the other hand. . . ." That's about all there is to the first shot. No lines. . . . That was my first day's work on the picture. That's *all* there was to the first day. That's not all *they* did, but that's all *I* did. You understand the motivation, you've read the script, you know the importance of establishing the thing with the girl, but still it's really not the most marvelous day's work you've ever done. Orson has the capacity as a director to somehow persuade you that each time is *indeed* the most important day in the picture, and that's kind of marvelous, and I applaud it.

Is he this way with all the actors? Minor scenes as well, bit parts?

I think so, yes.

Can we talk about the first shot? The famous first shot?

This first shot in *Touch of Evil* is, as I said, technically one of the most brilliant shots I have ever seen in any film. Among film buffs it has become a classic shot.

It's in all of the books.

Is it? Is it in some books? Well, for the record, it begins on a close-up insert of a bundle of sticks of dynamite, and it pans up just enough to apprehend an unidentifiable figure dashing out of the frame. As the pan continues, you see in the middle distance a couple coming out of the door of a bar, and going even deeper into the background, and turning around the back of the building and disappearing. Led by the couple's exit, the camera pans down the alley in the direction in which the figure holding the dynamite has fled, on the near side of the building, going in the same direction. You see the figure (and of course now you can't possibly identify him) dart behind the building. Following with the camera, but still too far away to tell who he is, he lifts the trunk of a car and puts what is obviously a bomb into the car, slams the lid, and disappears into the shadows just as the camera, now lifting above the car, picks up the couple coming around the other side of the building and getting in the car. You establish him as a fat political type and she a floozy blonde type. And they carry on—there's enough awareness of their dialogue to establish a kind of drunken nonchalance.

The camera booms up on a chapmain boom as the car drives out of the parking lot and out into the street. The boom sinks down, picks up the car, and picks up me and Janet Leigh walking along and talking. The camera then moves ahead of both us and the car, the car's progress being to some degree impeded by foot traffic, so as to keep us more-or-less in the same context. But first you pick up the car and then us walking, and in the course of our movement you establish that we are just married and honeymooning. All the time, on the sound track you hear the ticking of the bomb.

By this time we get to the border station and have a little dialogue that established me as a government official. We go through the Mexican station, and then through the U.S. station, and the car does too, and there's a little carrying-on that makes it clear that this fellow is a guy with some political clout. . . .

And the girl says, "My watch is awfully loud, I think I hear something ticking."

No. "There's this ticking in my head" . . . she's drunk. Then the car zooms past us out of shot, we now being in the United States, and there's some dialogue to the effect that we've just been married and I haven't kissed her in an hour, and I pull her into my arms and kiss her and of course as our lips touch the car explodes offscreen. That's quite a shot.

That is called Orson Welles.

It took *all* one night to shoot, as indeed it might. And the spooky thing about night-shooting, night exteriors, is that when the sun comes up that's all, you've got to quit. And we were shooting in Venice and we. . . . Oh, I don't know, laying the shot was incredibly complicated. The boom work with the chapmain boom was the major creative contribution. The men who ran the boom had a *terribly* difficult job, but they finally were getting so it was working well enough to do takes on it, and we did two or three or four takes, and in each take the customs man, who had just one line, would flub his line.

Oh Christ.

Cause he'd see this great complex of cars and lights and chap-main booms bearing down on him from three blocks away, and they'd get closer and closer, and finally there they would all be, and he would blow his line. I will concede that Orson did not do a great deal to stimulate his. . . . Orson said, "Look, I don't care what you say, just move your lips, we can dub it in later. Don't just put your face in your hands and say 'Oh my God, I'm sorry.' " And of course the fellow never did get the line. He finally managed to blow the line impassively. He just stood there moving his lips impotently.

At which point Welles gave him a medal and his walking papers. At this time, were you beginning to take a creative interest in the technical aspects of the films you were working on?

Well, you begin to, if you have any brains, the first time you work on a film. This was the first film on which I was quite as aware of the enormous creative composition of the camera, which is not surprising since Russ Metty was the cameraman. It was also the first film on which I spent any time in the cutting room. I sat and watched Orson fiddle with sequences with his cutter, and it was a very learningful experience.

That's the kind of experience that most of us would give our shirts for.

Yeah, it's valuable.

Is he a perfectionist?

No.

In terms of just putting things right?

I think that's the last thing Orson is. He probably has a larger measure of talent, whatever the hell that means, than anybody else I've ever met, but a perfectionist he is not. He can get an *incredible* idea about how to solve a scene, or a piece of casting, or a bit of writing, or an editing problem. But rather than polish it to perfection, he is likely to substitute still another idea that is nearly as good or maybe better. But, I would say, he is disinclined to sandpaper.

Does he get a lot of coverage? I know Sam Peckinpah sometimes uses eighteen or nineteen cover shots on one set-up.

No. Now mind you, at the time I made *Touch of Evil* I wasn't as sophisticated an observer of the mechanics of filmmaking as I am now. But, nonetheless, in my memory . . . well, the first shot is . . . what I've said to you. There is no cutting to that. They just got the slate off it and that's the first three minutes of the film.

The studio likes that kind of thing (both laugh).

Was Welles doing any rewriting when the film was being made? Or was he working straight through?

Not once we started shooting. I think that's one of the reasons *Touch of Evil* could be said to have turned out better than *Major Dundee.* Sam had to attempt to undertake his rewrite while shooting the film. Orson undertook his and accomplished it before shooting.

How would you describe the working relationship you had with him during the film?

Enchanted. Orson *seduces* you in a marvelous way. You know he's one of the most charming men in the world, if it's important to him to be charming. He is, at *minimum,* interesting—but if it's important to him to enlist your support and cooperation, he is as charming a man as I have ever seen.

And was he so with the rest of the crew as well would you say?

Oh yes. See, that's an important thing. Orson elicits remarkable support from his companies, he asks a lot from them, his crews too, but he jokes with them and recognizes what they're doing, their contributions, and it works *marvelously.* They put out a great effort for him.

It shows in the fact that he got tiny performances, one-scene performances, that are memorable.

Yeah, that's it. Sam, on the other hand, *requires* your commitment, and that's not quite the same thing as *eliciting* your support. Because you can choose not to deliver your commitment. Personally, in my own style of work, I prefer working as an individual film actor, in a somewhat more detached manner. I think you tend to get into a hothouse atmosphere. You're living in each other's laps anyway, and it's long days, and I frankly prefer a little more detached and cool relationship. But you've got to do to it the way the director wants. In both the case of Sam, who demanded it and required it, and Orson, who elicits it, that's the way you go. But some people won't make that kind of commitment to Sam.

On individual scenes when you'd be working with Welles—would he say do this and this and this and this—in a way some directors will—or is he a director who will let you create and then say "well, maybe this and maybe this?"

By and large, assuming the contribution of professional actors . . . in my experience on forty films the complexities of the mechanics of filming and the creative problems they present tend to preoccupy a director to a large degree. A good actor is likely to have a fairly free hand in the shaping of his—certainly of his character, possibly of the scene as well. I'm not speaking of a Wyler or Stevens or Lean, but most directors, even directors like those I've mentioned, who work in *incredibly tiny detail* in altering facets of a performance, they often tend not to do so in acting terms, if you follow me. I think Wyler, for example, has an absolutely *infallible* taste for a performance. If he says it's right—it's *right*. There's just no question. But I don't think he's particularly empathic with actors.

Orson probably taught me more about acting than any film director I've worked for. Which is not to say I necessarily did my best film performance for him, but he taught me a great deal about acting—the whole, acting generically. He's both specific in technical details, and in broad concepts about acting, and I found it an enormously stimulating experience.

The scenes you did with Welles—did you find those to be your most difficult scenes?

The most difficult?

The most difficult, Or the most draining, I would say. It's really the word I would use. Draining would also mean that when you were finished with them you probably felt the most satisfied.

I recall performing in the whole picture, doing the whole picture, as being as satisfying creatively as anything I've ever done. I don't recall it as being—the part was not an enormously difficult part. There was never a scene that you look on as a major jump—you know, a barrier that somehow you have to clear. Like the dagger speech in *Macbeth*. Or Antony's suicide. They were scenes that you did with as much creative juice as you could call on at that time. Orson helps you quite a lot.

The sequence with the shoebox is a brilliant scene. It's also brilliantly directed and photographed, again because the camera is constantly moving in that scene.

That's about thirteen pages. That was the first day's work on the picture. And Orson deceived the studio, and he conned them, because the scene was scheduled for three days of shooting, which is about reasonable, which would be a little over four pages a day—which is a respectable day's work in an "A" picture. He, in fact, had rehearsed the scene in his home with the actors over a Sunday or two. He proceeded to lay out the scene in terms of *one* shot with a crab dolly, that encompassed all the eight or nine performers who had lines in the scene. The action ranged through two rooms, a closet and a bathroom, and, as I said, thirteen pages of dialogue. It was quite a complex shot, with doors having to be pulled, walls having to be pulled aside—very intricate markings, inserts on the shoebox, and things like that. All of which were in one shot.

When you're shooting, the production office is informed when the camera turns over the first time, when the first print is made, and so on. And of course we never turned a camera until way. . . . Lunch went by, and uneasy little groups of executives began to huddle about in the shadows, not quite willing to approach Orson but increasingly convinced that they were on the brink of disaster, cause we hadn't turned a camera and it was, by now, three or four o'clock in the afternoon. Finally, at about 4:30, we turned. And of course it was tricky. We did several takes—seven or eight takes. Finally we got a print, just before six o'clock. And Orson said, "OK, that's a print. Wrap." He said, "We're two days ahead of schedule. We go to the other set tomorrow."

The executives must have been down on their knees.

Everybody thought it was marvelous. Of course he never did that again, you see, but they always thought he *might*.

It's a brilliant idea.

Just great. They never gave him any trouble again after that. They thought, "My God, he did three days' work in one shot!"

The little touches that he adds from scene to scene. Were they all in the script? The things like Akim Tamiroff's hairpiece which was a running gag throughout the whole film.

That was not in the script, no. And of course, I wasn't in those scenes, so I don't know how they were created, but I know they weren't—it wasn't in the script. The scenes are put together in a very loose atmosphere that makes for that kind of creativity.

Was there any ad libbing in terms of dialogue?

Orson has a marvelous ear for the way people talk. One of the many things I learned from him was the degree to which people in real life overlap one another when they're talking. In the middle of somebody's sentence you will, in fact, apprehend what he's talking about and you will often start to reply through his closing phrase. People do that all the time. Orson directs scenes that way—to a larger degree than most directors do.

There's a marvelously counterpointed scene in *The Lady from*

Shanghai in which the people sit in the dark—obviously he doesn't want a visual image to intrude—and you hear two conversations interwoven. He likes that, and I do too. I think it's very valuable, and I've tried to use it in scenes myself since. He not only changes dialogue, as . . . dialogue is changed all the time on film. It's some of the most creative work in putting a scene together.

All of Hawks.

Pardon?

All of Hawks had to be written on a daily basis.

It goes on all the time. Sure. Orson is, as I said, a very instinctive, intuitive creator, and he would restage whole scenes. I mean put them in different places. We were shooting in this crummy hotel in Venice, and at three o'clock in the morning—in the middle of night shooting—we were down in the basement of this old hotel, peeing in a drain in the corner of this old basement, and he said, "Gee, these pipes and this boiler. That's marvelous. You know this—we should do the scene with Joe Calleia here—where he shows you the cane."

He zipped up his fly and said to the first assistant, "Get Joe Calleia down here." They said, "Jesus, Orson, we were gonna do that scene on Friday; they've got it set up at the studio." He said, "That's terrible. That's no place. We're going to do it down here. We'll do it right now." And they said, "Well, we've got to finish this scene." He said, "I can finish this scene in one shot. It'll take you an hour to get Calleia out of bed. Get him down here and I'll have this scene finished by then." And he did.

That's beautiful.

And it is better there.

Cause that is the turning point of the film.

It's a great scene. And part of the reason it's good is he. . . . Here's Joe Calleia getting up out of bed in the middle of the night, and staggering down to Venice. They take him down in this stinking basement and they give him the cane, and they say "Joe, now do it." And he says, "What-what-what???" "The scene." "Where?" You know, and it's marvelous.

THE
TECHNIQUES

An Infinity of Mirrors

by RICHARD T. JAMESON

In the sensitive art of the Rosebud Movie Palace
there is a Message, and humor, strictly moral.
SINCLAIR LEWIS,
Main Street

1940: George Orson Welles, early in his twenty-sixth year, encases himself in the makeup of a seventy-year-old man and sleepwalks down a corridor of an American dream-palace called Xanadu. The camera watches his approach obliquely, then turns to the mirrored wall. The opposite wall is a mirror as well, and we are startled to perceive a rank of Charles Foster Kanes stretching to infinity. The visual reality is so compelling that we are doubly startled when the corporeal man catches up to and reenters the frame. A Welles is a Kane is a Welles. All of them pass out of view and the camera nudges ever so slightly inward, past the reality-establishing frame of the mirror itself. We remain faced with bottomless illusion as the scene fades out.

1966: George Orson Welles, in his fifty-first year, encases himself in the makeup of Jack Falstaff and his own flesh. Before him stands a nameless Spanish actor pretending to be an Englishman of Henry IV's day, unfit for military service. Falstaff challenges the recruit, who replies, "Oh sir, I am a diseased man!" Out of him comes the voice—*a* voice—of Orson Welles. Orson Welles spends a delightful moment conversing with himself on the soundtrack.

Even in a director-worshipping age, Welles constitutes the most thoroughgoing instance of, not film as the director's event, but rather, the director as film event. Discounting such sometime

Prepared for publication in this volume and published by permission of the author.

occupations as bullfighter, illustrator, editor of Shakespeare, magician, and pitchman for an airline and a bourbon, we are still faced with a great many Orson Welleses whenever we confront one of his movies. He acts in them, writes them, directs, edits, frequently selects or designs the sets and costumes, and increasingly dubs the voices of his co-players (at one point in *Touch of Evil*, even that of concealed guest star Joseph Cotten). Bits of his autobiography find their way into the scenarios (the character of Eugene Morgan in the novel *The Magnificent Ambersons* was allegedly based on Welles' father), and he imparts an only semi-private kind of sympathy to the heroic villains of *Citizen Kane*, *Ambersons*, *The Stranger*, and *Touch of Evil* by calling attention to their own/his own fatal tendency to fat. Although Welles is the sort of global celebrity whose force of presence guarantees the center of focus in any context, it is important to point out that all his films, to some extent or another, have dealt with the phenomenon of personal identity—dealt with it, moreover, in terms of media: his protagonists manipulate media, transcend media, sometimes *consist of* media effects. The best Welles films boast as many structural levels of self-awareness and self-examination as there are Welles/Kanes in that infinity-of-mirrors shot.

The definitive line in *Citizen Kane* is: "A toast, Jedediah, to love on my terms. Those are the only terms anybody ever knows—his own." The speaker is Kane (portrayed by Welles, of course), a master of media who spends his life trying to reconstruct the world in terms that suit his vision, and who at one point projects a light-and-shadow play upon a wall. Kane's creator and incarnator can hold himself at sufficient objective distance to observe the moral, ethical, and emotional limitations of this proposition. But aesthetically, and personally, it fascinates him. And why not? With a little twisting, Kane's remarks imply an essential definition of the film director: one who has the power to remake the world in precisely those formal terms that embody his own imaginative version of reality. The difference is that Welles the filmmaker hopes to have his terms recognized by others, and known, appreciated, perhaps incorporated into the viewer's own way of seeing.

Let's consider some of the terms in which Orson Welles realizes film-worlds.

LIGHT AND SHADOW

In his book *Movie Man* David Thomson interestingly suggests that "The whole of *Citizen Kane* might be Kane's own dreamed recollections in the last moment before his death. The fact that the film takes the form of investigations carried out by a representative of a newsreel company could be interpreted as showing the degree to which Kane's own publicity has conditioned his attitude to himself." *Kane* begins in the utter darkness and silence of an uncreated world and an uncreated medium. Then a chord shudders down under things and we begin to perceive abstract images: several kinds of wire mesh, dark grillwork of increasing complexity of pattern, set against an out-of-focus luminescence. These images fade into one another in funereal ascending shots, mount toward coherent narration of a landscape and, ultimately, a life. "Rosebud," Charles Foster Kane's dying word, bespeaks a reversion to childlike conceptualization at the moment of death; and the initial shots and shot-movements of Welles' first film constitute an introduction to the most elemental language of the cinema.

Light and shadow have traditional associations in our culture and in the cinema, but Welles' use of light and shadow, like his use of virtually any device, leads us away from clean-cut oppositions and toward ambiguity. Light is a life force; it awakens the screen of consciousness from darkness, but only to cast shadows. Light marks the advance of death: the movement of the sun shifts the shadows around Jed Leland as he tells his story in *Kane*, and morning comes up over a burnt-out El Rancho sign to be noticed by Susan Alexander Kane as she finishes her own account of Charlie Kane and tosses down a bolt of her particular brand of self-destruction. In *The Magnificent Ambersons*, the harsh sunlight that shines into the Major's carriage as he discusses the vulnerability of himself and the Amberson fortune seems to have the power to rot flesh; during another carriage ride the dying Isabel is cruelly blasted by the light, and so is Fanny Minafer as she sits with her back against the boiler in the all-but-deserted mansion. The shafts of illumination that pour through the projection-room ports early in *Kane* reduce the newsmen to sectors of jittery activity and selectively deny them any individual identity; but the chill beam that falls on the throne of the two Henrys in *Chimes at Midnight* sets royalty apart and condemns them to a terrible election.

Darkness is traditionally linked with death, and in this spirit Welles opens many of his narratives of dead or doomed men at night (*Kane, The Lady from Shanghai, Touch of Evil*) or in some stylized dimness (*Ambersons, The Stranger, Macbeth, Othello, Mr. Arkadin, The Trial*). Isabel Amberson Minafer and her father are both visually swallowed by shadows in their last moments of (screen) life, and so, even though he does not actually die, is George; the Amberson mansion, itself virtually a character, is filled with impenetrable black reaches even when lit up for the last of the great balls; and we are told and shown how the Ambersons' town, embracing modern industrialization, "befouled itself and darkened its sky." Yet the darkness of the vanished past is ambiguous. The dimness of the Amberson mansion, like the quaint impurity of its architecture, is inseparable from its reassuring spiritual comfiness, its personality; the same holds for Tanya's place, Quinlan's refuge in *Touch of Evil.* Their darkness stands in atmospheric and moral counterpoint to the "bright, guilty world[s]" of *The Lady from Shanghai* and *Othello.*

Death is the ultimate form of domination, and Welles frequently employs shadows as a means of demonstrating less-than-mortal ascendancy. Charles Foster Kane, who increasingly makes a mockery of himself by forcing his untalented wife Susan into the limelight of the opera, stands over her the morning following her disastrous debut, swallowing her in his shadow and compelling her to continue with her singing. Later he will repeat the tactic in their grand picnic tent in the Everglades, but by that time Susan is no longer impressed by his stylized behavior. Welles gives this over-shadowing ploy full-screen coverage in *Kane*; in *Ambersons* the effect is disposed over a comparatively small portion of the frame, yet by operating in the context of myriad other details it achieves greater subtlety while the precision of the gesture maintains its impact: standing amid his family in a sunlit garden, the pre-pubescent Georgie Minafer casts an utterly black shadow over his mother's perfect profile at the moment *she* seeks to impose *her* will on him. George retains control by appearing to accede to her request, verbally contradicting this impression only at the moment he passes off screen, leaving the astonished elder generations to reconstitute their complacent dignity.

As the mise-en-scène of Welles' work grows more complex in its suggestibility, shadows extend themselves across structural links in his films. In *Othello* the Moor and his Desdemona are photographed from on high, two light figures darting across a court below, while in the foreground of the scene the dark and as yet unarticulated Iago stands in near silhouette. Welles dissolves to another shot—of a lagoon, water, the medium of Othello's mastery as a hero—and over this Iago's figure continues to be prominently visible for a long while, as his manipulative power will extend itself over nearly every event to follow. Indeed, in formal terms *Othello* is based on elaborations of shadowplay: the dynamics of shadow and substance as Iago redirects reality according to his design to convince the Moor of cosmic falsehood; the shadow's association with the principle of the divided or shared identity, the *alter ego* and, again, the mirror, reversed face of reality; and the ambiguous uses of white and black as emblems of moral condition, with not only the black Moor and dark Iago but also the alabaster Desdemona in a characteristically Wellesian complicity.

The whitest white in the world is figured in the snows that decisively punctuate many of Welles' films. In *Kane*, the title character expires under a subjective overlay of artificial snow distributed across our vision after a closeup has placed us inside a glass snow globe in his hand. With mesmerized conviction the camera sweeps us along a line of Walter P. Thatcher's spidery handwriting until we white out through the very page into the proverbial snows of Kane's yesteryear. The soundstage environment of Charlie Kane's boyhood—an abrupt snowbank buttressed against a two-dimensional RKO infinity—is already a rarefied version of youthful innocence and is the more poignant because the longing we sense through the rapturous music and the delirious dissolve technique resists attachment to, is "disappointed" by, such an abstraction. We depart from this snow-world via a shot of the sled Rosebud, a distant train whistle telling us that Charlie has gone before. Rosebud is already freighted with enough snow to conceal its crucial identity from us at this point; the snow continues to fall and, by means of a match-dissolve, grows deeper on the sled. As it *falls*, it *rises* in preserving and also access-denying layers. The formation of a personality, a behavioral style, a film style—for the film opens with an ascent toward Kane's death chamber and the falling of the snow globe, and closes with the camera having descended back outside the fence at Xanadu as Rosebud's remains climb skyward in a great column of smoke.

If the snow of *Citizen Kane* ultimately assumes the coldest of values, it is used as an exquisite grace note in *The Magnificent Ambersons*. The luminousness of the winter outing sequence is not diminished by its being framed between a misty reflection shot, implying the evanescence of the Ambersons' world, and a screen-blackening iris-shot that puts an anachronistic period to their era without their realizing it. Indeed, the cold of the season enhances the warmth of interiors: Eugene and Lucy Morgan take us into the Amberson mansion through doors glazed with ice. The ice suggests the past rightly enough, and a kind of crystallization, containment in form; but when it is immediately echoed visually in the Ambersons' crystal chandelier and aurally in the tinkling of those crystals in the draught from the door, the effect is of sublime transformation, an oddly graceful ostentatiousness through which a peculiarly American lifestyle is achieved, one that accommodates itself to the stylistic splendors of the season. This suggestion that life itself can become art carries no hint of the desperation implicit in Charles Foster Kane's self-advertising, self-concealing tactics.

Snow marks a stage in the transformation of the world even in a minor Welles film like *The Stranger*. Transpiring as autumn gives way to winter in a New England college town, this thriller about the search for and destruction of an infamous Nazi war criminal is remarkable for its unimpeachable sense of place. Unlike many Welles pictures, *The Stranger* involves no suggestion of virtual identification between the dream-vision of its focal character and the actual landscape against and through which the drama is played out. Kindler/Rankin murders the former colleague who has unwittingly led the war crimes investigators to his hiding place and buries his corpse in a drift of leaves. Later, as part of the atmospheric background to another scene, we notice seasonal leaves being burned, their smoke hugging the ground like fog. At the climax of the film, the smoke is succeeded by snow. As forecast in a passage from Emerson that is quoted by the Nazi's chief pursuer, its shining purity will show up the track of any guilty thing.

SPACE AND TIME

There is a moment's pause, at the beginning of *Citizen Kane*, before Orson Welles provides us with any idea of what the opening NO TRESPASSING sign and the various layers of fence are guarding. Then we are vouchsafed a more rationally coherent, if rather dreamlike, landscape: a huge wrought-iron K atop a gate and, in the other half of the frame, a fairy-tale castle on a hill. The preeminent sense of ascension established in the dissolving fence shots gives way momentarily to a penetrating motion—not that of a camera moving, but shots themselves, editorial logic in motion, as a series of precisely matched *still* images samples the bizarre ground of an estate presided over by the castle, which maintains a territorial imperative over the same section of the frame in each shot. That the landscape should in fact consist largely of painted or miniature effects supports the surreality of this kind of progression through space: this space is an imaginative reality that, like the monogram and the castle and the man-made mountain it stands on, is contained within the dreaming mind of the man whose name is shared with the film and whose identity, far from being restricted to a characterization by a twenty-five-year-old actor or a Freudian inscription on a childhood sled, is defined by the terrible, irreconcilable stylistic tensions that *are* the movie. And if these vast spaces, like the cavernous interiors of Xanadu, can be contained within the inner space of a visionary sensibility, so can the movie be thought of as one suspended moment—a concept vividly particularized by the passage of the burning Rosebud through all the potential stages of its own mortality.

Space and time are often inseparable in Welles' film-world. The staggered chronology of *Kane* is realized through discrete, discontinuous scene-moments culled from various times and places: Walter P. Thatcher's "Merry Christmas . . . and a Happy New Year!" requires almost two decades, but only a single splice, to be completed; Jed Leland, delivering a political exhortation to a small street audience, has his line completed by Kane in a crowded meetinghall. *The Magnificent Ambersons* foregoes such pyrotechnics in the interest not only of a more muted narrative tone appropriate to a scrupulously genteel subject, but also of a more profound formality. Here long, fluid takes of several minutes' duration dominate and define the aesthetics of the film. During the early ballroom sequence, paths converge, people converse but don't always communicate, pass moments of decision that will determine the course of their futures; and yet still they have to finish crossing the room of the present, deal with the amenities, save face while behind the façade a heart may be breaking. Eugene Morgan says laughingly, "Old times? When times are gone they're not old, they're dead! There aren't any times but new times!" The mise-en-scène wishfully belies this—for a time—as real and potential lovers from different generations cross and re-cross over one another's temporary cinematic space. But later in the film the auspiciousness of this interpersonal confluence gives way to the fatal, frame-dividing machinations of character against character, and we are made to realize the ultimate implication of Welles' long-take aesthetics: that such integral comprehension of space and time produces documentaries of people dying.

"We have heard the chimes at midnight," Falstaff pronounces before the credits of the film of that name have even come on the screen. A number of Welles' films begin with the title character dead (*Kane*, *Othello*, *Arkadin*) or with the action otherwise already concluded or somehow foreseen (*Ambersons*, *The Lady from Shanghai*, *Macbeth* and, implicitly, in the parable of the law, *The Trial*). One that does not, *Touch of Evil*, begins with a dazzlingly integral shot that reaches fruition and conclusion only as it defines itself as a stylistic time bomb—the shot-equivalent of *Kane*'s overall narrative structure. *Othello* opens with the funerals of Othello and Desdemona and the incarceration of Iago, and we are reminded of the completedness of its story at several junctures. At one point the Moor lies outside the walls of Cyprus, his lips frothed, his eyes staring sightlessly at the shrieking birds wheeling overhead; he seems to be dead already though in fact much of the tale remains to be told. Another time, Iago promises Roderigo to turn Desdemona's "virtue into pitch / And out of her goodness make the net / That shall enmesh them all"; thus saying, he strides purposefully away, superior in his meticulous connivance—until Welles shows him moving under the silhouetted image of the cage that he will ultimately occupy, that we have already seen him occupy: like the dynamic Charlie Kane, his actions are foredooming himself as well as his target, the Moor. Iago too will be "enmeshed."

If time, as the supreme existential fact, is deadended in the chill of eternity, still the Wellesian characters' passage through time and space is not without value. "Human nature is eternal. Therefore he who follows his nature keeps his original nature in the end." So speaks Elsa, a most untrustworthy character in *The Lady from Shanghai*. Welles goes along with her up to a point, and with Gregori Arkadin's fable of the scorpion that stings the frog that is carrying it across a river even though it means that the scorpion too will die: " 'I cannot help it. It is my character, and there is no logic in character.' Let us drink to character." His people are true to their natures, their characters, and in being true discover what those natures are. This usually comes only at the end of their lives, or screen lives: Kane calling for Rosebud, George Amberson Minafer asking forgiveness at his dead mother's bed, Michael O'Hara—who "never makes up his mind about anything till it's over and done with"—observed in an ironically grandiloquent crane shot as he strides away from the shattered illusions in *The Lady from Shanghai* funhouse and into the proverbial new dawn, admitting that he hasn't really been "innocent—stupid's more like it." A few are given a chance to submit to the life-preserving domination of others—Macbeth to be led in chains before Malcolm, Joseph K to become "the advocate's dog"—but defend and define what's left of their integrity by going to their deaths. Others cop out: In *The Stranger*, Kindler/Rankin, Hitler's most brilliant young lieutenant and a chief shaper and mover of the Nazis' "Tomorrow the World" program, has his dominion reduced (theoretically) from the world to a small town, from the town to a churchtower, from the tower to the very clockwork room where he has symbolically tried to control time (a passion for clocks helps disclose his identity); as that room also begins to close on him, and before it ultimately expels him, he disclaims responsibility for his crimes: "I only took orders."

There are those who arbitrarily separate Welles' directorial output into art and trash: the former category including *Kane, Ambersons*, and the adaptations of Shakespeare, Kafka, and Dinesen; the latter, the thrillers. Even the most stodgy of commentators is willing to fudge on these: *Macbeth*, produced on a hectic schedule at the poverty-row Republic Pictures, may be seen as first proof of how the puerile diversions of *Journey into Fear, The Stranger*, and *The Lady from Shanghai* had subverted Welles' seriousness as a filmmaker, whereas the astonishing technical virtuosity of *Touch of Evil* and

director Welles' obsessively honest acknowledgement of actor
Welles' corporeal grotesqueness compel profound, if grudging,
respect. I invoke such subdivisions of Welles' oeuvre only to insist
that they have nothing to do with cinematic reality, or with an
understanding of his continuing and consistent development as a
film artist.

Journey into Fear, credited to Norman Foster but in part directed
by Welles and entirely influenced by him, was clearly a lark for the
Mercury Theatre company, but the stylistic and structural approach, however lighthearted, anticipates the blackly comic form of
Welles' later thrillers. Most of the action unfolds aboard a
run-down freighter, and Welles takes the confined space as cue to
cram the melodramatic complications of the Eric Ambler plot to a
comic overtenseness. This is reinforced by the film's very brief
running time (sixty-nine minutes). There is nothing tongue-in-
cheek about the nightmare atmosphere created in the opening
moments of *The Stranger*. In some South American night city of the
imagination an escaped war criminal is followed by Allied agents,
the peregrinations of all the characters traced by sinuous camera
movements snaking over a virtually three-dimensional landscape of
chiaroscuro. One backward-tracking shot is particularly significant,
the camera receding before the advance of a female agent who, at
the moment her crouched form emerges from a dark culvert, has
her body topped by the shadow-head of the man she is trailing; this
grotesque, seeming byproduct of the film's technical fluidity hints at
ambiguities of both character and morality to be developed in the
course of the movie and, beyond that, throughout Welles' work.

The Lady from Shanghai is the pivotal film of Welles' career. Under
the aegis of a major studio (Columbia) and not especially restricted
by the budget, the magician in Welles gained the ascendancy and
the director began inventing sleight-of-hand tricks whose successful
accomplishment would be remarked by hardly anyone but himself.
In his *The Films of Orson Welles* Charles Higham is at great pains to
explain how the finished movie constitutes a desperate attempt to
rescue ineptly shot footage that just wouldn't cut together in the
manner to which old-line film editors were accustomed. Certainly
there is nothing customary about it. A woman stands on a rock just
above sea level; she steps out of the shot and we cut to an image of
her diving off a cliff. Separated from a yacht by a hundred yards of
water, she apparently traverses the distance during one-and-a-half

lines of dialogue, while a man who pretends to depart the yacht by motorboat is revealed to be still in the vicinity several moments later. Two men have a conversation on the Acapulco cliffs; the event is comprised of dozens of minute shots—precipitous location work flamboyantly intercut with floaty process shots, lines of dialogue begun in one shot (location reality) and completed in the next (studio reality), the mad, taunting George Grisby dropping verbal bombs and then stepping out of frame leaving the bewildered protagonist to catch the suggestive charge; the ground is pulled from beneath both Michael O'Hara and the viewer. During a later conversation between George and Michael, seated in a waterfront bar, Arthur Bannister appears outside the window on the wharf; the bar is a set and Bannister is really a figment on a process screen (not too unusual) who calls out to the real people in the foreground (pretty unusual) and is invited inside for a beer (very unusual). Welles ignores the usual working distinctions between the various kinds of visual reality and employs film editing to create a brand-new, poetic, spatial logic. It is significant that, just before Elsa's dive from the rock that becomes a cliff, we are afforded a glimpse of her poised against the sky; what we are really seeing is a reflection in the lens of a monocular—properly so, for Elsa's stock-in-trade is deception, illusion; it is her very reality (she tells Michael, "I'm not what you think—I just try to be that way," to which he replies: "Keep on trying, you might make it!"). The monocular is glued to the eye of George Grisby, and Welles takes us into his point of view, presenting a middle-distant shot of Elsa climbing out of the water, the edges of the frame masked to suggest looking through the glass. Without cutting away or showing George moving nearer to Elsa, Welles dissolves to a close shot, also circularly masked, of Elsa reclining on a rock. The monocular is explicitly likened to a director's viewfinder, here and in a later scene wherein voyeur George "builds" a montage out of his fellow characters' movements on a beach. Directorial vision enjoys a primacy over and above the conventional logic of vantage and distance.

The Lady from Shanghai is an exciting and, in its way, harrowing excursion into illusionism. Irresistibly recognizable as an only half-wry psychodrama based on the director's marriage to and recent separation from his co-star (Rita Hayworth), the film shoots devastating glances behind the silver mask of a duplicit murderess and a glamor girl of dubious substance; when, after the whirlwind progression and dazzling imagery of the filmic adventure, Michael is brought face to face with Elsa in flatly luminous closeup, he perceives the coldness of her beauty, the deadness in the eyes. The slipperiness of the images, the uneasy truce between artifice and reality that is an integral aspect of the film's own physical being, culminate in a justly famous shootout in a hall of mirrors, with the participants unable to distinguish their proper targets from the reflections.

The most desperate irony of *The Lady from Shanghai* is that the tricks of showmanship Welles played almost for his private fun in Hollywood proved essential in just getting his films made thereafter. In realizing projects like *Othello, Mr. Arkadin, The Trial,* and *Chimes at Midnight* abroad, he has been forced into catch-as-catch-can shooting schedules, sometimes requiring a period of years over which footage would be shot when money, film stock, players (or acceptable standins) and workable sets were available. Visually, aurally, and psychologically, his movies have grown increasingly off-kilter, off-key. *Arkadin* is a sort of remake of *Citizen Kane* as continental gangster film, but symbolically it might almost be a documentary on the making of *Othello*, its trans-global locations (many of them glimpsed only instantaneously, as some of the characters are seen but momentarily) so diverse as to defy being pulled into the neighborhood of a single movie. When Van Stratten, the film's counterpart to *Kane*'s inquiring reporter, asks one of the colorful weirdos "Where's Sophie?" the man understandably responds: "Where is anybody?" At the beginning of *Arkadin* a peg-legged man commits a murder and vainly attempts to flee; his silhouette recedes into the distance but his shadow, huge and mocking, remains fixed in the foreground of the scene. In *The Trial* the distinctive fixtures of the abandoned railway station where Welles was forced to shoot most of the film poke into the corners of every set, regardless of its ostensible location, as the vague but ominous bureaucracy seems to reach everywhere. And in *Othello* the Moor drives Iago to the very edge of a rampart overlooking the sea, as Grisby and O'Hara ended their surreal encounter at the brink of the Acapulco cliffs; we cut to Othello, who advances one step further; and to Iago, who retreats yet another step. There could not be room for either to have taken these final steps without pitching into the surf—but there is. The film says that there is.

DIRECTORS AND DIRECTIONS

There's a tantalizing structural pun (and I'm not greatly
concerned whether Welles intended it or I'm inferring it) in those
opening images of *Citizen Kane*. The rising pattern shots that suggest
the first sentient gropings of a new consciousness are, literally,
pictures of fence, wire, mesh: a *screen* which simultaneously evokes
Kane's desperate penchant for walling his private self (Rosebud,
etc.) off from the world's eyes, and the two-dimensional surface on
which Welles will explore Kane's (and his?) definition-resisting
identity in terms of three-dimensional space and the fourth
dimension of time.

Welles' latest completed film, *?* (or *Fake*, as it is called more
handily), reportedly combines documentary footage about an art
forger with explicitly Pirandellian scenes celebrating the director's
expertise as various kinds of conjurer. Until prints of *?* become
accessible to us (the film has had but a single festival-style screening
in this country), *Citizen Kane* must stand as Welles' most relentlessly
media-conscious movie. The newsreel following Kane's demise is an
orgy of cinematic effects savored for their own sake as much as
employed for purposes of verisimilitude: the grossly dissimilar film
stocks (a dim, blocked-up shot of a body-clogged swimming pool
setting off the narrator's line about Kane's "private pleasure-
ground"); the deliberately scratched and underexposed or overde-
veloped new footage interspersed with actual newsreel; the delicious
recreation of media inadvertencies (the jump cut from a longshot of
Thatcher offering to read a statement, to a closeup as the first word
is all but pinched off; the union man doubly blowing his
denunciation: "He is today what he has always been, a—and
always will be—a fatshist!"); the melodramatization of Thompson's
voiceover that parodies *The March of Time*; the construction of
Xanadu represented by scenes of an RKO crew building the
cathedral for *The Hunchback of Notre Dame*; and the musical theme
for Kane's empire, which originally accompanied the guru's
Napoleonic speech in *Gunga Din*. We see many specimens of plastic,
graphic, and literary representation: photographs of Kane and his
mother, a woodcut of the Kane boardinghouse, architect's sketches
of the Chicago Opera House, statues of Walter P. Thatcher and a

dame without a head, posters for Susan's operas, memorial paintings of Thatcher and Kane, a declaration of principles, a rejected political cartoon, alternative newspaper headlines . . . We see a photograph of Kane, his wife and his son; an hour later we see it being made. Emily Monroe Norton Kane and Jim Gettys make their separate ways out of the shot of 185 West 74th Street and we anticipate that this housefront will resolve into the scandal-sheet halftone we have already observed in the newsreel. We watch history become history, time have a stop.

People's behavior, their very lives, resolve themselves into media effects. We are afforded an almost subliminal glimpse of the door to Susan's room at Xanadu as the maid closes it behind her: the pattern on it is not unlike one of those jigsaw puzzles she fills her life assembling. Similarly, the cold, smooth, characterless portal that slams behind Thompson at the Thatcher Memorial Library memorializes Kane's guardian more aptly than he could have appreciated. According to Jed Leland, Kane builds the Chicago Opera House for Susan Alexander to remove the quotation marks from the headline KANE MARRIES "SINGER"; during the marriage/breakfast montage he completes Emily's sentence "People will think—" "—what I tell them to think" and adds a period with his coffee cup, as he will carefully adjust a typewriter carriage from mid-line to the margin so he can follow his "Sure we're speaking, Jedediah—you're fired" with a slammed exclamation point. But sometimes the world gets bigger than Charlie Kane, other people cease to play supporting roles in his private drama, and when he bellows a hollow threat after Jim Gettys to put him in Sing Sing, his line is cut off by a door and mockingly completed by a distant auto horn.

If lifestyle is defined by film style in Welles' work, so is death. Kane's snow globe explodes. Jed Leland is wheeled off into the shadow, leaving the film as he entered it, trying to borrow a cigar. Susie, as Salammbo, dies at the end of the opera and just as surely "dies" as a performer. Eugene Morgan, in *Ambersons*, begs Isabel not to "strike my life down twice" while George, who expresses surprise through the jointly suggestive phrases "That's a horse on me" and "I *will* be shot," ends as a near-anonymous off screen accident statistic: "G.A. Minafer . . . both legs broken." The fall of images and the fall of bodies are coequal in *The Lady from Shanghai*, while the decapitation of Macbeth is figured in the mutilation of the witches' voodoo-like doll. Indeed, associative objects are so expressive in Welles' films that only total destruction will serve in the later works: as Hank Quinlan remarks in *Touch of Evil*, the killer "didn't just want Rudi Linnekar dead, he wanted him *annihilated*"; and dynamite, rather than the ceremonial knife, does for *The Trial*'s Joseph K.

It is entirely appropriate that the main title of *Mr. Arkadin* should be formed out of newspaper cuttings. Gregori Arkadin first appears as a figure in a limousine, his head swallowed in shadow; he is next introduced as an airplane flying overhead and interrupting a conversation between his daughter and his fellow protagonist, or antagonist, Van Stratten; then he's a castle on a hill, then a robed and disguised figure at a masked ball, and last a surreal closeup with shockingly artificial hairline and beard. His power is drawn from his surroundings, the size of his work force, the low wide angles that enable him to loom over us and the others in the film, the hectic, hurtling movement and cutting of the picture. The film that bears his name is composed of irredressible imbalances and vast lacunae bleakly filling with snow, discordant Christmas carols, the detritus of history (disused cannon in Jacob Zouk's courtyard, an inverted portrait of Hitler, a fallen swastika), corrupted artifacts and near-corpses who seem artifacts as well. His identity is spurious several times over. One of the wealthiest and most influential men in the world, he claims to be an amnesiac with no idea of who or what he was before one snowy night in 1927. He engages Van Stratten, an adventurer and petty crook, to carry on a Thompson-like investigation of his past. The quest is based on deception—Arkadin knows very well who and what he was—and on the need to conceal; for above all, Arkadin fears that his daughter Raina will learn he was once something less than Gregori Arkadin, and he intends to kill off anyone who could tell her.

Arkadin appears to enjoy an ascendancy in the film. He can toy with Van Stratten by pretending to call him long distance from Europe while actually sitting in plain view a couple hundred feet away in the Mexican sun; as his yacht pitches on a restless sea and the walls appear to roll and his companion lurches about the cabin, Arkadin, "a phenomenon of an age of dissolution and crisis," remains stable. But in the end Arkadin is unable to cross Munich for want of his own car, which Van Stratten has appropriated in Arkadin's own powerful name, and he stands behind a chain watching Van Stratten and dozens of other commoners board a plane belonging to an airline of which he is a major shareholder. "I am Gregori Arkadin!" he booms at the crowd, but Van Stratten deflates that identity by calling back "Yeah, and I'm Santa Claus" (a role sardonically attributed to Van Stratten at the beginning of the film and momentarily assumed by Arkadin shortly before the airport scene). Arkadin commandeers a private plane and races after his employee who, to save himself from the fate of all others privy to the great man's secret, intends to reveal it to Raina, with whom he has become romantically involved. She meets him at the other end of the flight and he has only time enough to beg her to tell her father she has got Van Stratten's message. Arkadin's voice roars from a loudspeaker; Raina lifts a microphone and says, as instructed, "It's too late." There is only static in response. We cut to the cockpit of Arkadin's plane, now empty. Looking up at the speaker on the ceiling, Raina cries, "Father! Father!" but it is as though the God of this particular universe, unmasked as a charlatan, had simply evaporated. We do not even see his body fall from the plane.

Welles claims that this is the most mutilated of his films, so one hesitates to insist on any interpretation. As it stands, however, this wildly disjunctive work is based on the principle of the vacuum. The secret of Mr. Arkadin holds it together, and the secret of Mr. Arkadin is that there is no "Mr. Arkadin." It is the force of that central conceit that prevents the film's diverse elements—the far-flung locations, the myriad grotesques who inhabit them, the preposterously jarring camera and editing techniques—from flying off into space.

If, as David Thomson has suggested, Charles Foster Kane is dreaming the newsman's investigation of Kane's life, we should mention here that Arkadin, having hired Van Stratten to file a confidential report on his history, himself embarks on a parallel quest. (In a deceptively structured sequence we observe Arkadin interrogating one of the witnesses, the Baroness Nagel, and are led to believe he has got to her before Van Stratten—an assumption that proves false a moment later.) The director, as it were, is not content to sit in his "ogre's castle" while his cast plays out their parts. Moreover, he has no sooner set Van Stratten on the trail than he attempts to call him off—an act which strengthens Van Stratten's resolve to continue, speculating "Maybe *I*'ll end up an

Arkadin!" Many such references link the two men, but it is their mutually exclusive love for Raina that dooms both of them and, indeed, dooms her as well. She chooses for her lover a junior version of her father and, as so often in Welles' work, extra-filmic considerations suggestively enhance our experience of the film: Arkadin's daughter is played by Welles' own wife. In the end, the original sin that both necessitates and explodes the world order of *Mr. Arkadin* may be incest.[1]

Dual and slurred identities are common in Welles' films. George Amberson Minafer does not decisively intervene in his mother's affair of the heart until Aunt Fanny starts functioning as on-screen director, eliciting from her young and inexperienced co-star a performance he may have had in him all the while but might never have delivered without her histrionic midwifery. Time and again Fanny lays her version of reality on George and he repeats it as though it were a verbal blueprint to be learned by rote (Fanny capping her act with a carefully belated "Why, George, didn't *you* know that's what people are saying?"). There is no necessity save cinematic necessity in Fanny's leaning forward during the luncheon scene in mid-*Ambersons* to goad George about Lucy's absence (George will momentarily take out his frustration by insulting Eugene's invention)—she is sitting right beside George and, as far as the geography of the table is concerned, can see him very well—but the angle from which this action is photographed makes Fanny seem to lean *out of* George.

George and Fanny become one in the form of Iago, who exercises great directorial potency over the Moor in *Othello*. At one point Iago stations Othello where he may observe a supposed rendezvous between Desdemona and Cassio; Othello's vision is circumscribed by a frame (he looks through a hole in the wall) and his hearing is impaired by echoes as well as the pounding surf and screaming gulls nearby; "Watch Cassio's gestures," Iago instructs, and then in effect plays the scene himself, interpreting reality selectively for Othello's increasingly susceptible eye and mind. Iago begins by announcing "I hate the Moor," yet he must frequently protest his love for Othello and at base does express love in the form of a cosmic envy:

[1] The rafters of Susan Alexander Kane's bedroom at Xanadu are decorated with juvenile decals of cuddly animals, which remind us of the real-life zoo maintained outside and convey Kane's ultimate vision of the bedroom as nursery.

he destroys what he wishes he were, and in the process destroys himself. This is consistent with a character who possesses a mirror reality—the sharp-focus replica of truth and yet a precisely reversed version of truth—and defines himself by saying, "I am not what I am."

Othello begins with a shot of the dead Moor's head tilted toward the bottom of the frame; *The Trial* opens with a similar view of Joseph K, who may or may not awaken from his dreams to find officers of the law entering his apartments. In Kafka and Welles we may see both the absurdly available females and the dubiously masculine figures of circumstance who always interrupt K's dalliances as projections of K's own psyche—respectively, of his libido and his superego. At film's end K confronts Hastler, the most individuated of the law's representatives—played by Welles—who is flashing illustrative panels of the parable of the law on a screen. The shadows of both men fall on that screen, and in reverse cuts of their faces we observe only half-faces in harsh chiaroscuro, ready to merge *Persona*-like. K comes to recognize his trial as an act of self-accusation. In his moment of greatest self-awareness, he casts no shadow on the screen; he is a whole man. But when he moves away he pauses, and his executioners appear, seeming to step out of either side of him. K attempts to hurl away the dynamite they would kill him with, and an odd, conspicuous lapse between his drawing back his arm and the ensuing blast makes it problematical who kills whom. Yet it would be uncharacteristic of Welles to suggest that anyone could escape from, or do more than come to recognize, his demons. A freezeframe of a mushroom cloud evokes not only memories of the cremated Rosebud but also the notion of an entire world dying with its dreamer.

Orson Welles takes no role in *The Magnificent Ambersons* but that of an off-screen narrator. Yet the film is called out of *Kane*'s uncreated darkness by his voice. That darkness closes down again after the Ambersons' story has been told. Welles' voice speaks: "Ladies and gentlemen, *The Magnificent Ambersons* has been adapted from the novel by Booth Tarkington"—and we see the book. "It was photographed by Stanley Cortez"—a movie camera; "Mark-Lee Kirk designed the sets"—sketches, "Al Fields dressed them"—a chair. And so on through to the cast: "Eugene—Joseph Cotten," and there is Cotten in costume, lovingly lighted in cameo against a solid black background; "Isabel—Dolores Costello," and so through the principal players. A microphone hangs in space, an ironically bombastic image: "I wrote the script and directed it. My name is Orson Welles. This is a Mercury Production." And the boom swings up and away into a beam of light. The device operates as more than a clever way of writing finis. We have watched an entire film that chronicles the fading of the magnificence of the Ambersons and their way of life—and even Eugene Morgan, the romantically disprized inventor who helps end that way of life, is a prime example of its gentility and grace. We have seen these people pass on, some of them dying during the course of the film, others suffering a stylistic negation. Yet here they are, all of them, as in a living album, while the men of the present who made this film celebrating their quaint pastness are nowhere to be seen: only their machines are their—camera, sound meters, editing spools—machines not unrelated to the inventions that toppled the Amberson dynasty as much as the Ambersons' own flaws. Yet through these machines this celebration has been made possible, as have been the realization of all the forms with which Welles has sought to define the compelling imperfections of eternal, imperfect human nature. The facelessness of the machinery really expresses one face of Orson Welles. He is the true protagonist of *The Magnificent Ambersons*, and of every film he has ever made.

Orson Welles's Use of Sound

by PHYLLIS GOLDFARB

Sound and space are immutably related, whether they comple-
ment one another or, as is often the case in the movies of Orson
Welles, they conflict. Welles' early films, especially *Citizen Kane*,
were remarkable for the way in which sound was used to elongate
space. The screen was forced to give up part of the flatness of its
nature. In later films, sound is put to a variety of uses, not the least
of which is a negation of reality. What we hear no longer works in
conjunction with what we see. Eisenstein might have called it
harmonized counterpoint. The sound is temporally synchronized
with its source, but at the same time mismatched—not in terms of
direction (since, in most theaters, there is a single loudspeaker), but
of distance and surroundings. As a result, there is a tension created
between the space and the sound, between our aural and visual
perceptions. If this tension remains unresolved, a partial fragmenting of our senses takes place. Sound becomes disembodied and
takes on a force and presence of its own.

Every time a movie is projected on a screen in front of us, we
relinquish part of the power we have over our psyches. The
narrative film invites us to participate in a fantasy, and to a certain
extent we always do. The creative artist is able to take advantage of
the vulnerable position in which the moving picture medium places
its audience, in order to present a previously unavailable experience. Orson Welles is such an artist. He gains control over our
ability to organize the barrage of stimuli that is constantly
assaulting us. A careful study of *Citizen Kane, The Magnificent
Ambersons, The Lady from Shanghai,* and *Touch of Evil* reveals a
progression toward manipulation of the viewer's powers of concen-

Originally published in Take One *(Vol. 3, No. 6), Box 1778, Station B,
Montreal, Canada H3B 3L3.*

tration, his visual and aural perception, and disorientation of his spatial and temporal organization.

If there is a progression toward fragmentation and disorientation in these four films of Welles, it is not to be found within the narratives; in these four movies the narratives move away from fragmentation, toward consolidation in terms of time, place, and structure. *Kane* moves forward and backward through time and space; it covers perhaps three generations. While *The Magnificent Ambersons* is composed of a number of moments just before and during Georgie Amberson's life, with an extended examination of one experience (his reaction to the Morgans), the narrative is limited to forward movement in time, and the action takes place within the perimeters of one city. The geographic area covered in *The Lady from Shanghai* is quite extensive, but in a dramatic sense the narrative movement is more limited than it would be if it took place within the confines of a small town. The drama's settings are forced upon the hero—first as an employee, then as a prisoner. He doesn't have the freedom that Georgie and Kane are allowed. In addition, temporal and structural elements are incontestably consolidated. There is a beginning, a middle, an end, a climax and a denouement—all of which take place within one year. Finally, *Touch of Evil* is the most compact of all. Its narrative is so tightly interconnected it unravels rather than unfolds. It is wholly contained within a twenty-four-hour period, and all the action takes place around one point on the Mexican-American border.

Disorientation is accomplished not within the narrative structures of the films, but by fragmentation of our perceptions and manipulation of our responses. In order to understand how this comes about, it is necessary to have a clear conception of the role that sound plays in film, and of the processes of aural perception.

There are three basic classes (or "uses") of cinematic sound: spatial sound, ideational sound, and music. Everything we hear falls into one of these categories—or is a combination of two or three.

Spatial sounds obey the laws of real sound. Our ears place the source of the sound within space. We're not limited, aurally, as we are visually by the flat screen. If the soundtrack of a movie accurately conforms to the behavior of natural sound in space, we receive aural cues with which we can determine the surroundings, direction, and distance, of the sound source. This results in a definition of space.

Surroundings are determined by volume and quality of sound. For example, a sound made and heard in a closet full of clothing will be appreciably different in quality from the identical sound made in a cave. Compare the quality of Kane's voice in the halls of Xanadu to that of his voice in the car on the way to the picnic. The reason for this is that various objects absorb and reflect different amounts and frequencies of sound. It follows, then, that sound heard from inside a room won't register exactly like the same sound heard from the other side of a glass partition, or a closed door—a variation Welles carefully manipulates when Quinlan enters the hotel room to strangle Joe Grandi in *Touch of Evil*.

The reason I have concerned myself with something that seems so obvious is that when this factor is ignored, or purposely used to distort the duplication of real sound, the mismatch makes us vaguely uncomfortable, slightly dislocated, usually without knowing why. The reaction is very subtle. A sort of floating tension is created which can be used, by the filmmaker, in directing audience response. Welles uses this device, in *The Lady from Shanghai* and *Touch of Evil*, but leaves the tension unresolved. The voices in the post-explosion confusion in *Touch of Evil*, for example, sound as if they were being emitted within a confined area, but the scene takes place in the open air. The disembodied quality of the voices sets a pattern that is reinforced throughout the movie. It has the effect of partially disorganizing our perceptions: the visuals and aurals don't fit.

Direction is understood biaurally. Our ears are incredibly sensitive: we can detect a time difference between the two ears, if the onset of the sound is sharp, of 0.65 milliseconds. This, coupled with the minute difference in volume due to the sound shadow the head casts, and one ear catching the sound wave at a different point in its compression-rarefaction phases, accounts for the accuracy with which we can determine direction. Unfortunately, the closest we can come to experiencing it in the cinema (a monaural medium) is by interpreting visual cues. We know where a voice is coming from because we see the speaker's lips moving. If the source of sound is outside our visual field, we follow the gaze or reaction of a character on the screen.

Distancing is the one aural space-defining factor that all filmmakers are aware of. Amplitude (or loudness) increases as the source of sound moves toward us, but because there are so many variables in sound production, and because of our poor aural storage and/or retrieval systems, we aren't able to make more than a crude approximation of absolute distance. That's why movies, which have dialogue varying from close-up to medium shot, don't expend much effort modulating the volume as the camera, or characters, move.

Sound, then, opens up and makes us aware of space. The accurate and creative use of volume alone has the effect of giving depth to the flat screen image. Using sound in this way is one of the most impressive innovations of *Citizen Kane* and is also prominent in *The Magnificent Ambersons.* There may be no scene in the history of film that is more two-dimensional than the good-bye at the train station between Georgie Amberson and his uncle. Visually, we perceive depth on a flat surface by certain cues—such as lines diminishing to a vanishing point, objects in the distance getting smaller, objects cut off by others in front of them, etc. In this scene, with the two men surrounded by mist, there are no visual cues—so there is really no feeling for depth until the older man turns and walks diagonally across the screen. Even then, it is only the sound of his receding footsteps that gives us a sense of space.

Welles wasn't satisfied with merely defining space. In *The Lady from Shanghai* and *Touch of Evil* he deliberately undermines space perception by mismatching the sound and its source. The roar of the jalopies is heard in close-up long before they approach the motel in *Touch of Evil.* In the middle of an intimate scene between Mike and Elsa in *The Lady from Shanghai*, Grisby's voice intrudes in close-up while the sound of the launch he's in is distanced correctly. Grisby is nowhere near the couple. In fact, his voice always seems a little too loud, a little too close. The sound takes on a presence of its own.

Welles goes beyond undermining aural reality. By substituting and confusing sound with its reproduction, and objects with their reflections, silhouettes, and shadows, Welles manages to separate sound from its source, and from space. By the end of *The Lady from Shanghai* we have no idea from what direction the sound is coming. By the end of *Touch of Evil* we have not only lost all sense of distance and direction, we are also confused about the source itself. Quinlan and Menzies' voices physically separate from their bodies, as the soundtrack is taken, in part, from a small radio receiver/tape recorder which is picking up transmissions from a concealed microphone carried by Menzies. We hear the voices in tinny close-up, off the radio receiver, at the same time as we see the two men moving in the distance.

At one point, as they are crossing the bridge into Mexico, sound becomes directly involved in its own disassociation: Quinlan hears his voice coming from the receiver—a sound which is twice removed from the filmic reality, but which has a central place within the narrative. It leads directly to Menzies' death. We don't see the actual shooting—we only experience it second-hand, through sound: we see a close-up of the tape as it records the events that are going on above, on the bridge. Moments later, we hear the playback—with the camera again focused on the recorder. This repeat is no different from our first experience, and no more closely related to real filmic space, time, or character.

The fragmentation of the relationship between a sound and its source is such a dominating feature throughout *Touch of Evil* that we don't even notice all sorts of anomalies in sound, space, and narrative. We don't find it peculiar for Vargas to turn his back on the blind lady so she won't hear him telephoning his wife, nor are we disturbed by the fact that he doesn't hear Suzy's shouts from the hotel fire escape, even though we hear her voice booming across the crowd that has gathered below her, and through which he drives in search of her. His visual and aural dislocations aren't questioned, because our own are so pronounced.

Most of the time the kinds of sounds that define space are sound effects and background noise. Straight dialogue usually draws and holds our attention away from the spatial dimension: we are more concerned with what is being said than the relationship between the source and space. Dialogue has the effect of taking us out of space and placing us in the realm of ideas. The transition is completed by the sound editor's toning down of background noise. Normally, we have the ability to disregard distracting stimuli and focus our attention on whatever we choose. Cinema usurps that power. It may be the speed at which images are presented, or the rapidity with which we are shifted about in time and space, but whatever the cause there is a pronounced impairment of our ability to tune out surrounding stimuli and the sound editor has to do it for us. Reintroducing, or increasing the level of, these effects takes us back to the spatial dimension. Our attention is caught by the aural change and the switch is made.

This gives us a whole new perspective for appreciating the courtroom sequence in *The Lady from Shanghai.* Welles has no intention of allowing us to focus on the trial proceedings. Thus, he makes escape to the ideational difficult by constantly reintroducing spatial elements. Coughing and whispering in the jury box are typical of this effort, as are the cutaways to audience reactions. There's something particularly interesting about these. The first few times Welles cuts away, he synchronizes it with sound. The later cutaways have no track, but they have a noisy effect. We can almost hear the rustling. When Elsa finally admits to having kissed O'Hara in the aquarium, the camera doesn't cut away, but we hear the silence and feel the weight of the courtroom bearing down on her.

To say that conversation removes us from the spatial and places us in the ideational is not to say that it can't be used to define space. Speech works on both levels. Mrs. Kane closes the window on little Charlie, playing outside, when she gets ready to discuss her decision to send him away. It's not as if she does this just because she is concerned about his over-hearing. Welles is making sure that we don't miss these important details of Kane's life, since distance and its concomitant definition of space tends to distract us from what is being said.

If conversation takes us out of space, what is the effect of narration? The narrator is twice removed from spatial reality. Not only are his words ideational, and consequently flattening to the screen image, but his intrusion upon the story reminds us of the unreality of the whole filmic experience. The result is a reflexivity that is increased in Welles by his deliberate flouting of narrative convention. The narrator is supposed to set the scene, and perhaps fill in some background, but it is clearly against the "rules" for his words to be synchronized to the character's lips. " 'Fine weather we're having,' I said to break the ice," says O'Hara, *as narrator,* over a medium close-up of O'Hara walking and talking beside Elsa's carriage. Convention dictates that we already be within the scene. The character can, and should, speak his own lines. Anything that goes against a convention (and our expectation) calls attention to itself, and reflects on the medium that has promulgated that convention. We end up, momentarily, conscious of the film as a vehicle of fantasy.

There are a number of forms narration can take. Welles

apparently prefers to fade the narrator out during the first quarter of the film, and then in again toward the end. He uses this method in both *The Magnificent Ambersons* and *The Lady from Shanghai.* This would ordinarily leave a large center portion virtually without moments of reflexivity. Welles lets this happen in *Ambersons,* but in *Shanghai* and *Evil* where there is no narrator at all, Welles forces us to become aware of film as a medium by manipulating our expectations of musical convention.

Background music in a Hollywood movie sometimes has its source within the ongoing scene; usually it is just mood music added in the sound mix. It is never supposed to compete for our attention. Such is not the case in *Shanghai* or *Evil.* Typically, the music and visual start out simultaneously, with the music in the background. All of a sudden we are made to realize that the music is *real* music within the film's narrative. It eventually slips back into the background. The first shot after Elsa's singing scene in *Shanghai* is of Elsa sunning herself on the ship's deck. O'Hara is at the wheel. On the soundtrack is brassy popular music of the forties. It is brought to our attention because it is so loud, and so incongruous with the rather idyllic visual. Suddenly the music stops, and a disc jockey starts to talk. It is only Elsa's radio. The disc jockey goes off, and soft music comes on. This becomes background music which is toned down when Elsa and O'Hara begin to talk.

In an earlier scene in the same film, a juke box and its music is brought to our attention when the record ends. Goldy turns to a waiter and says, "Would you put these in crank number four? That's all we want to listen to." After this, the music returns to its place in the background until it is again referred to in the conversation. By constantly surprising us with new methods of presenting this pattern—from background to foreground—the effect remains fresh. The music has been brought to our attention, and has served the movie reflexively.

In *Evil* our awareness of music is so intense that it takes on an ideational quality. We respond to it directly, rather than to a mood it creates. The volume and persistence of the irritating music in the motel scenes invade our consciousness much as it does Suzy's. It is a pervasive force in her presence, and seeps into Vargas' as well by way of his car radio, but it belongs by association to the teenage hoodlums. This isn't the only association of character and music that exists in the film. Mexican nightclub music belongs to Joe

Grandi and player-piano to Tanya, the Marlene Dietrich character. Most of the time, although not always, these sounds also conform to spatial limitations. There are times when what had been real music swells to reinforce a climax in the narrative, and other times, especially with the player-piano music, when the sound is toned down under conversation that is put into aural foreground.

Music, dialogue, effects, any type of aural signal can also be used ideationally, as a transitional element when the narrative is moving through time and/or space. When Elsa leaves the nightclub in Acapulco, the orchestra music follows her and continues, reduced to a single guitar, when she meets O'Hara. In *Kane* Susan's singing in the parlor is heard, without a lapse, over the dissolve which moves us to the parlor at a later date. Then Kane's applause turns into light clapping heard behind Leland's campaign speech. Leland's voice, in turn, becomes Kane's heard over the microphone in a large auditorium.

The transitions between scenes become tighter through the four movies. In *Evil* almost every scene has some element to bridge the gap to the next. Grandi's nephew decides to call his uncle for instructions, and we cut away from him at the phone to Quinlan and Grandi in a bar. A few seconds later the telephone in the background rings. We leave these two men when Grandi puts a coin in the juke box, whose music is associated with the Grandi boys, who are at the motel, where rock and roll is being piped into Suzy's room. That's where we end up.

The transitions in *Shanghai* aren't as tight as they are in *Evil*, and in *Ambersons* they are rarely anything but straight cuts. In *Citizen Kane* the aural equivalents of match dissolves are used in conjunction with visual dissolves to move us across spatial-temporal coordinates, but the process is different in the later films. In *Kane* the sound is a technical device used to make the transition smoothly. In *Evil* an element integral to one scene is present in, and brings us to, the next.

Spatial definition is one of two perceptual contributions to the aural experience. The other is an attention-focusing mechanism. We are perpetually surrounded by noise, but we're only aware of part of it. The rest is toned down by our mental processes and remains on a lower level of consciousness. Generally, our attention is drawn to an object that is producing sound, especially if it is moving, or given visual prominence in some other way. There's an interesting maneuver in *Shanghai* that manipulates and moves our attention by changing only what we hear. As Elsa enters the courtroom, we follow her movement down the aisle. On the soundtrack we hear the noise that surrounds her. The camera stops as she finds a row with a seat, but the sound continues forward, carrying our attention with it, away from Elsa to the courtroom proceedings at the far end of the room. These are sounds that were previously unheard.

Loud or unremitting sounds force themselves on our attention, as in the motel scenes in *Evil*. Any change in volume or quality also attracts our attention, so we could be diverted by a new sound, especially if it was coming from outside our visual field. This probably stems from a survival instinct: anything that makes a noise within hearing distance is a possible threat, especially if we were previously unaware of its presence, and we respond involuntarily to such a stimulus. This reaction is used in *Ambersons* as a means of splitting our attention. We watch the grandfather, in close-up, contemplating death, while we listen to a discussion of the estate Elizabeth has left. In another scene, we are paying attention to Fanny and Georgie arguing when, from off-screen, comes the voice of the Ray Collins character complaining about noise and finally saying, "I'm going to move to a hotel."

Welles is extremely conscious of the mechanisms of attention. Early in *Kane* there is a scene of Thompson, the reporter, after his unsuccessful attempt to interview Susan. Just before he leaves, he makes a call from a telephone booth in the extreme foreground. He should be the center of attention, as we usually attend to that which is producing a sound. Furthermore, he is close to us, and he is heard in aural close-up. The nightclub music is in the background, partially shut out when he closes the door. Nevertheless, a substantial portion of our attention is drawn away from the sound, through the left window of the phone booth door, and across the room to Susan—where she slumps in a pool of light. If sound attracts our attention, so does light. The result is that we are unable to focus completely on either one of the stimuli presented to us. In this case, the two are compatible: the telephone call has to do with Susan. Furthermore, one is completely visual and the other is completely aural, as Thompson is in a shadow; there isn't too much competition between them. In *Shanghai* and especially in *Evil* there is often so much confusion and competition between the elements within the frame that the audience finds itself unable to organize and process it normally. Consider the scene immediately after the explosion in *Evil*. There are many people, all being introduced to one another and to us talking and milling about. Characters critical to the narrative pop onto the scene and, just as quickly, disappear. We aren't given any signals as to what we should attend. The result is a diffusion of our faculties—and a feeling of relief when we finally leave with Vargas' wife.

In a later scene the fragmenting is done somewhat more delicately. In the scene where Vargas is talking on the blind woman's telephone, his turning away does bring the sound to our attention. We think about what an unnecessary movement he has made. By calling attention to itself it works reflexively, so we become aware of the film medium. At the same time another part of our attention is drawn out the window, where we see Menzies and Grandi. These two characters are seen in longshot, fussing and arguing with one another. The elements in this example, and the previous one, work against each other to split our focusing abilities.

When Welles does give us something to concentrate on in *Shanghai* and *Evil*, it is often something that seems peripheral to the narrative. The water glass and pills, in *Shanghai*, are forced on us well before they play any part in the narrative. Similarly, in *Evil*, the camera is on Vargas while Quinlan is interrogating his suspect about "finding" the dynamite. It's a critical moment until we realize that it's Vargas' reaction to this evidence that's important. We are continually left mildly disconcerted and dislocated by the conflicting demands on our attention.

Welles doesn't limit himself to psychological means when it comes to playing with our perceptions. He takes advantage of other, more complex social responses. We can't help but attend to Bannister as he laboriously leaves the witness stand in *Shanghai*. How often are we allowed to stare unabashedly at someone who is crippled? We are hardly aware of the calling of his wife, even though the prosecuting attorney who calls her is standing in the extreme foreground. His words carry the plot forward, and ordinarily his voice and position in the frame would be attention-getting devices, but Bannister steals the show. There's also the ringing telephone in the judge's chamber as O'Hara fights to get away. That's a sound to which we have a conditioned response, and Welles uses that response to assure our diversion—and a certain building up of tension which is turned to comic relief when the judge reacts for us and answers the phone.

Persons suffering from schizophrenia complain of being bombarded by sensations, and of a lack of control over their consciousness. Paranoid types often believe that outside forces have taken over their thought processes. Such claims would not be totally irrational for the moviegoer—especially if he's watching a movie by Welles. In such a situation his perception of reality is torn apart. Sound no longer defines space. Unable to focus his attention, he becomes dislocated within the narrative. If art is a re-experiencing of our mental and emotional conditions within a new context, Orson Welles is one of the world's supreme artists.

THE FILMS

Welles Before Kane

by JOSEPH McBRIDE

Orson Welles has never mentioned to interviewers that he did
any experimentation in film prior to his coming to Hollywood—un-
doubtedly preferring the world to think that he burst full-blown on
the scene with *Citizen Kane*. To an interviewer who asked him
recently how he arrived at *Kane*'s "cinematic innovations," he
replied airily, "I owe it to my ignorance. If this word seems
inadequate to you, replace it with innocence." But Welles was far
from being a filmic innocent. There have been a few furtive
mentions, largely unheeded by film historians, of a film he shot in
1938 for use in a Mercury Theatre stage production, William
Gillette's farce *Too Much Johnson*, which ran for two weeks at the
Stony Creek Summer Theatre in New York before Welles decided
not to bring it to Broadway. He reportedly shot a twenty-minute
silent prologue to the play, and ten-minute films to introduce the
second and third acts. Included in the cast were Joseph Cotten,
Edgar Barrier, Marc Blitzstein, and Virginia Nicholson, Welles'
first wife. I have not been able to see a print of *Too Much Johnson*.
Welles has one, but he says that it is not worth seeing without the
play. He also shot a film as prologue to his 1939 vaudeville show,
The Green Goddess, "depicting an air crash in the Himalayas,"
according to his associate Richard Wilson. This also has so far
proved impossible to locate.

But I have been able to unearth an extremely interesting little
silent film called *The Hearts of Age*, preserved in a private collection,
which apparently was Welles' first venture into film. It runs about
four minutes and stars Welles and Virginia Nicholson. The copy I

© *1970 by The Regents of the University of California. Reprinted from* Film
Quarterly, *Vol. 23, No. 3, Spring 1970, pp. 19–22, by permission of The
Regents.*

saw, until recently probably the only one extant, was the original 16mm print. It was donated, as part of the Vance collection, to the Greenwich (Conn.) Public Library. The sound of the splices clicking through the projector was nerve-wracking—though the film is in remarkably good condition—but my apprehension about projecting it was more than assuaged by the excitement of discovery. It was like finding a youthful play by Shakespeare. Access to the film has now been given to the American Film Institute, and a duplicate negative for preservation is lodged in the Library of Congress, which has also made a study copy that can be viewed by scholars on Library premises. (A study copy can likewise be seen at the Greenwich Library.) It will probably also be included in the AFI Welles retrospective in Washington this spring.

The credit cards list only the title and the actors, but they are in Welles' handwriting. Another person who has seen *The Hearts of Age* called Welles when he was in Hollywood recently and asked him about it. At first he didn't remember it, but when assured that he appears in the film, he recalled that, yes, it had been made in the summer of 1934, when he was nineteen, at the drama festival he sponsored at the Todd School in Woodstock, Illinois, from which he had been graduated three years before. He denied that he directed or edited it, claiming that it was just a "home movie." The Vance collection records, however, state that Welles co-directed the film with William Vance (who produced it and makes a brief appearance), and there is much internal evidence to support this.

The late Mr. Vance was a college student when he met Welles; he later went on to produce and direct television commercials. I saw a ten-minute adaptation of *Dr. Jekyll and Mr. Hyde*, made in 1932, which he stars in and directed. It is nothing more than a crude and rather risible student movie. *The Hearts of Age* is something more, however. Though it is afflicted with facile symbolism and flippant obscurity, there are many directorial and photographic flourishes which point unmistakably to Welles' later work. A few of the shots are eerily prophetic of *Kane*, and the film shows even more than *Kane* the extent to which Welles was influenced by German theatrical and cinematic expressionism, particularly by F. W. Murnau's *Nosferatu*. And if some of the camerawork is perfunctory (especially when Welles is not on the screen), many of the shots are beautifully lit and composed, and the general lack of coherence is almost offset by the humor of Welles' performance.

At first the film seems hopelessly obscure, one of those bastard children of 1920s French avant-gardism that still afflict us today, but a pattern gradually emerges. It becomes clear that the film is an allegory of death. The first shot is of a spinning Christmas tree ball, later repeated and echoed again when a white-robed figure walks past stroking a globe; *Kane* of course. After the opening shot, we see a quick montage (much too quick for comfort, with that projector churning away) of bells ringing, some of the shots in negative. Then we see an old lady—Virginia Nicholson in grotesque make-up—rocking back and forth. The camera, smoothly hand-held in contrast to the jerky camerawork in *Dr. Jekyll*, pulls slowly back to show that she is suggestively straddling a ringing bell. The next shots reveal a man in black-face, wigged and dressed in lacy little boy's costume incongruously completed by football knickers, pulling the bell rope, with the old lady on the roof above him. After the second shot of the spinning ball, we see a tilted shot of a grave stone with three elongated shadows moving slowly on the ground behind it, and then a grave marker tilted in the opposite direction with a hand grasping around it.

A shadow hand rings a shadow bell, hazy latticework lighting all around it; we are reminded that Welles, by the age of nineteen, had already directed and lit more than a score of plays, both with the Todd School's student company and in Dublin, where he had been an actor with the Gate and Abbey Players and a director at the Gate Studio. There is nothing in *Dr. Jekyll* to compare with the suppleness of this film's lighting. The hand bell falls harshly to the ground in the next shot, no longer a shadow now, and we return to the old lady riding the bell with an obscenely pained expression as the black-faced man tugs spiritedly away. She opens an umbrella over her head (Welles was also fond of Keaton, who liked to fool around with umbrellas when it wasn't raining). We see a hand spinning a globe in close-up and then a striking shot, worthy of Murnau: a gray tombstone, dizzily tilted, with a shadow hand creeping up it (a *white* shadow, because the shot is in negative) and beckoning with a long finger, while a corporeal hand crawls along the edge of the stone. We see a piano keyboard—a flash-forward, as it turns out—and then Orson Welles opening a door over a rickety flight of stairs.

It is always a strange experience to stumble back upon the first screen appearance of one of the *monstres sacrés*. The shock of that first entrance is not only the shock of recognition, it is like a glimpse of a platonic form. We are watching a privileged drama; every step, every gesture is hazardous and exciting, because what is at stake is the formation of a legend. Sometimes we are startled, as when we see Chaplin without tramp's costume as a suave, top-hatted villain. Does he know what we know? Or are we witness to the very moments in which the great secret makes itself known? Enchanting to see Katharine Hepburn sweep down a staircase in *A Bill of Divorcement*, Cukor's camera whipping across an entire room to intercept her flight; but how would we react if we could see Garbo in the advertising film she made for a department store, demonstrating how not to dress? With a bravura that will come to be known as his, Welles the director delays Welles the actor from appearing until we are sufficiently expectant of a grand entrance, an apparition that will transfix our attention and conjure up our unquestioning awe.

Whatever doubts we might have as to Welles' self-awareness are immediately dispelled by his appearance, mincing and leering, in a sort of comic Irishman costume, his face grotesquely aged like the lady's, his hairline masked and a wispy clown wig protruding from his temples. He starts down the stairs, bowing to the old lady. He carries a top-hat and a cane—later to be the talisman of other Wellesian characters, from Bannister in *The Lady from Shanghai* to Mr. Clay in *The Immortal Story*. He descends the stairs, seen from a variety of angles, intercut with the old lady watching warily. Then Welles shows the character walking down the steps three times in succession, a common enough avant-garde affection but appropriate here to underscore the fateful nature of the character's arrival. Presently we are treated to quick appearances of Miss Nicholson as a Keystone Kop and Mr. Vance as an Indian wrapped in a blanket (making a face into the camera as he passes), neither of which has much connection with the already rather tenuous story.

It seems that Welles' character is a figure of death, for he disturbs the indefatigably rocking old lady by appearing all over the rooftop of an adjoining building—and making a choking gesture with his cane for the man in black-face, a gesture echoed twenty-five years later by Quinlan in *Touch of Evil*. One of those quaint inserts dear to Griffith and Stroheim interrupts the action: a hand pouring coins from a shell, and a broom sweeping the money away. (Later we will see a hand dropping a crumpled five-dollar bill to the floor, but nothing else will come of it.) Death appears at the window, leering coyly and dangling two heart-shaped lollipops, tortuously wrapped around each other. These especially infuriate the old lady, who accelerates her rocking. From the smiling Death, Welles cuts to a skull, to a yanking rope, to a pair of feet hanging in mid-air, and to the head of the black-faced bellringer, dangling in a noose. Then we see a drawing of the hanged bellringer, and soon a hand enters the frame and draws a little bell as signature in the corner.

There is a startling transition to Death walking into a darkened room (the underworld?) carrying a candelabrum. He places it on a piano and starts to play, the camera tilted wildly to the right as he pounds furiously away: very much *The Phantom of the Opera.* We see his fingers coming closer and closer to the camera. Abruptly the pianist hits a wrong note and stops. He plunks at the keys, bending his head owlishly to test the sound (a good job of miming by Welles). He gets up and discovers that the old lady is lying dead inside the piano. Death opens the piano bench and takes out, instead of sheet music, a pile of thin slabs, shaped like tombstones. He shuffles through them: "Sleeping," "At Rest," "In Peace," "With the Lord," and "The End," leaving the last behind. He sits down again to play, undulating deliriously. We see the bell again, and then his hands playing the piano. Then the slab, "The End."

It would be pompous to claim that we can look at *The Hearts of Age* and see that its maker must have become a great director, just as it would be to extrapolate Chaplin's greatness out of *Making a Living.* But we can see, through the young man's melange of styles, the conglomeration of postures both congenial and unassimilated, a vigorous, unguarded, *personal* approach to even the most second-hand of ideas and motifs. It would be foolish to try to justify *The Hearts of Age* as a self-sufficient work. It is juvenilia, and Welles might be rather embarrassed by it today. But *Citizen Kane*, we should remember, is also the product of youthful eclecticism. That is part of its charm; its strength, like that of the first *nouvelle vague* films, comes from the integration of these divergent styles into a coherent framework, each part appropriate to the drama. We can see in *The Hearts of Age* that Welles, like all young artists, had to work a penchant for gratuitous allusion and self-indulgence out of his sytem before being able to create a unified work.

Citizen Kane

by DAVID BORDWELL

The best way to understand *Citizen Kane* is to stop worshiping it as a triumph of technique. Too many people have pretended that Orson Welles was the first to use deep-focus, long takes, films-within-films, sound montage, and even ceilings on sets when these techniques were child's play for Griffith, Murnau, Renoir, Berkeley, Keaton, Hitchcock, Lang, and Clair. To locate *Kane's* essential originality in its gimmicks cheapens it; once we know how the magician does his tricks, the show becomes a charade. *Kane* is a masterpiece not because of its tours de force, brilliant as they are, but because of the way those tours de force are controlled for large artistic ends. The glitter of the film's style reflects a dark and serious theme; *Kane's* vision is as rich as its virtuosity.

The breadth of that vision remains as impressive today as thirty years ago. *Citizen Kane* straddles great opposites. It is at once a triumph of social comment and a landmark in cinematic surrealism. It treats subjects like love, power, class, money, friendship, and honesty with the seriousness of a European film; yet it never topples into pretentiousness, is at every instant as zestful, intelligent, and entertaining as the finest Hollywood pictures. It is both a pointed comedy of manners and a tragedy on a Renaissance scale. It has a Flaubertian finesse of detail and an Elizabethan grandeur of design. Extroverted and introspective, exuberant and solemn, *Kane* has become an archetypal film as boldly as Kane's career makes him an archetypal figure. "I am, always have been, and always will be only one thing—an American," he declares, and the contradictions in *Citizen Kane* echo those of an entire country. No wonder the film's

David Bordwell, "Citizen Kane," Film Comment, *Summer 1971, Vol. 7, No. 2.* © *1971 Film Comment Publishing Corporation. Reprinted by permission.*

original title was *American*: like the nation, the film and its protagonist hold contraries in fluid, fascinating suspension.

To unify such opposites, *Kane* draws together the two main strands of cinematic tradition. As both a mechanical recorder of events and a biased interpreter of the same events, cinema oscillates between the poles of objective realism and subjective vision. This tension, implicit in every film (and, as Pasolini points out, in every image), is at the heart of *Citizen Kane*. Faithful to the integrity of the external world, the film is simultaneously expressive of the processes of the imagination. As the ancestor of the works of Godard, Bergman, Fellini, Bresson, and Antonioni, *Kane* is a monument in the modern cinema, the cinema of consciousness.

Since Lumière, motion pictures have been attracted to the detailed reproduction of external reality. Still photography, the literary school of Naturalism, and the elaborate theatrical apparatus of the nineteenth century gave impetus to the documentary side of film. Thus most of the films made before 1940 reflect this sort of objective realism in their mise-en-scène. But running parallel to this documentary trend is a subjectivity that uses film to transform reality to suit the creator's imagination. From Méliès' theatrical stylization and cinematic sleight-of-hand come the distorted décor of *Caligari* and the camera experimentation of the European avant-garde.

This tandem line of development highlights the significance of Eisenstein in film aesthetics. He demonstrated that montage could assemble the raw data of the Lumière method in patterns which expressed the poetic imagination. Dialectical montage was an admission of the presence of artistic consciousness in a way that Griffith's "invisible" cutting was not. The audience was made aware of a creator's sensibility juxtaposing images to make a specific emotional or intellectual point. Eisenstein claimed to control montage of attractions "scientifically" (sometimes to the point of reducing metaphor to rebus), but after Eisenstein, a less didactic, more associational montage became a dominant poetic style of the avant-garde.

In its own way, *Citizen Kane* also recapitulates and extends film tradition. On a primary level, it makes sophisticated allusions to several genres: the detective thriller, the romance, the musical, the horror fantasy, the hard-boiled newspaper film, the big-business story, the newsreel, and the social-comment film. But *Kane* is more than an anthology. Testing the Lumière-Méliès tension, Welles, like Eisenstein, gives the cinema a new contemplative density by structuring his material on the nature of consciousness. What Eisenstein does between individual shots, Welles does in the film's total organization. *Kane's* great achievement, then, is not its stylistic heel-clicking, but its rich fusion of an objective realism of texture with a subjective realism of structure. Welles opens a new area to the cinema because, like Eisenstein, he not only shows what we see, but he symbolizes the way we see it.

Kane explores the nature of consciousness chiefly by presenting various points of view on a shifting, multiplaned world. We enter Kane's consciousness as he dies, before we have even met him; he is less a character than a stylized image. Immediately, we view him as a public figure—fascinating but remote. Next we scrutinize him as a man, seen through the eyes of his wife and his associates, as a reporter traces his life story. Finally, these various perspectives are capped by a detached, omniscient one. In all, Kane emerges as a man—pathetic, grand, contradictory, ultimately enigmatic. The film expresses an ambiguous reality through formal devices that stress both the objectivity of fact and the subjectivity of point of view. It is because the best contemporary cinema has turned to the exploration of such a reality that *Kane* is, in a sense, the first modern American film.

The opening twelve minutes of *Citizen Kane* capsulize its approach and scope. At the very start, Welles uses a basic property of film to establish *Kane's* method and pays homage to the two founts of cinema—the fantasy of Méliès and the reportage of Lumière.

The camera glides slowly up a fence. NO TRESPASSING, warns a sign. Immediately, the camera proceeds to trespass. It is a tingling moment, because the driving force of cinema is to trespass, to relentlessly investigate, to peel back what conceals and confront what reveals. "The camera," writes Pudovkin, "as it were, forces itself, ever striving, into the profoundest deeps of life; it strives thither to penetrate, whither the average spectator never reaches as he glances casually around him. The camera goes deeper." Cinema is a perfecting of vision because the eye of the camera, unlike that of the spectator, cannot be held back by fences or walls or signs; if anything interferes with the steady progress into the heart of a scene, we know it is an artificial and temporary obstacle. Thus it is this forward-cleaving movement, begun in *Kane's* first scene, that is completed at the climactic track-in to the Rosebud sled.

Immediately, the imagery becomes dreamlike: a castle, a light snapped out and mysteriously glowing back to life, a man's lips, eerily sifting snow, a shattered crystal, a tiny cottage. Dissolves languidly link huge close-ups; space is obliterated; the paperweight smashes but makes no sound; a nurse enters, distorted in the reflection. We then see the deathbed dark against an arched window, and the shot fades out. The sequence is a reprise of the dream-structure of the European avant-garde films, especially *Caligari*, *Un Chien Andalou*, and *Blood of a Poet*. Welles celebrates the magic of Méliès and stresses, in both the content and the juxtaposition of the images, the subjective side of cinema.

But suddenly, in one of the most brilliant strokes in film, the "News on the March" sequence bursts on our eyes, history fills the screen, and we are confronted with the Lumière side of cinema, reality apparently unmanipulated. The stentorian announcer, the corny sensationalism, the *Time* style, and the histrionic music announce the newsreel's affinity with the popular *March of Time* shorts. (It is still the funniest parody of mass-media vulgarity ever filmed.) Furthermore, since each shot looks like period footage, "News on the March" virtually recapitulates the technical development of cinema from 1890 to 1941. Scratches on the emulsion, jerky movement, jump cuts, overexposures, handheld camerawork, insertion of authentic newsreel clips, the use of different filmstocks and cameras—each frame is historically persuasive. Glimpses of Chamberlain, Teddy Roosevelt, and Hitler are immediately and indelibly convincing. Thus as the first sequence had given us a private, poetic image of Kane, so this sequence supplies the public, documentary side of him. In clashing the two together, Welles immediately establishes the basic tension of *Kane* (and cinema itself): objective fact versus subjective vision, clearness and superficiality versus obscurity and profundity, newsreel versus dream. By making us question the very nature of experience, this clash of forms and styles produces the tension between reality and imagination that is the film's theme.

"News on the March" does more, though. Jumping, skittery, grainy, the sequence is the narrative hub of the film, the argument of the story, simultaneously running through Kane's life and

Orson Welles as Franz Kindler in *The Stranger*.
Man as monster, time as retribution.

Agnes Moorehead as Aunt Fanny and Tim Holt as George
Minafer in *The Magnificent Ambersons*. Space as arena for
psychic struggle.

Tim Holt as Georgie Minafer in *The
Magnificent Ambersons*. The problem
of identity: Man as statue, shadow,
image and reflection.

The bibelot from *Citizen Kane*.
Expressionism as surrealism.

Orson Welles as Michael O'Hara, Rita Hayworth as Elsa
Bannister and Everett Sloane as Arthur Bannister in *The
Lady from Shanghai*. The search for identity and the shat-
tered self.

Orson Welles as Macbeth in *Macbeth*.
Costume as theme.

Jeanette Nolan as Lady Macbeth in *Macbeth*.
Mis-en-scène as actor.

From *Othello*. Darkness made visible.

Michéal MacLiammoir as Iago in *Othello*.
Man caged, man divided.

Orson Welles as *Othello*. The face as field of action.

Orson Welles as Hank Quinlan in *Touch of Evil*. Maculate man.

Anthony Perkins as K in *The Trial*. Man as a much
diminshed thing.

Jeanne Moreau as Doll Tearsheet and Orson Welles as
Falstaff in *Chimes at Midnight*. The face as field of action.

Keith Baxter as Prince Hal in *Chimes at Midnight*.
Mis-en-scène as theme.

outlining the story we are about to see. It builds our curiosity, plants a handful of clues, establishes the film's leaping, elliptical form, and, anticipating a major tendency of contemporary films, reminds the audience *à la* Brecht's "A-effect" that it is an audience and that it is watching a film.

Structurally, "News on the March" is the whole of *Citizen Kane* in miniature, a subliminal preparation for the narrative to come. It opens, as does the film proper, with shots of Xanadu—this time giving us detailed background information. Abruptly, Kane's death is referred to in the shots of pallbearers, and a montage swiftly reviewing Kane's wealth suggests the summarizing function that the newsreel itself serves in the entire film. Then we are shown two faded photographs, one of Kane beside his mother (hinting at the importance of their relationship) and another of Mrs. Kane's boarding house: these parallel the moment in Kane's childhood when his parents sent him away with Thatcher. That man himself is seen immediately, condemning Kane as "nothing more nor less than a Communist," suggesting his distrust of Kane, which is explored later in the film.

Instantly we are shuttled to Union Square, where a demagogue denounces Kane as a Fascist; and immediately Kane himself asserts that he is only an American. The quick linkage of these various opinions of Kane establishes the method of the film—a comparison of colliding viewpoints, the conflicting judgments that portray Kane and his life. Bernstein's story, primarily centering on Kane's journalistic career, is paralleled by the section, "1895 to 1941—All of these he covered, many of these he was." We see Kane's support of the Spanish-American war and Roosevelt's campaign, corresponding to the era presented in Bernstein's story.

The newsreel goes on to cover the material in Leland's narrative: Kane's marriage to Emily, his affair with Susan, and his political career. Then we see the 1929 closure of several Kane papers and Kane's trip abroad in 1935; these shots plug the gap between Leland's narrative and the final stage of Kane's life. Shots of Xanadu return and suggest Susan's narrative. Finally, glimpses of the old hermit on the grounds of his estate evoke the years of decay and loneliness which Raymond's story will verify later. The newsreel closes with the Times Square marquee: "Latest News— Charles Foster Kane is dead."

Thus in eight-and-a-half minutes and 121 shots, the entire

progress of the ensuing film is mapped out and an enormous amount of information is given—about Kane, about the climate of the country, about the method of the film. Interestingly, this extraordinary device is prefigured in the "War of the Worlds" radio play, in which Welles and writer Howard Koch molded their narrative to the specific shape of the radio medium. At the beginning, a conventional music program is interrupted by a bulletin announcing a meteorite's landing; the music show resumes, to be cut off again by an on-the-scene-report, and so on. This device made the fantastic plot plausible enough to jam highways with fleeing listeners. Just as "The War of the Worlds" mimicked the form of radio broadcasting to persuade its audience of a Martian invasion, "News on the March" imitates the uniquely cinematic form of the newsreel to corroborate the existence of Charles Foster Kane.

We accept the newsreel's argument too quickly, though. Welles immediately points out that the Kane of "News on the March" is literally only an image. The newsreel's final fanfare is abruptly cut off, the screen goes blank, and we are yanked into the screening room, where we are privy to the shadowy manipulations of 1940 media-men. Their talk dispels the hypnotic authority of the newsreel, reminding us that facts are not the truth, that data can be shuffled in any order. One side of us shares the boss's demand for a key that will impose a pattern on life; the other side suspects that life will not submit to tidy arrangement. Objective fact invites subjective interpretation, and several such interpretations will be supplied in the rest of the film.

Henry James described the structure of *The Awkward Age* as "a circle consisting of a number of small rounds disposed at equal distance around a central object. The central object was my situation . . . and the small rounds represented so many distinct lamps . . . the function of each of which would be to light with due intensity one of its aspects . . ." If we substitute "character" for "situation," we have a good description of the structure of *Citizen Kane*. The film is like one of Susan's jigsaw puzzles; each piece contributes something essential, but some pieces are missing.

Two parts of *Kane's* structure act as summations. The first, the "News on the March" sequence, maps out the course the film will take. But by the end of the film, the personality depicted in the newsreel has been reduced to mere objects. The second summation, the final scene in Xanadu, balances "News on the March." We already know Kane's life story, but Welles gives us a reprise—the piano Susan played, the "Welcome Home" loving cup, the statuary, the bed from the *Inquirer* office, the stove in Mrs. Kane's boarding house. The camera tracks ominously over these from the most recent to the most remote, backwards through Kane's life, to settle on the symbol of his childhood: the Rosebud sled. The uninterrupted flow of this extravagant sequence reassembles the life that has been presented in so fragmented a fashion.

Between these two summations the film rests. Told from the viewpoints of five different people, the movie uses the thread of the reporter Thompson's search for the meaning of Rosebud to stitch the stories together. The sections are for the most part chronological and overlapping; with the exception of Thatcher, each narrator begins his story a little before his predecessor ended and carries it past the point from which the next narrator will begin. Some events, then—such as Susan's rise and fall as an opera singer—are shown twice, but from different perspectives.

Kane's multiple-viewpoint form has a simpler but startling antecedent in William K. Howard's *The Power and the Glory* (1933). In that film, after the burial of Thomas Garner, a railroad tycoon, his story is told by Henry, his best friend—but not in chronological order. When Henry's wife makes an accusation against Garner, he counters with a remembered incident in Garner's defense. As a result, chronology is violated—a scene of Garner ruling his board of directors precedes a scene of young, illiterate Garner working as a track layer—and we are shown the play of conflicting opinion surrounding a famous man's career. Like Kane, Garner is a grand figure, both loved and hated, and Henry is qualified to reveal the private side of a public man. Scripted by Preston Sturges from an original idea, *The Power and the Glory* remains a daring experiment in the narrative method Welles and Herman Mankiewicz would refine.

But Welles brought to *Kane* his own special interest in point of view. His first, never-realized project for RKO was to be Conrad's *Heart of Darkness*, in which the narrator Marlow was not seen on screen. It may not be too much to see in this the genesis of the moral complexity Welles infuses into *Kane's* subjective points of view. "I believe it is necessary to give all the characters their best arguments," he has remarked, ". . . including those I disagree with."

But *Kane* should not be seen as a *Rashomon*-like exploration of the relativity of fact. At no point does Welles suggest that Kane's story is being distorted, wilfully or unconsciously, by any narrator. In fact, we are sometimes made to feel quite differently from the narrator (as in Thatcher's and Leland's narratives) and the narrator's presence is so little stressed during each segment that sometimes scenes are included which the narrators were not present to witness. There is thus no doubt about the *facts* which are revealed.

The film's complexity arises from the narrator's conflicting *judgments,* their summing-ups of Kane. Each one sees a different side of him at a different stage of his life, yet each takes his estimate of Kane as definitive. To Thatcher, Kane is an arrogant smart aleck who became "nothing more nor less than a Communist." Bernstein's Kane is a man of high principles, with a sharp business sense and a love of the common man. Leland's Kane, only "in love with himself," is a man of no convictions, a betrayer of the masses. Susan sees Kane (in imagery that recalls Caligari and Svengali) as a selfish but piteous old man. And Raymond's story of Kane as a lonely hermit betrays the cold detachment of his own nature. Each narrator judges Kane differently, and each judgment leaves out something essential. As T. S. Eliot puts it in *The Confidential Clerk*: "There's always something one's ignorant of about anyone, however well one knows him: And that may be something of the greatest importance."

The effect of seeing so many conflicting assessments is to restrain us from forming any opinions of Kane we might take as definitive. As each character tells his story, the reporter's search for an accurate judgment is taken up by the audience as well. Thompson, whose face we never see, is a surrogate for us; his job—voyeuristic and prying, yet ultimately disinterested and detached—is the perfect vehicle for the curiosity without consequences that film uniquely gratifies. The more we see of Kane, the harder it becomes to judge him; understanding passes beyond praise or condemnation. This complex frame of mind in the audience is central to much of contemporary cinema, from *Vertigo* to *La Chinoise*, and is a major source of *Kane's* originality. Its multiple-narration structure warns us not to look for conventional signals of recognition and resolution. A film that opens and closes with NO TRESPASSING and that completes its dialogue with "I don't think that any word can explain a man's life" suggests that the authors mean no simple judgment can be final. The portrait of Kane that has emerged is contradictory and ambiguous. "The point of the picture," Welles has remarked, "is not so much the solution of the problem as its presentation."

The problem may have no solution but it does have a meaning. The structure of the film, while discouraging easy judgments, leads us down a path of widening insight. The newsreel surveys Kane's public career but does not penetrate to his soul. Thatcher's narrative offers us our first clue, hinting at matters of love, childhood, and innocence. Bernstein's story renders Kane sympathetically, suggesting that Rosebud may be "something he lost." Leland's narrative prickles with his urge to puncture Kane's reputation, but his invective doesn't obscure a further clue: "All he ever wanted was love." Finally, Susan's narrative demonstrates that Kane bought love from others because he had no love of his own to give. Thus we are led, step by step, to confront an ego bent on domination; like Elizabethan tragedy, the film proposes that action becomes an egotistical drive for power when not informed by love.

Love is the key to *Kane* and Kane. Sent from home as a child, raised by the cold Thatcher, Kane lost forever the love symbolized by the Rosebud sled and the snowstorm paperweight containing that little cottage that resembles his mother's boarding house. The sled isn't really the cheap Freud some (including Welles) have claimed; although it stands for the affection Kane lost when he was wrenched into Thatcher's world, the sled is clearly not to be taken as the "solution" of the film. It is only one piece of the jigsaw puzzle, "something he couldn't get or something he lost." The Rosebud sled solves the problem that Thompson was set—"A dying man's last words should explain his life"—but by the end Thompson realizes that the problem was a false one: "I don't think that any word can explain a man's life." The appearance of the sled presents another perspective on Kane, but it doesn't "explain" him. His inner self remains inviolate (NO TRESPASSING) and enigmatic. The last shots of the sign and of Xanadu restore a grandeur to Kane's life, a dignity born of the essential impenetrability of human character.

Part of Kane's love problem is bound up with his mother. Hinted at throughout, this is made explicit in the scene in which Kane, having just met Susan, talks with her in her room. Here, for the first time in a character's narrative, the snowstorm paperweight is seen—on Susan's dressing table, among faded childhood snapshots. Kane tells her he had been on his way to a warehouse "in search of my youth," intending to go through his dead mother's belongings: "You know, sort of a sentimental journey." But now, with Susan's reflection behind the paperweight, he decides to remain here; all the elements are present for a symbolic transfer of Kane's love to this new mother figure. And when Susan tells him that her desire to sing was really her mother's idea, the transfer is complete. Kane quietly agrees that he knows how mothers are.

Kane seeks love from anyone—Leland, Bernstein, Emily, Susan, "the people of this state"—but the film traces a growing-apart, through imagery of separation, as Kane's life, from the moment he leaves home, becomes haunted by lovelessness. His relations with his wives typify this: the intimacy of the honeymoon supper yields to the distance of the long breakfast table and, eventually, to husband and wife shouting across the halls of Xanadu. The movement is from crowdedness (the busy *Inquirer* office) to emptiness (the hollow vaults of Xanadu); from cheerfulness (Kane as a young editor) to despair (after Susan has left); from true friendship (Bernstein and Leland) through gradually materialistic relationships (Emily and Susan) to sheerly mercenary companionship (Raymond); from a quick tempo (the liveliness of the *Inquirer*'s crusades) to a funereal one (the picnic cortege and Kane's final, deadened walk); from self-sacrifice to selfishness; from the brash openness of youth to the cancerous privacy of NO TRESPASSING, from intimate joking with Leland to shouts in a mausoleum and long silences before a huge fireplace. Kane's degeneration parallels these shifts in relationships: his contacts with people slough off in proportion to the accumulation of his material goods until, solitary and friendless, only cherishing a cheap snowstorm paperweight, he is engulfed by infinite extensions of his ego.

In the central portion of *Citizen Kane*, then, the various points of view balance the stream of consciousness of the opening and the detachment of "News on the March." Charles Foster Kane is observed from various angles, making the film more kaleidoscopic portrait than straightforward plot. But the matter is complicated because Kane's character changes with time, as does that of each narrator. Thus the clash of fact and bias, objectivity and prejudice, interweaving through the history of a personality, creates a world that is nearly as complex as reality and yet as unified as great art.

That complexity and unity are achieved in large part by the use of symbolic motifs, which both reinforce the realism of the milieu and accent the subjective flow of the narrative.

Whiteness, for instance, takes on strong symbolic associations. From the beginning, the white window of Kane's castle is a focal point toward which our eye is relentlessly drawn. The white of the window dissolves to the snow in the paperweight. Later, the white of Thatcher's manuscript dissolves to the whiteness of Kane's winter childhood days. The beloved sled is covered slowly by snow at the end of that winter scene; cut to the whiteness of a package wrapping as Charles receives a new sled from Thatcher. Bernstein tells his story of a girl dressed in white, with a white parasol: "Do you know, I bet there hasn't been a single month when I haven't thought of that girl." White suggests a lost love and innocence— "something he couldn't get or something he lost"—but it is also the color of death. The cold whiteness of the marble and alabaster of Xanadu contrasts ironically with the nostalgic warmth of the whiteness of Kane's childhood, and the women in his life—Emily and the blonde Susan, both of whom are first seen dressed in white—have given way to the professional nurse in her white uniform.

Accompanying the whiteness motif is that of the snowstorm paperweight, first seen as it falls from the hand of the dead Kane and smashes on the floor. The paperweight enters Kane's life in that crucial scene in Susan's apartment on the night he first meets her. Later, on the morning after Susan's premiere, the paperweight can be glimpsed on the mantelpiece, but no attention is called to it. We see it for the last time when Kane, after wrecking Susan's room, stumbles up to it, clutches it, and mutters, "Rosebud". Thus the paperweight links three crucial scenes in the Kane-Susan relationship, in the meantime becoming a symbol of Kane's lost childhood. Kane's treasuring of the paperweight suggests that it recalls both the night he first met Susan and the day he lost his innocence.

In making a film about a man possessed by an overriding egotism, Welles uses acting and dialogue to suggest the legend that the character fabricates around himself. But he also embodies

Kane's myth in arresting visual symbols. Xanadu is the primary one: decaying, uncompleted, hollow, filled with objects and empty of love, it embodies the grandeur and tragic shortsightedness of Kane's vision. Its name suggests he is "Kubla-Kane"; Xanadu is indeed "a sunny pleasure dome with caves of ice." *Kubla Khan* and *Citizen Kane* are both about the recreation of reality by the Imagination; like Coleridge's narrator, Kane tries to incarnate his vision of "a damsel with a dulcimer." The process works for Coleridge and Welles, and the result is "a miracle of rare device"; it fails for Kane, and "the pool becomes a mirror."

Thus the vault of mirrors that encases the aged Kane at the end of the film is the culmination of the K-images which enclose him throughout. A K surmounts the gates of Xanadu, and is carved in ice at the *Inquirer* party, wrought in metal as a stickpin, sewn in gilt monogram on a bathrobe, and stitched into campaign ribbons. Even Kane's son is seen only as a miniature version of his father. The name, in itself harsh, crisp, and powerful, is constantly pounding at the spectator, from the first sight of the screen-filling title to the final shot of Xanadu with the K gate looming in the foreground. Welles utilizes every chance to flood the screen with a picture of a man filled with his own importance.

Welles also uses musical allusions and motifs to make thematic points. For example, Susan's singing "Una voce poco fa" from *The Barber of Seville* economically evokes the play's themes of youth imprisoned by age and of the abuse of personal authority. Another example is the recurring tune, "It Can't Be Love." Sung at Kane's Everglades picnic, its melody is heard earlier as a mournful piano version in the two scenes with Susan at the nightclub. The repetition ironically links three bleak scenes.

One could trace other motifs: Bernstein in front of a small fireplace over which hangs a portrait of Kane—Kane in front of a larger fireplace on the morning after Susan's premiere—Kane in front of the colossal fireplace at Xanadu; the repeated associations of Susan and rain; the waltz music accompanying Kane's return from Europe which is heard again, mockingly, in the breakfast-table sequence; the movement from the chilliness of the opening to the blazing furnace of the finale. Each detail, entirely realistic in itself, gathers meaning and force as a symbol.

By now it should be clear that *Kane's* stylistic pyrotechnics are not just meaningless virtuosity, but rather aural and pictorial expressions of the tension between reality and imagination at the heart of the film. Objectively, the wide-angle lens renders every plane of a shot, from the nearest to the most distant, in sharp focus. Thus there is no stressing of one image by throwing its context out of focus; ambiguity increases when all characters and objects are equal in definition. As André Bazin puts it, "The uncertainty in which we find ourselves as to the spiritual key or interpretation we should put on the film is built into the very design of the image." There are scarcely a dozen true closeups in the film, and most appear at the very beginning, as an abstract procession of images which contrasts with the spatial authenticity of the rest of the film. Montage, which stresses the juxtaposition of images more than the images themselves, always implies the shaping hand of a creator, but the compression of multiple meanings into one shot can seem to efface the director, giving the illusion of unarranged reality. Thus the compositional detachment of each shot corroborates the film's pull toward realism.

Keeping all the action in the frame may suggest a kind of objectivity, but camera angle belies the detachment by expressing attitudes toward the action. For instance, when Kane is a child, the viewpoint is usually that of the adult looking down. But as Kane's career progresses, he is often shot from an increasingly low angle, not only to indicate his growing power but also to isolate him against his background as he becomes more and more lonely. In Xanadu, though, Kane is again seen from a high angle which points out his smallness within the cavernous crypt he has erected. Within the objectivity of the single frame, Welles' angles (unlike, say, Hawks') suggest subjective bias and point of view.

Welles' *mise-en-scène* modulates the drama's flow with great subtlety, using angle to indicate patterns of domination. Recall the climactic scene when Kane confronts Boss Jim Gettys in Susan's apartment. Gettys' entrance is as thunderous as a kettledrum roll: Kane, Emily, and Susan are on the staircase, light is pouring out of the doorway, and quietly Gettys' silhouette steps into the shot; for once someone has the upper hand over Kane; Nemesis has caught up with the hero. (In Welles' *Macbeth*, Macduff storms out of a smoking beam of light on a similar mission.) Inside Susan's bedroom, the angles crisply build the tension. First, a shot frames Emily in the foreground, Susan in the middle ground, and Gettys and Kane facing each other deep in the shot. But as Gettys explains the power he has over Kane, he advances to the foreground, dwarfing his rival; Emily says that apparently Kane's decision has been made for him; Kane, in the distance, seems overpowered by circumstance. But when Kane decides to assert his will, the shot cuts to an opposite angle: he dominates the foreground, and Gettys, Susan, and Emily taper off into the background. Then, a head-on shot, with Kane in the center, Susan on the left, and Gettys on the right, capsulizes his choice: he can save his mistress or fight his opponent. Welles' arrangement of actors in the frame and his timing of the cuts brilliantly articulate the drama of the scene. The material seems to be objectively observed (no close-ups or first-person points of view), but the structure of each shot and the pacing of the editing inject subjective attitudes.

Welles can also use the moving camera to efface the director's controlling hand by choreographing the material in fluid, unobtrusive patterns. Take, for instance, the scene in which the boy Charles is sent from home. (1) In long-shot we see the boy playing in the snow. (2) A snowball hits the sign over the porch. (3) The camera travels back from the boy in the snow through the window as his mother closes it, and back from her, Thatcher, and Mr. Kane as they advance to the desk, where the papers are read and signed; the camera then follows them back to the window. (4) We are now outside the window, and after the camera travels back to the snowman and Charles, the scuffle between the boy and Thatcher takes place in the same shot. (5) A close-up of Charles and his mother closes the scene. In a sequence of several minutes, we have five shots, two of negligible length. Yet the shots seem realistically observed because Welles has intricately moved his actors and his camera; despite the complexity of the set-ups, we gain a sense of a reality—actual, unmanipulated, all of a piece.

Yet the moving camera can suggest the drift of subjective interest too, because it is also a tool of discovery. Again and again the camera probes like an inquisitive reporter, nosing relentlessly to the center of a scene, gradually stripping away extraneous dramatic matter. Welles' tracking shots imitate the process of investigation itself—a gradual narrowing of the field of inquiry—so that the progress *inward,* toward the heart of a mystery, becomes the characteristic camera movement. The opening dissolves which draw us deeper into Xanadu; the slow dolly up to the flashing "El Rancho" roof sign and then between the letters to the skylight; the imperceptible closing in on Bernstein as he begins his narrative; the diagonal descent to Susan and Kane meeting on the street; the sudden, curious rush to Susan's door when Kane shuts it; the traveling shot over the heads of the audience at Kane's speech; the implacable track to Kane and Emily standing at the door of Susan's house—all these are preparations for the portentous tracking shots through the costly rubbish of Xanadu, coasting slowly over Kane's belongings to settle on the Rosebud sled—the answer to the quest.

Welles' use of sound is indebted, intentionally or not, to Lang's *M* and Clair's *A Nous La Liberté*. In the latter film, a policeman outdoors saying, "We must all—" cuts to a teacher in a classroom saying, "—work." Welles called these "lightning mixes," in which the sound continues (although from a different source) while the scene cuts or dissolves to a new locale and time. A shot of Susan at the piano in her shabby rooming house dissolves to a shot of her, much better-dressed, at a finer piano in a more elegant house, while she continues to play the same piece. Kane's applause immediately dissolves to a crowd's applause of Leland's harangue. Thatcher says to the child Kane, "Merry Christmas, Charles," the boy answers, "Merry Christmas—" and the story leaps ahead seventeen years to Thatcher saying, "And a Happy New Year." Leland's promise to a street crowd that "Charles Foster Kane . . . entered upon this campaign—" cuts to Kane himself in a huge auditorium bellowing, "—with one purpose only. . . ." Scenes Eisenstein would have linked by visual metaphor Welles links by the soundtrack. Eisenstein would have announced the presence of a manipulating directorial intelligence, while Welles suggests the interlocked imagery of mental-association processes.

We should not overlook Welles' celebrated *tours de force*, those moments of sheer cinematic pluck that everyone cherishes in *Kane*. When Kane, Leland, and Bernstein peer in the *Chronicle* window, the camera moves up to the picture of the *Chronicle* staff until it fills the screen; Kane's voice says, "Six years ago I looked at a picture of the world's greatest newspaper staff . . ." and he strides out in front of the same men, posed for an identical picture, a flashbulb explodes, and we are at the *Inquirer* party. Another famous setpiece is the breakfast-table sequence, in which the deterioration of Kane's marriage is traced in a number of brief scenes linked by a whirling effect (swish pans over the windows of the *Inquirer* building). The music pulsates in the background, rising in tension, and the mounting pace of the cutting gives impetus to the final surprises: Mrs. Kane reading the *Chronicle* and the length of the breakfast table.

These, then, are the techniques Welles drew on in *Kane*. Exciting in themselves, they coalesce into a unified style by expressing the film's juxtaposition of reality and imagination. The spatial and temporal unity of the deep focus, the simultaneous dialogue, the reflections and chiaroscuro, the detached use of the moving camera, the intrusion of sounds from outside the frame—all increase the objectively realistic effect. These are correlatives for the way we seem to see and hear in life. The inquisitive camera movements, the angled compositions, the "lightning mixes" of sound and image— these suggest subjective attitudes and the workings of narrators' memories. They are stylistic equivalents for the way we seem to channel our thoughts in life. The cinematic traditions of Lumière and Méliès become surrogates for an epistemological tension. Here are the facts; here are subjective interpretations. Alone, neither has value. Can we then ever know "the" truth? Thompson's final remark "I don't think any word can explain a man's life," the enigma of the Rosebud sled, NO TRESPASSING, the black smoke drifting into a gray sky—these, finally, unmistakably, convey the film's answer.

At bottom, the film's reality/imagination tension radiates from the hero's own nature. *Citizen Kane* is a tragedy on Marlovian lines, the story of the rise and fall of an overreacher. Like Tamburlaine and Faustus, Kane dares to test the limits of mortal power; like them, he fabricates endless *personae* which he takes as identical with his true self; and, like them, he is a victim of the egotism of his own imagination.

Up to a point, Kane's career rises steadily. He is a rich, successful publisher, he has married well, he has a chance to become governor. But his flaw is that he sees love solely in terms of power. His friends, Leland and Bernstein, are also his employees; his wife Emily is the President's niece. He expands his idea of love to include "the people," his aspiration to public office is a confirmation of his confusion of love with power. Thus his liaison with Susan (whom he calls "a cross-section of the American public") represents the pathetic side of his desire, the need for affection which his mother aroused and which Emily could not gratify. Ironically, it is this weakness which undoes him, for in the end, Kane's immense vision of love as power falls tragically short of basic humanity.

The turning point of Kane's life is the confrontation with Gettys in Susan's room. It is the climax of his personal life (Emily or Susan, which will he choose?) and of his political career (the love of "the people" or the love of his family and mistress?). Surprisingly, Gettys turns out to be more sensitive and humane than Kane. He was led to blackmail Kane by the newspaper cartoons Kane printed of him, which humiliated him before his children and, significantly, his mother. Unlike Kane, Gettys distinguishes between attacking a man personally and attacking him politically; thus he gives Kane a chance ("more of a chance than he'd give me") to avoid personal embarrassment. Gettys assumes that Kane places the same value on personal relations that he does.

He is wrong. Up till now Kane has always defined himself by telling others what to do, by bossing Mr. Carter, Leland, Bernstein, Emily, and Susan. Now morality demands that Kane give in and for once define himself by placing others' welfare above his own. But Kane cannot relinquish the role of an autonomous power: "There's only one person who's going to decide what I'm going to do, and that's me." It is the voice of the bully, but also that of the tragic hero. By sacrificing others to his delusion of moral omnipotence, Kane commits his energy to an idea of himself that has become divorced from human values. How can he accept "the love of the people of this state" when he will not show love for his family and mistress? This refusal of imagination to recognize reality constitutes tragic recklessness, but Kane's punishment brings no recognition. Gettys is prophetic: "You're gonna need more than one lesson, and you're gonna get more than one lesson."

After his defeat at the polls, Kane's career declines. His image shattered, he constructs a new one: Susan's singing career. He announces, "*We're* going to be a great opera star"; as his alter ego, she may find the public acclaim in art that he couldn't find in politics. At the opera, Kane in the balcony dwarfs the tiny Susan onstage like a harsh god overseeing his creation. From singing lesson to opera rehearsal, Susan is not an identity in her own right, only an extension of himself. But again Kane fails to win the love of "the people"; the public's response to Susan's premiere is symbolized by the judicious grimace of the stagehand high in the flies. So, when Susan attempts suicide, Kane must change his *persona* again.

The next image Kane constructs is on a mammoth scale. He builds Xanadu, a miniature world, which he stocks with every kind of animal. This parody of God's act of creation gives a blasphemous dimension to Faustus-Kane's galactic vision of power. Yet in the end this god is swallowed up by his own universe. Since he can breathe no life into his creations, he gradually becomes an object like them. Appropriately, the last time we see Kane is as an *image:* a zombie moving stiffly against an endlessly receding tunnel of mirrors, mocking duplications of his own self-absorption. Dying, he can only clutch the icon of love and innocence: his last moment becomes a final assertion of imagination in the face of the ultimate reality of death.

Kane may not be able to reconcile the tragic discord between his inner vision and the outer world, but Welles' creative imagination is larger than Kane's sterile one. The conflicts we noted at the start—between social realism and surrealism, tragic seriousness and comic high spirits, rich detail and complex superstructure—are contained by Welles' broad vision of aspiration and waste.

To my way of thinking, that vision was not permitted utmost scope again until 1965, when Welles completed *Chimes at Midnight.* He has called Falstaff "the most completely good man in all drama," but the film's hero is far from the sentimentalized sack of guts of a (happily, dying) critical tradition. Like Kane, Falstaff is admirable because of his appetite and his imagination, but his fall is observed with no less objectivity. Welles (and Shakespeare) have it both ways: Falstaff is both the Pan of mythology and the Vice of the morality plays, and Prince Hal may love him but he must reject him.

Chimes at Midnight is as morally complex as *Citizen Kane*, but here cinematic traditions are not analogues for epistemological modes. *Chimes'* style and form are translucent, like *The Immortal Story*'s, but without that later effort's crude parody of the reality/imagination theme. In *Chimes at Midnight*, Welles concentrates straightforwardly on a set of characters symbolizing the alternatives surrounding the problem which obsessed Kane: the connection between personal and political power.

Prince Hal must choose among three ways of life—that of king, warrior, and roisterer—as represented by his father King Henry IV, his distorted mirror-image Hotspur, and his adopted father Falstaff.

Henry, though regal and commanding, struck in a chilly shaft of light that suggests divine authority, is nonetheless aloof and solitary, entombed in cold gray stone. Hotspur is vigorous and manly, but also crude, hotheaded, and notably solitary. Falstaff is a vulgar buffoon, but he inhabits a glowing world of comradely merrymaking. The three worlds rotate on the same axis: Falstaff lives by robbing, Henry has usurped the throne, and Hotspur seeks to steal the crown from Henry. By a music motif (Henry summons musicians to salve his illness, Hotspur's trumpeters blast pompously and phallically while he ignores the blandishments of his lovely wife, and Falstaff calls for music to ease his melancholy), Welles suggests that each way of life has become sterile. The whole of medieval England—king, fighter, and déclassé—is sick, barren, dying.

Hal, man of the Renaissance, becomes almost cynically adept in all three worlds. He bests Falstaff at thieving and lying; he wins his father's respect by stately eloquence; and he vanquishes Hotspur in battle. Supreme in all three arenas, Hal becomes their synthesis. Like the sun he compares himself to, he is a source of the power that will revivify England.

Still, he cannot live permanently divided. He must choose among the court, the battlefield, and the tavern. Since possessing the crown permits him to legislate his wisdom in the other areas, he must sooner or later renounce his dissolute life, which comes down to renouncing Falstaff. Hal's "I know you all" speech is a soliloquy in the original play, but Welles makes it Hal's direct warning to Falstaff. Henceforth, fat Jack should expect to be abandoned. And when, in the comic crowning scene at the Boar's Head, Falstaff begs not to be forgotten—"Banish plump Jack and banish all the world"—Prince Hal reminds him of his fate in a reply that reverberates like a thunderclap: "I do, I will."

Since *Chimes at Midnight*, like *Kane*, is about personal and political authority, Welles again creates the drama of power within the shot by means of camera angle. When, at Justice Shallow's house, Falstaff has been meditating on his death, a deep shot shows Falstaff sitting stonily in the distance, for once positively miniscule. Pistol bursts in to announce Henry's death, and suddenly Falstaff lumbers into the foreground, filling the frame, towering like a colossus as he gasps, "What? . . . Is the old king—*dead?*" The shot depicts his vision of the power he has dreamed of. But after the coronation and

Hal's repudiation of him, in which angle shots have expressed the new king's sovereignty over his former companion, Falstaff leaves Shallow, walking off into a distant corridor—like Kane, dwarfed by real forces his imagination could not control.

Welles' imagination, though, is large enough to make great art of his heroes' defeats. Joseph McBride has argued that Hal's rejection of Falstaff and his declaration of war with France label him a villain and Falstaff a victim.* This underestimates Welles' irony. Hal is a practical politician. Like Kane, he must eventually choose between political and personal virtue, but (more sensitively than Kane), Hal struggles to keep them distinct, publicly humiliating Falstaff only to aid him privately later. Hal will mock him with Poins, but he will hide him when the king's men come. He will burlesque him before the tavern crowd, but he will give him a post in his army. And even after the rebuff at the coronation, Hal privately (in an inserted text from *Henry V* that originally did not refer to Falstaff) orders his counselors to "enlarge" (!) Falstaff: "If little faults, proceeding on distemper/Shall not be winked at, how shall we stretch our eye/When capital crimes, chewed, swallowed, and digested/Appear before us?" He tempers the inevitable wickedness of his repudiation with a measure of regal mercy. Welles sees public ethical problems as private ones writ large, yet between the two is an irreconcilable tragic tension. Nym summarizes the complexity of the problem as Falstaff lies dying: "The King is a good King. But it must be as it may."

Thus the final words from Holinshed, ". . . and so human withal that he left no offence unpunished, nor friendship unrewarded," reverberating over the shot of Falstaff's coffin, constitute not a sarcastic dig but a sublime irony. *Chimes at Midnight*, like *Citizen Kane*, shows both sides—public good and private misery, heroic ambition and tragic necessity, pragmatic reality and alluring imagination—sympathizing with each but, finally, presenting both honestly. The irony is the richest and most basic one of man's experience, so vast that usually we must split it into tragedy and comedy. That Welles art is able to serenely contain and transcend both might be the final estimate of his genius.

* [See McBride's essay, pp. 178–186 of this volume. Editor's note.]

"The Magnificent Ambersons"

by STEPHEN FARBER

Although *The Magnificent Ambersons* was not the last film Welles made in America, he never again took on such large, quintessentially *American* themes as he did in his first two films. *The Magnificent Ambersons* deals with the price of technological "progress"—the contamination of the city and the influence of the automobile on modern American life, an extraordinary subject for a 1942 movie. Perhaps it seems even more important today than it did to audiences barely aware of the menace of freeways, noise, and air pollution.

The attempt is impressive, but the film has never struck me as an entirely satisfactory study of the emergent nightmare city of the twentieth century. The dying aristocratic world of the Ambersons is drawn with great affection and complexity, but the urban industrial world that will take its place is only a shadow; the contrast of nineteenth and twentieth century is asserted rather than explored dramatically. Eugene Morgan's speech about the influence of automobiles ("With all their speed forward, they may be a step backward in civilization. It may be that they won't add to the beauty of the world or the life of men's souls. . . .") has to carry a great deal of weight, more than the film can really bear. What Eugene talks about is never shown. According to Charles Higham's descriptions of the material cut from Welles' version of the film (*The Films of Orson Welles*), the original included many more scenes about the city rising around the Ambersons, scenes that might have effectively corroborated Eugene's bleak prophecy. The one scene that remains—George's last walk home through the altered, disfigured city near the end of the film—is brilliant, an example of

Film Comment, *Summer 1971 Vol. 7, No. 2.* © *Film Comment Publishing Corporation, reprinted by permission.*

Welles' astonishing resourcefulness and economy; thanks to the lucid, carefully chosen images and the evocative narration, in just a few seconds we think we've seen more of the expanding city than we actually have. Outside of this scene, however, the swelling city is an off-screen character, and it needs to be a stronger *presence* in the film for the erosion of the Amberson style to be fully comprehensible.

Even Welles' original version may have been slightly out of balance in this regard. The Booth Tarkington novel (published in 1918), which Welles follows closely, gives much more emphasis to the bewitching nineteenth-century world of the Ambersons than to the industrial megalopolis that Eugene Morgan helps to usher in. And judging from Welles' other work, he seems to be more attracted to the past than to the future. His characters inhabit great cavernous houses cut off from the world, castles that easily turn into mausoleums; those magnificent, magical houses represent Welles' intoxication with imaginatively created, self-enclosed private worlds where one can retreat from the chaotic pressures of the present. One thrilling dolly shot in *The Magnificent Ambersons*—in which the doors of the house are opened on the night of the last great ball, and the camera sweeps us inside—perfectly captures the luxury of immersion in a world of vanished elegance and grace.

The tranquillity savored in Welles' films is not, admittedly, the first thing one notices in watching them. The other side of his work, especially pronounced in the first two films, is the youthful energy of his style. Just as one is immediately struck by the tremendous *élan* of the *March of Time* parody or the newspaper party in *Citizen Kane*, the sequence in *The Magnificent Ambersons* that is most dazzling on first viewing is the hilarious, breathtaking scene of the automobile ride in the snow—the staccato rhythm provided by the overlapping dialogue gives the film a burst of exhilaration. It is the one moment in the film when the nineteenth and twentieth centuries seem to come together, and when Welles acknowledges his attraction to the machine, and to the speed and volatility of modern life.

One would also expect the youthful Welles to be drawn to the figure of the automobile inventor, Eugene Morgan, a man with the audacity to take on the future. But the casting of Joseph Cotten as Morgan is curious. *The Magnificent Ambersons* is the only Welles film in which Welles does not appear, and so there is no representation of the charismatic, superhuman, power-mad tyrant (Kane, Macbeth, Quinlan in *Touch of Evil*, Clay in *The Immortal Story*) who provides a focus for so many of his films. In *The Magnificent Ambersons* the Welles hero is split in two—the arrogant, domineering, but childish man of leisure, George Amberson Minafer (Tim Holt), and the gentle, self-effacing entrepreneur, Eugene Morgan (Joseph Cotten). William Johnson, in an article ("Orson Welles: Of Time and Loss," *Film Quarterly*, Fall 1967) that still strikes me as the most sensible, helpful introduction to Welles' films, has noted the paradoxical nature of these two characterizations: "George, who stands for the innocent age that is dying, is the film's most objectionable character; Gene Morgan, who is helping create the age of noise and crowds and air pollution, is its most likable." It's an interesting concept, but *too* neat a paradox, too schematic. If Welles had played Eugene Morgan, the film might have developed a richer kind of tension. Cotten is difficult to accept as a business genius; he's too gentlemanly, almost too fastidious. Welles would have given the character more hardness, energy, and drive; and, if Gene Morgan were a more complex character, we really wouldn't need any more images of the blemished industrial landscape, because all of Welles' ambivalence toward the rise of the modern city could be contained within that one characterization. Welles would have played the role with great spirit, ambitiousness, and ruthlessness, as well as with the elegant charm that Joseph Cotten relies on. He might have evoked the excitement of the new industrial age and some of its truly disturbing implications. A stronger actor in the role might have given us an idea of how the thrill of power and technology could be coarsening. Then Gene's speech about the profound danger of the automobile would have worked dramatically, instead of didactically.

But if the film lacks sharp dramatic focus, its lyrical portrait of the dying aristocratic world is masterful, enhanced by Stanley Cortez's lovely, mellow photography. Many of Welles' films are set in the past, but *The Magnificent Ambersons* is a different kind of journey backward in time—a journey back to childhood, a study of the claustrophobic intensity of family life. The film is full of painful family separations; the central one, as in *Citizen Kane*, is the separation of mother and son. *The Magnificent Ambersons* has the power of a dream formed in boyhood, a spell that can never be broken. Welles pays attention to the perversions of feeling within the suffocating cocoon of the family mansion—George's inhuman pride, his destructive, vaguely incestuous relationship with his mother, the neurotic repression of Aunt Fanny.

Welles follows Tarkington closely in all of this, but he sometimes extends the novel's implications. The most obvious variation is in the characterization of Fanny, whom Agnes Moorehead makes one of the first truly *modern* characters in American films, an archetype for all those hysterically repressed, neurasthenic spinster heroines of the next decades. This characterization is not conceived in conventional, realistic terms. There's no apparent logic to many of Fanny's outbursts—they surprise us and make us uncomfortable. Even *within* a scene, her quicksilver shifts of emotion are startling and alarming. Here is an example of a subtle difference between text and film. The scene near the end of the film in which George and Fanny argue in the now-desolate mansion, and Fanny sits down against the boiler, is drawn directly from the novel. George tells her to get up, afraid that she may burn herself. " 'It's not hot,' Fanny sniffled. 'It's cold; the plumbers disconnected it. I wouldn't mind if they hadn't. *I* wouldn't mind if it burned me, George.' " In the film she doesn't "sniffle" those words, she spits them out in enraged, hysterical laughter; Agnes Moorehead makes Fanny's breakdown truly horrible to watch. No one who has seen the film will forget the intense, frightening close-up of Fanny at her brother's wake—an image that seems to take us *inside* her troubled mind; her grief contains a fierce, frantic desperation just barely under control.

Though Welles never appears in *The Magnificent Ambersons*, his presence as narrator is crucial to the conception of the film. *The Magnificent Ambersons* contains the most beautiful, pertinent use of narration I have seen in movies. The narration is not used simply to provide information; it adds to the sensuous atmosphere of the film. The language itself, eloquently spoken by Welles, has a rich, lyrical quality that seems to belong to the aristocratic past; its literary cadences are part of the vanished courtly style that the film mourns. But in an even more important sense, the narration calls attention to the nostalgia that is the film's *subject* as well as its dominant mood. We are constantly aware of a voice reflecting on the past, wistfully invoking its mysteries. From the very start the hushed but intense tone of Welles' narration suggests the recreation of a child's fairy tale. The storyteller, the dreamer who calls up the past for us, haunted by the world he brings to life, becomes a character we want to evaluate along with the others. We want to test his voluptuous nostalgia against what we see, and within the film nostalgia is criticized rather than celebrated. For the characters who cannot break the spell of the past—George and Isabel and Aunt Fanny—are doomed, while Eugene Morgan, who comes from a background similar to theirs, has found a way of accommodating himself to the future. He seems freer, healthier, more mature than any of the Ambersons, and he will survive.

It's too simple, then, to say that *The Magnificent Ambersons* is no more than a film of nostalgic reverie but there is no denying the melancholy intensity with which the film dwells on the Ambersons' decline. Not too long ago I saw *Citizen Kane* and *The Magnificent Ambersons* as a double feature, and the thing that intrigued me in seeing them together was that while both films were the work of a very young man, and contain plenty of evidence of youthful exuberance, both are overwhelmed by images of old age, dissolution and death. Some young artists probably want to deal with death because it's so foreign, and they approach tragedy out of intellectual curiosity rather than out of any genuine sense of weariness and despair. It *is* there that some of the Gothic scenes of decadence and old age in *Citizen Kane* have a self-conscious, theatrical quality that seems slightly adolescent. But I don't think that is any longer true in *The Magnificent Ambersons*. The scenes of Isabel's death, Major Amberson's death, the parting of George and Uncle Jack in the railway station, Aunt Fanny going hysterical in the empty old house, George's last walk home are unusually sharp, poignant moments. One cannot account for the film's distinctive qualities by saying that Welles was simply being faithful to his source. What is inescapable on watching the film is the graceful, persuasive feeling he has for the material. This film contains some of the strongest, most haunting, and desolate images in any of Welles' work. The same mournful sense of loss and regret in much later films like *Falstaff* and *The Immortal Story* seems easier to understand.

But how does one explain this obsession with rot and decay in a man of 26, who seemed to the world to be the most youthful and vigorous of artists, the "boy genius"? The scenes of death in *The Magnificent Ambersons* seem to transfix the young Welles. Is this the famous "self-destructiveness" of the Welles legend evidence of a morbid, irresistible attraction to decadence? I don't know the answer to that question, and clearly the sources of any artist's work are extraordinarily complex. I can only describe what is on the screen: that, among great films, *The Magnificent Ambersons* is the one you remember for the sad, lush, seductive poetry of death.

Style and Theme in
The Lady from Shanghai
by *JAMES NAREMORE*

Much of the footage Welles wished included in the release print of *The Lady from Shanghai* was revised or left on the cutting room floor, a victim of Columbia's desperate attempt to "save" the project.[1] Yet what remains is filled with bizarre visual dissonances, Welles' fascinating camera work and imagery coexisting with banal material that seems to mock the Hollywood studio movie. Again and again a brilliant moment will be interrupted with gauzy close-ups or over-the-shoulder editing, awkwardly composed and badly acted. The real locales of Acapulco and San Francisco are inter-cut with retakes containing obvious studio settings or process screens, and students of Welles can actually make a game of distinguishing shots that are authentically Wellesian from the ones Columbia inserted. To some extent the game is futile; Welles himself has noted the impossibility of determining exactly who did what under the old studio system.[2] Nevertheless, it is a game worth playing, if only because it enables us to talk about the typical features of Welles' style, and about the relation between style and theme in this particular film.

Prepared for publication in this volume and published by permission of the author.

[1] See Charles Higham, *The Films of Orson Welles* (Berkeley and London: The University of California Press, 1970), pp. 111–115.

[2] "Under the American system, no one is capable of saying whether a film was or was not directed by a director." Juan Cobos, Miguel Rubio, and J. A. Pruneda, "A Trip to Don Quixoteland: Conversations with Orson Welles," trans. Rose Kaplin, *Cahiers du Cinema* (English), No. 5 (1966). Reprinted in part in *Focus on Citizen Kane*, ed. Ronald Gottesman (Englewood Cliffs, N.J.: Prentice-Hall, 1971), p. 23.

A logical place to begin is with Welles' habit of animating the environment, using it to express the emotions of his players or to comment on their behavior. Welles is a master of mise-en-scène, and he will seldom do one thing on the screen when he can do three or four. Typically he gives us as much information as possible, playing off the most subtle exchanges among characters against two or more levels of action. Even the kitchen dinner scene in *The Magnificent Ambersons* is not so restrained as is commonly supposed: The camera barely moves, but, as Georgie Minafer (Tim Holt) wolfs down strawberry shortcake, a Gothic storm rumbles outside the windows of the big kitchen, and the actors keep stepping on one another's lines. Welles depends heavily on this multiplication of stimuli, so that he not only expresses psychology through the settings, but gives us the feeling of many actions, visual and aural, occurring simultaneously. It is this richness, this seven-layer cake profusion, that most distinguishes his work in Hollywood.

The Lady from Shanghai offers many examples of such density, only the most obvious of which is the climatic encounter in the funhouse mirror maze. The gun battle among the mirrors functions beautifully within the plot of the movie, compactly expressing the ruthless ambition and the self-destructive mania that has been evoked verbally in O'Hara's story about the sharks. It is also characteristically Wellesian in its extreme of dynamization, producing an infinite depth of field and more information than we can absorb in a single viewing. Not satisfied with the simple phenomenon of reflections in mirrors, Welles complicates the spectacle with a split-screen: we see two images of Arthur Bannister and his cane at either side of the frame, in between them two gigantic portraits of Elsa's blond head. In a later shot, two Bannisters are superimposed over Elsa's eyeball. Toward the climax, Bannister lurches to the left and produces three images of himself; the camera pans and three more Bannisters approach from the opposite direction, the two converging groups separated by a single image of Elsa holding a gun; Bannister now takes out his own pistol, and as he points it his "real" hand enters the foreground from offscreen right. All this time the actors are delivering crucial speeches—in fact, so much happens so rapidly that only a studied analysis can lead to a full understanding of the sequence.

Several viewings reveal that the episode contains a complex set of symbolic visual conflicts between Bannister and Elsa. If the ugly, crippled male is reflected many times in a single shot, the unreal sex goddess will be seen alone; if both characters are multiplied, one will be very much larger than the other. The audience, of course, does not have to make this sort of analysis in order to respond to the dazzling series of events, but most viewers feel they have to "meet the film at least half way," as Herman G. Weinberg once said, in an effort to assimilate all the information.[3] Thus one of the pervasive qualities of this sequence and of Welles' movies in general is *wit,* which means not only a sense of humor but what the OED defines as an appeal to the mental faculties, especially to "memory and attention."

Of course, the typical studio film does not have much to do with wit; its chief desiderata are clarity and simplicity, and it usually tries to conceal the presence of artisans. That is perhaps one reason why Columbia tried to efface Welles's idiosyncracies. Luckily, they did not succeed completely, but in some cases they considerably upset his plans. Notice, for example, the scene in which Grisby calls O'Hara aside to make a "proposition," and the two men stroll along a hillside above Acapulco Bay. The longshots filmed on location are held on the screen only briefly, but they suggest a conception that is nearly as impressive as the party scene in *Ambersons* or the elaborate track at the beginning of *Touch of Evil.* As Grisby and O'Hara climb the hillside, the whole social structure of Acapulco passes them by, from the impoverished peasants at the bottom of the hill to the American tourists and their Latin retinue at the top. The atmosphere at the bottom is dirty, crowded, and hot, but at the parapet above a sea breeze is blowing and Acapulco sparkles in the sun like a "bright, guilty world."

Welles apparently planned this episode as a series of elaborately choreographed traveling shots that express O'Hara's state of mind while at the same time showing the effects of Yankee capital. He uses a wide-angle lens, which gives the movement of camera and actors a dramatic sweep, and he fills the screen with several layers of action; the camera spirals up the hill, picking up additional people moving past at different angles, creating a busy, swirling effect. Notice also that some of these location scenes are cut on movement in order to preserve the flow of action and dialogue;

---

[3] Welles himself agrees with this comment. See "A Trip to Don Quixoteland," p. 11.

Welles tries to evoke a subtly dizzying sensation, which culminates in the final shot—a high-angle, fisheye view of Grisby and O'Hara standing over the sea. When Grisby steps out of the screen, O'Hara seems to be hanging vertiginously in midair.

In the completed film, however, the episode has been substantially revised. Charles Higham has suggested that some of the Acapulco scenes were filmed so clumsily they "would not cut." [4] The painstaking blocking of the sequence makes it difficult to accept this charge, but in any case retakes have been introduced, consisting chiefly of closeups of Welles and Glenn Anders. The lighting in these studio shots does not match Charles Lawton's strikingly naturalistic location photography, and when the close-ups are inserted all the restless movement ceases; the two actors are shown as big, static heads, isolated against a grey, indeterminate backdrop.

A similar intrusion can be seen in the courtroom sequence, which remains one of the most grotesquely funny in the film. The defendant, O'Hara, is supposed to be completely ignored by everybody; in fact, Welles purposely keeps the camera off himself, shooting from a bewildering variety of angles and contributing to the maelstrom of activity. The camera leaps back and forth from harshly lit closeups to equally harsh wide-angle views of the room, showing Bannister parading before the jury on crutches or the courtroom crowd breaking into spasms. Dialogue overlaps, a juror sneezes, the judge cracks jokes, and nearly everybody deliberately overacts. Now and then, however, the sequence is interrupted by shots of Welles and Rita Hayworth, done in a style that is utterly conventional and radically different from the surrounding imagery. Presumably someone felt the trial would make no sense without "reactions" from the protagonists; whatever the cause, the movie seems to have been made by two different hands, or by a director who, out of indifference or contempt, chose to deface his own work.

I raise the possibility of Welles' indifference here because certain defects in the film could have been repaired by any competent technician. For example, after the cataclysm in the mirror maze we are given a shot of Everett Sloane coiled up and dying, viewed through jagged edges of glass at the corners of the frame. As Elsa dashes from the room, the camera pans and the "glass" moves with

[4] Higham, *The Films of Orson Welles*, p. 112.

it. The shards in the extreme foreground are revealed as a painting mounted to the front of the camera, and the decision to use a panning movement is clearly a director's error. On the other hand, there is no way of knowing what opportunities Welles had for retakes, and it is obvious that the studio interfered with his more ambitious efforts. Some of his characteristic long takes have been cut to pieces, including the ride through Central Park that opens the film.[5] The long takes that do remain are expecially witty moments, indications of what he might have accomplished elsewhere. For example, a complicated and extremely funny shot shows O'Hara learning he has been framed: he drives up in Grisby's car, climbs out, and is met by the zaniest swarm of policemen since Keaton's *Cops*. In lightning succession they discover a murder weapon and a signed confession; officer Peters reads the confession aloud, Arthur Bannister limps into the picture, Grisby's corpse is wheeled under O'Hara's nose, and Elsa drives up in her convertible. The only cut is here at the end, where we are given a soft-focus closeup of Hayworth, surely intended as a parody of the *femme fatale* (as the earlier shot of her pinned to the deck is a parody of the glamour pin-up).

But these interesting moments might have become mere curiosities if the film had not retained a certain integrity of purpose. What is surprising is the degree to which it remains whole, despite the confusing plot and the many alterations. As it stands, the movie has a considerable degree of formal narrative unity. The story covers roughly a year, beginning with a shot of New York harbor and ending at San Francisco Bay. O'Hara's voyage takes him around the continent, with pauses at seaports, as if he were a tourist on a grand tour of American corruption. Because he is a sailor, even his adventures on shore are filled with references to the sea: the fantastic aquarium scene, for example, or the long take in Grisby's office played off against South Sea island music coming from a radio.

Furthermore, there is a sense in which all Columbia's tampering has not been so disruptive to the tone of the film as RKO's revisions of *Ambersons*. This is because *The Lady from Shanghai* is essentially a dark, grotesquely stylized comedy, a film that takes us beyond expressionism toward absurdity. (In one of his best exit lines, Glenn

[5] Ibid., p. 113.

Anders steps close to the camera and whines, "Silly, isn't it?" He then moves out of the frame, leaving O'Hara sitting there looking as bewildered as usual.) The peformances are deliberately exaggerated, so that the sinister moments keep verging on farce—an effect similar to the motel scenes in *Touch of Evil* or K's interviews in *The Trial*. Hence the vulgarity of the revisions sometimes adds to the feeling of satire; as several critics have indicated, the bad closeups of Rita Hayworth, which seem to have been forced on Welles to give the picture a "star" quality, often serve as a commentary on Hollywood's synthetic sexuality. Welles turns Hayworth (his second wife) into a vaguely Sternbergian Circe, or into a calendar girl who lures a stage-Irish Ulysses onto the rocks with her wet black swimsuit. He poses her like a figure in an advertisement—a smiling figure in a bathing suit, reclining, her toes nicely pointed and wind blowing her hair, much as she appeared in *Cover Girl* (1944). He cuts from her awful siren song (which turns O'Hara into a zombie) to a Glosso Luxo commercial; or he views her through Grisby's telescope, suddenly lowering the glass and confronting the audience with Grisby himself, who is sweating and leering voyeuristically back at the camera.

These touches are not out of keeping with the mood of the film as a whole. In fact one could argue that Welles' career during this period had begun to move more and more away from realism to fantasy, from the investigation of consciousness to the daring exploration of subconsciousness, from ports to crazy houses. His style, with its fantastic distortions, its complex plays of light and shadow, its many levels of activity, had always been suited to the depiction of corruption and madness. But *The Lady from Shanghai*, probably out of sheer necessity, combines the extremes of this style with the extremes of Hollywood convention; in the process it becomes one of Welles' most delirious films, and perhaps his most misanthropic treatment of American life. Indeed, the movie can almost be read as an allegory of his Hollywood adventures, depicting his simultaneous fascination with and nausea over the movie industry. Hiding behind a phony Irish brogue instead of the putty nose he would later adopt, Welles enters the film as a wanderer from another country, a man who finds himself in a world of dog-eat-dog (or shark-eat-shark) individualism. In such a world, which is ruled by what a shipmate calls an "edge," the good characters are powerless; at best they philosophize while the bad destroy one another.

This doomed world is, of course, basic to the *film noir*, and to most other pictures by Welles—the only difference is that here he has cast himself as a naive idealist instead of a tyrant, a proletarian Jed Leland instead of a Kane. As always with Welles, however, the central character is ambiguous. We are told that Black Irish O'Hara can "really hurt a guy" when he's angry, and he certainly recognizes the evil around him quickly enough. In fact, the only way to explain his behavior is to say that he is either more foolish or more complicated than we expect him to be. In the opening voice-over, he says he is "foolish," and adds, "If I'd been in my right mind. . . . But once I'd seen her I was not in my right mind for some time." This reference to insanity prepares us for the radical distortions in the movie, and for the trip to the crazy house at the conclusion. At the same time, it emphasizes the temptations underlying the consciousness of the progressive, presumably rational O'Hara.

At its deepest level, therefore, *The Lady from Shanghai* concerns O'Hara's own potential for evil—an "exchange of guilt" formula that interested Welles from the time he came to Hollywood to adapt *Heart of Darkness.* Essentially a humane and liberal man, Welles has always been aware of the perils of humanism (to say nothing of the perils of California); like Conrad, he suggests that dark impulses are concealed within the most rational and benign of men. O'Hara feels these impulses from the beginning of the movie, and he unsuccessfully pretends that he does not understand them. Therefore, when he walks the moonlit streets of Acapulco with Elsa, we can see the hovels of the poor in the background; and when he walks with Grisby above the bay, he remarks that the brightness can't hide hunger and guilt. The guilt, however, is perhaps his own as much as the Bannisters'. That is why he finds himself descending into nightmare, coming out of it all resolving to grow older, wiser, and perhaps less complacent. His story has been a comedy, a fantasy, and something of a cautionary tale. For all its imperfections, it manages to retain many of the qualities of Welles' best work.

Orson Welles' Macbeth: Script and Screen

by MICHAEL MULLIN

Welles' *Macbeth* is a paradox. When the film came out in 1949, the critics damned it. When it is revived today, it provokes an odd mixture of disappointment with what Welles did and admiration for the *ideas* he sought to express.[1] The reasons for disappointment are obvious. The whole production *seems* confused and technically incompetent. The soundtrack is often unintelligible. The acting, especially Jeanette Nolan's Lady Macbeth and Alan Napier's Holy Father, is often ludicrously inept. The script garbles Shakespeare's text with interpolations, omissions, and rearrangements that frustrate anyone who comes to see the *Macbeth* Shakespeare wrote. Yet, like a master artist's unfinished painting, Welles' *Macbeth* remains interesting both for what it can tell us about the artist and for what it can tell us about the subject.

Prepared for publication in this volume and printed with the author's permission.

[1] The best digest of the film's critical reception appears in Donald S. Skoller's unpublished dissertation, "Problems of Transformation in the Adaptation of Shakespeare's Tragedies from Playscript to Cinema," New York University, 1968, pp. 550–555. Charles Higham, *The Films of Orson Welles* (Berkeley and London: The University of California Press, 1970), p. 134, speaks for the film society, museum, or university audience: "It is impossible to deny that Welles' *Macbeth* is a failure; but its concept was a noble one. It remains an authentic *film maudit*, worth reseeing today." It was first released in 1948, then withdrawn and re-released in 1949 with an "improved" sound track.

I

The conditions under which the film was made account for its most glaring shortcomings. Before Welles made *Macbeth*, Hollywood believed that Shakespeare meant spectacle, and that spectacle cost too much to pay its way at the box office (Reinhardt's 1935 *Midsummer Night's Dream*, for instance, cost $1.5 million). To challenge the belief that good Shakespeare films did not come cheap, Welles set out to make his low-budget *Macbeth* as much in hope that others would follow as in hope that his venture would fully succeed.[2] In April 1947 he sold the project to Republic Studios at a budget of $700,000, an arrangement that yielded eventual profit to the studio.

To stay within the budget, Welles cut production costs to the bone. The actors prepared for the camera by staging the play at the Utah Centennial Festival in Salt Lake City. To further economize, Welles used a single sound stage on which he rearranged papier-mâché cliffs and caverns for each new scene. He recorded the sound track in advance, then tried to keep the actors in sync by playing it over a loudspeaker during the filming. All these preparations and simplifications were designed to compress actual shooting time into twenty-three days. With three film crews at work—often simultaneously—Welles scrambled from one crew to another, directing, acting, and somehow getting enough footage to finish on schedule. Not surprisingly, there were problems. With little time for trials and retakes, the acting was often poor, sometimes terrible—the England scene (IV, iii) being probably the worst. At other times, while the acting was acceptable, the actors' lips were out of sync with the soundtrack. Editing took care of some of these botches by keeping

[2] Reinhardt's costs are given in Roger Manvell's *Shakespeare and the Film* (New York: Praeger, 1972), p. 26. From 1936, when MGM rivaled Reinhardt's *Dream* with its spectacular *Romeo and Juliet*, until 1948, when Welles' *Macbeth* came out, no American Shakespeare film was made. "My purpose in making *Macbeth* was not to make a great film," Welles said, "I thought I was making what might be a good film, and what, if the twenty-three day shooting schedule came off, might encourage other filmmakers." (Manvell, *Shakespeare and the Film*, p. 60.) Of course, since he was speaking several years after the film was made, Welles may well have only been rationalizing his failure.

the actor who was speaking off-camera, or, as in the case of Macbeth's soliloquies, by having the voice come through unspeaking lips. Yet, with little margin for error in the shooting or the soundtrack, errors abounded in the film, which, as mentioned, was finally released in 1949.[3] Stung by harsh reviews, by that time Welles had dismissed it as an "experiment."[4] And in fairness to Welles, the film ought to be judged as an experiment, a workshop production of the play made to test Welles' production methods, his interpretation of the play, and the play's possibilities as a film script.

II

Welles approached *Macbeth* unconventionally. Typically, films of Shakespeare's plays take the text as given, then find ways to "illustrate" its settings and actions, as when, for example, Polanski shows the execution of Cawdor, the banquet for Duncan, and the witches in their cavern. Although often cut and re-ordered, the text still directs performance. For Welles, however, the film came first, and the text was made to fit his resources and his interpretation of the play. "I use Shakespeare's words and characters to make motion pictures," said Welles, and the films "are variations on his themes."[5]

Welles' film script, which appears in abbreviated form in the appendix, shortened one of Shakespeare's shortest tragedies by two-thirds. Whole scenes are left out: the Hecate scene (III, v), for instance, and the meeting between Lennox and another lord (III, vi). The remaining one-third of Shakespeare's *Macbeth* is utterly changed by omissions, additions, and rearrangements. Scenes

[3] For accounts of the film in production, see Harold Leonard, "Notes on *Macbeth*," *Sight and Sound* (March 1950), pp. 15–17; Manvell, *Shakespeare and the Film*, pp. 55–61; and Higham, *The Films of Orson Welles*, pp. 125–134.

[4] Welles insisted on its unfinished state. To the attacks of French critics, he replied in his own defense: "Nobody seems to judge the picture on its own grounds; as an experiment achieved in twenty-three days on an extremely low budget" (quoted by Francis Koval, "Interview with Welles," *Sight and Sound*, December 1950, p. 316). By the time the film was being edited, Welles was acting in the film *Black Magic*, and he could only cable instructions from Italy to his cutter in Hollywood. See Higham, *The Films of Orson Welles*, p. 127.

[5] Quoted by Joseph McBride, *Orson Welles* (New York: Viking, 1972), p. 109.

appear in a new order, events from one scene are inserted in others, new characters and new scenes are added.[6] Consider Welles' treatment of Duncan's scenes. Shakespeare presents him three times; first, in the field receiving battle reports (I, ii), then in his court (editors call it "Forres," I, iv), and, finally, at Inverness to be greeted by Lady Macbeth (I, vi). Welles brings parts from each of these separate scenes into a single long scene at Macbeth's castle, rearranges the parts, and intersperses them with Macbeth and Lady Macbeth plotting. The short speeches come as patches of dialogue or asides set against a larger background of action: the beheading of the traitor Cawdor, the assembling of Duncan's retinue in Macbeth's courtyard, their ritual renunciation of Satan, and their climb up to the chambers above. People and events that Shakespeare kept separate, Welles brings together, exploiting film's ability to alternate rapidly from a large, public event in distance shots to the private words and thoughts of individuals in reaction shots and close-ups.

Whereas Shakespeare's narrative moves from one group of characters to another, Welles concentrates on Macbeth throughout the film, until the last battle scenes, where the action alternates between Macbeth's defense and his enemies' advance. Before Duncan's murder, Welles follows Macbeth's movements almost without interruption. Macbeth and Banquo, already introduced in the prologue as "riding homeward from victorious battle," meet the witches at once. Macbeth receives his new title. We next see him dictating his letter to Lady Macbeth, the image dissolves to her reading it, and, as she prays that the spirits unsex her, Macbeth rushes in. A noise, a glimpse of horsemen, and Lady Macbeth exclaims "King Duncan." The king has come to Inverness. From now until the king retires to bed, Macbeth remains part of the action, seen either in long shot as part of the king's retinue, or in close-up as the traitor in league with Lady Macbeth, the brooding man apart whose thoughts we hear. During the murder scene, deep focus shots with Macbeth standing behind the speaker keep him ominously present, even when he does not speak. Welles keeps Macbeth in view (or just off-camera) all the time, following him

---

[6] For clarity and simplicity, throughout this essay I use "scene" to mean not only the divisions of the text, but also parts of the film that might more precisely be termed "takes," "shots," or "sequences of shots."

into Duncan's bedchamber, where his shadow falls across the
sleeping king, and later into the grooms' chamber, where his knife
dispatches them.

In the banquet scene we move from a concentration on
Macbeth's actions to his very consciousness. The film shifts from
shots of a crowded banquet table to shots of one deserted except for
a ghost—at first the glowering Banquo, then, the silver-haired
Duncan. Immediately afterward, the cauldron scene confirms the
notion that the apparitions came forth from deep within Macbeth's
psyche. At first standing atop a crag, his black robes torn by the
wind, Macbeth conjures the witches. Suddenly, all is calm.
Surrounded by blackness, Macbeth's white face comes slowly
nearer, as he intones responses to prophecies that come from
nowhere visible. To this point in the film, Macbeth has been a
visible part of the action continually, and except for some reaction
shots after the murder, his thoughts and movements have directed
what the camera looks at. In the scenes that follow, although the
film continues to concentrate on Macbeth, this concentration is
interrupted with increasing frequency by scenes in which he is
spoken about, but not present—the conference in England, the
gathering of Malcolm's forces, and the final assault on the castle. In
the Lady Macduff scene (IV, ii) and in the sleepwalking scene (V,
i) Welles brought Macbeth into the action. Jackbooted and garbed
in leather, Macbeth leads Lady Macduff's murderers. As Lady
Macbeth cries "to bed, to bed" at the end of her dream, Macbeth
comes to her, holds her, and kisses her. She starts, wakens, and
screams as she realizes whom she is kissing. Even though Macbeth is
not present when she falls to her death or when the soldiers batter
down his gates, his cavernous fortress—the physical form of his lust
for power—contains the action.

The overall result of Welles' concentration on Macbeth is an
interpretation of the play in which Macbeth's consciousness con-
trols the action, absorbs space, time, and other characters. As, in
different ways, Kane dominates those around him in *Citizen Kane*,
and Falstaff overshadows even the prince in *Chimes at Midnight*,
Welles' Macbeth towers above those who surround him. Shakespeare's play balances our fascination with Macbeth against our
concern for those he harms. In Welles' film, Macbeth's victims are
first of all his *enemies*, as we can see from the way Welles portrays
them. Duncan may be an old man and a rightful king, but he is also

cruel. The beheading of Cawdor to the savage throb of a great drum and the corpses dangling from the gallows attest to the ruthlessness of the king's justice. Banquo may be Macbeth's companion, but he is not his friend. Everything he says in the film conceals a threat, and the threat becomes open when he confronts Macbeth after the murder. As Welles portrays them, the deaths of Duncan and Banquo do not move us. And sympathy for Macduff is mitigated when, deserting his wife, he flees with Malcolm immediately after Duncan's murder.

Leading Macbeth's enemies is the Holy Father, Welles's new character. Lines from the Old Man, Angus, Ross, Lennox, and other attendant lords give the new character words of greeting, command, and admonition. As proclaimed in Welles' prologue, he represents "Christian law and order." Those he fights, continues the prologue, are "agents of chaos, priests of hell and magic, sorcerers, and witches." The Holy Father's emblem is the cross, he leads Duncan's court in an abbreviated baptismal rite ("Dost thou renounce Satan?" . . . etc.), and he meets with Malcolm and Macduff in front of a huge stone cross in England.

As an *idea*, Welles' attempt to stress the holiness of those who oppose Macbeth makes sense. Even Macbeth acknowledges Duncan's goodness, and the innocent Malcolm shares the sanctity of Edward the Confessor, the "good King" whose court shelters Malcolm (IV, iii). Yet Alan Napier's Holy Father seems anything but holy, his bushy eyebrows and long braids making him look, said Charles Higham, "like a cross between Boris Karloff and Heidi." [7] Ominous in appearance, the Holy Father keeps turning up when least expected. He drives off the witches, he listens to Macbeth's examination of conscience, he takes down Macbeth's letter to Lady Macbeth, he pokes his head in to eye Macbeth just after the grooms die, he warns Lady Macduff, he tells Macduff about her murder, and, in the end, he rides with Malcolm's troops, to die at last (audiences cheer) when he catches Macbeth's spear in the chest. Everyone knows that in *Macbeth* there is a larger and holy power working against the weird sisters. Yet the great discrepancy between what the Holy Father is meant to be and what he looks like—an interfering, greasy prelate—makes Welles' idea ludicrous, a grotesque caricature of the Christian sanctity he is meant to embody.

[7] Higham, *The Films of Orson Welles*, p. 132.

Equally grotesque, but far more credible, are the witches. The prologue identifies them with heathen cults, and Welles associates their control over Macbeth with voodoo rites.[8] At the opening, three figures, backlit and barely discernible, crouch on a rocky ledge. A close-up shows three pairs of hands kneading a slimy lump of clay in their cauldron. They form it into a voodoo doll and place a chain round its neck, as they plan their meeting with Macbeth. They crown it as they hail Macbeth "King that shalt be." Their powers are confirmed at once when we see Cawdor's chain and medal of office pulled from his neck and given to Macbeth. Later, just before Macbeth sees the air-drawn dagger, we see an image of the witches holding a dagger in front of the voodoo doll. Although the witches never show themselves in Welles's cauldron scene, their control over Macbeth's mind has already been made clear. At the end, just before Macbeth is beheaded, they shriek and we see the voodoo doll's head lopped off. Identifying the witches' power with voodoo considerably simplifies their nature, and it diminishes Macbeth's responsibility for his crimes. Yet it also, helpfully, translates Elizabethan superstition into terms that a modern audience can easily comprehend and find credible.

III

Shakespeare, said Welles, "wrote melodramas which had tragic stature." [9] The film bears him out. Welles' concentration on Macbeth, his portrayal of Banquo and others as enemies, and his depiction of Macbeth as the victim of the witches' powerful malevolence—all these reduce the play's complex moral issues to the neat black-and-white ethics of melodrama, a danger inherent in the script, which sometimes overwhelms it in performance. Yet Welles' filming adds dimension that, in its best moments, transcends the limitations of melodrama. Forsaking realistic conventions, Welles adopts an expressionistic or subjective mode in which the consciousness of the hero colors the world around him. Consider, for

[8] Welles had used the same idea in his all-black *Macbeth* at the Lafayette Theatre, Harlem, 1936.

[9] Quoted by Peter Cowie, *A Ribbon of Dreams: The Cinema of Orson Welles* (New York: A. S. Barnes, 1973), p. 109.

example, the way the camera treats Macbeth. Many of the shots are from waist level or lower, so that his figure seems to tower over us, and, when his hand is extended, it looms grotesquely large as it nears the camera.[10] At other times, as if to share Macbeth's point of view, we look down from great heights at his enemies or at the stone courtyard below. Many of Macbeth's lines are spoken as the camera looks elsewhere, the most striking instance being the swirling mists and clouds into which we look with Macbeth as he utters his despair: "Tomorrow, and tomorrow, and tomorrow . . ." (V, v, 19–28). Tricks of lighting (Welles at times appearing as a white outline against a black background, as in a negative), visual shocks in the cutting and montage, and images of the voodoo doll being formed and then broken as Macbeth traces his fall—all these combine to shape the world in which Macbeth finds himself cabin'd, cribb'd, and confin'd.

The mind of the speaker, the world around him, and the world we see, are all one. That world is unfamiliar if not unknown, a castle that is a labyrinth of caves, their walls oozing with slime, while outside lies a barren wasteland. "Gigantic, distorted cardboard sets," writes Peter Cowie, "dwarf the protagonists with their harsh shadows, their strange, writhing shapes, deformed windows, stairways, arches, and parapets." [11] The primitive era suggested by the sets, by the costumes, and by Welles' dirge-like prologue looks back to a time when mankind was emerging from the dark mists of devil worship.[12] In this warped, surreal world, Macbeth's visions are not hallucination but clairvoyance, a second sight truer than mere physical sight. His perceptions of the otherworld are validated by the technique of the film, as, conversely, they would be invalidated were the technique highly realistic.

In this world, too, images and objects have powers that go beyond

---

[10] Henry Raynor writes: "The hands that will incarnadine the multitudinous seas are held out, waist height, towards a low-placed camera, and appear huge, knotted, and ugly" ("Shakespeare Filmed," *Sight and Sound*, July–September 1952, p. 14).

[11] *The Cinema of Orson Welles* (Amsterdam: Zwemmer, 1965), p. 98.

[12] Raynor, "Shakespeare Filmed," p. 12, oddly thought "the almost Mongolian costumes suggest Ivan the Terrible," a film that has nothing to do with Mongolians. My colleague John Frayne suggests that the costumes, and especially the forest of spears at the end, are reminiscent of Eisenstein's *Alexander Nevsky*. The complete prologue appears in the appendix.

their literal meaning. At times they set an emotional tone. Usually it is fear—the fear of things unseen in the mist, of entrapment in the caves of Dunsinane, and of the dizzying vertigo induced by strange camera angles, movement, and montage. At other times, they go beyond the emotional to take on conceptual meanings, becoming emblems with abstract significance. On the simplest level, each side in the conflict between good and evil has its emblem: opposed to the cross is the spiky emblem of the witches, a thin Y formed by two spines sticking out from a long, thin pole. Besides these explicit emblems the whole tenor of the film endows natural objects with emblematic significance, leading critics like Peter Cowie to conclude that Macbeth's "barbaric mind is mirrored in the scenery." [13] Thus, when Malcolm's cross-bearing army covers the barren landscape of Macbeth's Scotland with the trees of Birnam Wood, the moving trees become an appropriate visual emblem for the victory of life over death, of good over evil. Such a reading of Shakespeare's play is a commonplace of modern criticism, which sees a symbolic dimension in the play's imagery; and, despite Welles' often clumsy results, his work deserves attention for trying to visualize that dimension through the unique capabilities of film.

Yet Welles' surreal mise-en-scène contains no realm of goodness from which Macbeth exiles himself. Despite the Holy Father, the Christian symbols, and the baptismal rites, we never see anything like the world of justice and heroism that Shakespeare embodies in Duncan and his court, later in Malcolm and the English court. Nor does Welles endow his Lady Macbeth with the force of character that in part must keep us in sympathy with Macbeth as a man misled. Nor, despite the business of the voodoo doll, do Welles's witches help expose Macbeth's better nature because there is no goodness in him for them to overcome. Welles' Macbeth is a vicious monster from the outset, a grotesque mutation, adapted to an unnatural world. Even the great soliloquies of despair, meant to pull us back into sympathy with Macbeth in the final act, ring hollow because there has been nothing good—no honor, love, obedience, nor troops of friends—for this Macbeth to lose. In short, by allowing Macbeth's nightmare vision to control his setting and his cinematic technique, Welles kept much of the play's eerie atmosphere, but almost wholly lost the sense of good and evil warring within a man's soul.

[13] *The Cinema of Orson Welles*, p. 98.

This is a great loss. Yet, to ignore accepted film production procedures (by prerecording the sound track, for instance) and to change utterly a classic play requires great daring and a great risk of failure—even foolhardiness. It is not really surprising that Welles' experiment did not wholly succeed. Nonetheless, his treatment of the play is true to the major concerns of his art, in both style and substance: his simplification—or clarifications—of moral complexities, his obsession with a single, superhuman character (Kane, Falstaff, and Othello, to name only three others), and, ultimately, his need to break with the conventional in everything he did. In his *Macbeth* Welles suggests an expressionistic alternative to the realism that makes many Shakespeare films (I think here especially of Schaeffer's *Macbeth*) seem bad mixtures of intense poetry and prosaic filming. At its best moments, Welles' *Macbeth* leads us deep into the nightmare realms where Macbeth lives, where nothing is but what is not, where fair is foul and foul is fair. Although a reduction of Shakespeare's great tragedy, it is a reduction through intensity, a grim vision of man as "death-infected"—to use Ian Kott's apt phrase—trapped in the wasteland.*

* Professor Mullin prepared as an appendix to his essay a detailed record of the film script's dialogue as it compares with Shakespeare's text, but space limitations made it impossible to reproduce this aid.

Welles' Othello:
A Baroque Translation

by JACK J. JORGENS

Orson Welles' *Othello* is one of the few Shakespeare films in which the images on the screen generate enough beauty, variety, and graphic power to stand comparison with Shakespeare's poetic images, in which the visual imagery compensates for the inevitable loss of complexity and dramatic voltage accompanying heavy alterations in the text. Full of flamboyant cinematography, composed and edited in what has been called the "bravura style," [1] *Othello* transcends categories, blending the deep focus "realistic" photography hailed by Bazin with the expressionist montage of Eisenstein. What the film lacks in acting—subtle characterization and emotional range—it makes up in rich, thematically significant compositions. If it destroys the play's narrative continuity, it succeeds in creating a stunning subjective portrait of Othello's heroic world in disintegration. Plagued with garbled and poorly synchronized sound, it is filled with haunting and marvelous aural collages. In short, *Othello* is a comparatively rare thing in film—an authentic flawed masterpiece.

In Stuart Burge's film of Olivier's *Othello* (1966) the interpretation is a realistic one: the story has racial and political overtones, and its core is the searing, shocking spectacle of a man reverting to savagery, eaten up with jealousy until he murders the woman he loves. By contrast, Welles depicts a whole world in collapse (cf. *The Magnificent Ambersons*), a world that is a metaphor not just for

This essay is a shortened portion of a chapter from Jack J. Jorgens' forthcoming book Shakespeare on Film *to be published by Indiana University Press.*
[1] *Time*, June 6, 1955.

Othello's mind, but for an epic, pre-modern age. For him, *Othello* is mythic; it portrays another lost Eden, another fall from innocence in which the serpent fractures unity, harmony, love, and beauty, destroys man with terrible knowledge. The mad, nightmarish world of *The Trial* is born when Iago succeeds in undermining Othello's faith in Desdemona.

The visual style of the film mirrors the marriage at the center of the play—not of Othello and Desdemona, but the perverse marriage of Othello and Iago. Part of its cinematic language is born of Othello's romantic, histrionic, hyperbolic character. His heroic nature is embodied in Welles' low-angle shots, vast spaces, monumental buildings, and large groupings. The sky, sea, and rocks, the tracery of Venetian architecture, the brute fortress, the networks of arches express Othello's downfall. "These walls, these vaults and corridors echo, reflect and multiply, like so many mirrors, the eloquence of the tragedy." [2]

Although the film's grandeur, hyperbole, and simplicity are the Moor's, its dizzying camera movements, tortured compositions, grotesque shadows, and insane distortions are Iago's, for he is the agent of chaos. In Shakespeare's verbal terms, Iago's masterpiece is to reduce Othello's lyricism and verbal expansiveness to bursts of confused logic, shattered syntax, obsessive repetitions, and unconscious puns.

Lie with her? lie on her?—We say lie on her when they belie her.—Lie with her! Zounds, that's fulsome.—Handkerchief—confessions—handkerchief!

In Welles' visual terms, the paranoia Iago generates and the violence he unleashes are expressed in staccato rhythms and shadowy surfaces.[3] Iago isolates his victim, plays on his weaknesses, and fills his mind with troubled images, deceptive shapes, and contradictions until he loses all sense of orientation and continuity. His satanic artistry, in other words, is not unlike that of Welles.

The conflict of Iago and Othello is apparent in the opening

[2] André Bazin, "A Review of *Othello*," *Focus on Shakespearean Films*, ed. Charles W. Eckert (Englewood Cliffs, N.J.: Prentice-Hall, 1972), p. 78.

[3] See Donald Skoller's unpublished dissertation "Problems of Transformation in the Adaptation of Shakespeare's Tragedies from Playscript to Cinema," New York University, 1968, p. 352.

images of the funeral procession (we begin with the end; there is never any possibility of escape). After the disorienting opening shot in which the camera booms up from and then down again toward Othello's lifeless face, the corpse moves away on a bier. There is a jarring shift in scale as a vast horizon is filled with processions of mourning monks following the caskets of Othello and Desdemona. Against the slow, horizontal flow left to right of the funeral processions are set the spasmodic jerks and vertical movement of Iago as he is pulled by a chain around his neck right to left, caged in iron, and suspended from a huge tower. Against the solemn mourning chorus and massive low chords from an amplified harpsichord are set the shouts of a crowd hungry for revenge. The swaying point of view shot through bars that form a cross (echoing the cross in the procession) as Iago peers down from his cage is the first of many shots creating a sense of vertigo, a feeling of tottering instability culminating in Othello's epileptic seizure, the murder of Roderigo, and Othello's dizzying final fall.

Shots of great beauty reflect Othello's commitments both to Desdemona and the "plumed troops": the fluid gliding gondola in which they ride, the joyous silhouette of the ship with billowing sails against the fortress, and the spiralling ascent of Othello (to triumphantly rising chorus and trumpets) to greet Desdemona against a sky full of white clouds and wind-blown banners. A marvelous scene in which Othello and Desdemona consummate their marriage begins with a pan over silhouettes of mechanical figures striking a huge bell, the spires of the cathedral and misty St. Mark's square lying in the distance. In each case, however, the beautiful and the lyrical are shadowed by impending doom. The slow, horizontal movement of the gondola recalls the inexorable motion of the funeral processions. Othello's upward climb echoes the earlier descent of Brabantio's spiral staircase by torch-bearing householders as a harpsichord races down a scale—a "symbol of the spiralling rush down to doom." [4] In the love scene, framed by Iago's ominous "I am not what I am" and the fierce storm at Cyprus, Othello's shadow on the curtain foreshadows a similar effect later as he enters her bedroom to kill her; and behind the two lovers is the grillwork motif initiated by Iago's cage in the opening scene.

Shakespeare uses setting to express theme as well as character,

[4] *New York Herald-Tribune*, September 13, 1955.

and his symbolic geography is skillfully realized by Welles. In Venice, Iago's attempts to sow discord are frustrated. He is but a shadow on the canal or a lurking whisperer in the cathedral—a threat, a possibility. The civilized order is embodied in rich harmonious architecture, sculptured figures of heroic man, placid canals, and symmetrical altar at which Othello and Desdemona are married. Visually, people are dwarfed by an old and massive order that, if it cannot eliminate human suffering, can prevent injustice and at least provide a framework for happiness. In Venice Othello is completely in command of himself. He moves and speaks to his own rhythms. Unlike earlier rapid cuts, his speech to the senators describing how he won Desdemona is rendered in lengthy takes of his handsome profile, and the film again comes to rest in his lyrical love scene with Desdemona.

In Cyprus, at the frontier of the civilized world, the restraints of Venice are lifted. Art, luxury, and institutions are taken away. The armaments and the fortress represent a crude, and in the end hopelessly inadequate, way of dealing with the "Turk" in man. The group leadership of white-haired civilians is replaced by the individual generalship of Othello. The citizens are not the rich merchants of Venice, but soldiers, whores, and impoverished Cypriots. The glassy canals are replaced by vicious seas that pound at the foundations of the battlements. The longer we are in Cyprus, the more the involuted Iago style triumphs over the heroic and lyrical Othello style. Inside the town, water becomes more subtle, more dangerous: reflecting the vaults under which Cassio and Montano fight, rushing down through the board floor of a Turkish bath to drown Roderigo. Venetian Christianity is overpowered by paganism. Christian images appear but are put to perverse use: Iago kneels before a Madonna and Child to bow to aid Othello in his revenge. Othello's killing of Desdemona is a dark ritual recalling the wedding in Venice, but now he puts out the candles at the altar, the organ music is discordant and fragmented, and the vows are murderous. Sounds in Cyprus—wind, shouts, echoing footsteps, slamming doors—become surreally loud. The shapes on the screen are less and less easily recognizable. Compositions are tense, full of diagonals. Faces are obscured, crossed with shadows or bars, harshly side-lit, set askew in the frame. Moving shadows distort the human figure (Othello, Iago, the revelers). Labyrinthine corridors entomb Othello and Desdemona. "The bubbling, seething baths are a brilliant reminder of that 'cistern for foul toads to knot and gender' in that Shakespeare speaks of through Othello's mouth." [5] Characters are separated by tremendous distances, vertical and horizontal, and yet there is an increasing feeling of confinement. Ceilings bear down, walls become overpowering, the world seems to be closing in. The screen is sometimes masked to focus our attention on a face compressed into a small space. The exhilaration, the sense of freedom and infinite possibility experienced on the battlements, now seem an illusion; the reality, revealed by the inspired prophet Iago, is the tortured, solitary, eerily lit face of Othello surrounded by darkness.

The bed and the handkerchief, the two central symbolic props in theatrical productions of the play, constitute two of the recurring images in the film. The bed, emblem of the sexual union of Othello and Desdemona, is set contrapuntally against Brabantio's ornate bed, and later the grotesquely shadowed bed of suspicion and death in Cyprus. The handkerchief, symbol of the faith and trust between them as well as her honor, is stepped upon by Othello as he rushes away from her, and is seen on Cassio's bed and in Bianca's hands before, in carrying out his terrible brand of justice, Othello smothers Desdemona with it, creating a hideous death mask. But Welles' significant imagery is not limited to theatrical properties. Often he reaches for the resonant, multi-leveled images of Shakespeare's dramatic poetry. Some of the images, such as the opposition of black and white, are visual equivalents of poetic images. From the torches hopefully lit by Brabantio's followers, to Othello's sustained speech before the Duke where he moves from light to shadow to light as he speaks; from the flashes of lightning in the dark Cyprus storm, to the white of Desdemona's handkerchief and dress; from the emblem of the sun on Othello's black cloak, to the lighted window in the huge tower at Cyprus; from the extinguished candles at the killing of Desdemona, to the pit of blackness in which Othello dies, the opposition and interpenetration of dark and light is stressed.

In the play, one of Iago's favorite images is that of the net, the snare, the web, making him a fisherman, a hunter, a spider. "With as little a web as this will I ensnare as great a fly as Cassio." "Will

[5] Peter Cowie, *A Ribbon of Dreams: The Cinema of Orson Welles* (New York: A. S. Barnes, 1973), p. 352.

you, I pray, demand that demi-devil why he hath ensnared my soul and body?" Welles holds the image before our eyes, plays variations on it. We see it in the grate through which Desdemona passes to escape her father, the net that holds her hair in Cyprus, the ships' rigging, the rack of spears in the fortress, and the windows and doors of Othello's bedroom. In the end Iago is caught in his own mesh; always hovering above him is the iron cage where the sun will scorch him and the gulls will peck away his flesh. Similarly, through an image, Welles anticipates Othello's line in Act V: "Here is my journey's end, here is my butt and very seamark of my utmost sail." Following Othello's farewell to his occupation, a dark ship moves toward the walls of the fortress, its sail slowly coming down. Furthermore, like Shakespeare, Welles emphasizes through imagery the animalistic mentality into which Iago drags his victims: he leads Cassio and Roderigo past braying asses, treats Roderigo like his own little puppy ("drown cats and blind puppies"), and leads Othello among goats ("exchange me for a goat") and screaming gulls.

Not all Welles' imagery is drawn directly from the language of the play, however. Some of it evolves from dramatic situation. Mirrors into which Othello and Roderigo peer reflect Iago's technique of turning his victims in upon themselves and playing upon their impulses toward doubt or self-destruction, of showing them distorted images of reality. Iago's power over the other characters is repeatedly stressed as he casts a huge shadow, looks down at them from steep angles, makes sudden appearances, appears fully dressed and armed while others wear towels in the bath, and strips the armor from Othello as he works on his fears and latent suspicions.

Welles' *Othello* is impressive in the *range* of its images as well as their expressiveness and density. The tone may be light, as when Roderigo's dog bites his finger and follows him as he attempts to murder Cassio. Or it may verge on black humor, as in the little stick of soap dangling by his head in the bath, which resembles a little human figure hanging by its neck. Some of the best effects are simple ones: the *Seventh Seal*-like silhouettes of the funeral processions against the horizon, the spears piercing the delicate figure of Desdemona as she walks toward Othello, the slamming of the trap door at the top of the huge vault above the dead lovers. But some effects are only apparently simple, as in the centerpiece of the film—a traveling shot nearly one and one-half minutes long of Othello and Iago walking stride for stride along the ramparts of the fortress, Iago questioning Othello, pausing, refusing to reveal his thoughts, questioning him again. It is a good shot because the acting is good, and because the seeming endlessness of the walk is appropriate to the dramatic moment. It is a great shot because its overlaying of several aural and visual rhythms, all of them different, serves to build a sense of unease in the viewer: the regular beat of the boots on the stones and the tandem movement of the bodies, the rhythm of the waves beating the shore, the uneven bursts of speech and silence, the irregular appearance of cannon, notches, and squares of bright light, and the pattern of the irregularly spaced rocks in the sea beyond the ramparts clash with one another.

As in *Macbeth*, there are images in this film that are eloquent in a mysterious way, that have a suggestive vagueness about them like some of Shakespeare's best images. There is no simple way to account for the rightness of the uncomfortable moment when the soldiers stare up at Desdemona in her filmy white dress, the grotesque shape of a chandelier with lighted candles that masks Iago as he walks past, or the terror of the water blanking out the screen at the death of Roderigo. Often it is not the single image that works this way but a combination of images. Shot 1: an overhead long shot of Desdemona walking between two dark pillars onto a piazza with a hypnotic mosaic pattern (scales? shells?). Shot 2: dissolve from this abstract pattern to a rapid rush toward Othello accompanied by a loud roar on the sound track, his profile becoming obscured by a monstrous shadow as the camera follows him under an arch. Shot 3: cut to Iago's shadow lengthening on wet cobblestones as he approaches Othello to urge him to kill Desdemona. In these three shots the major triad of the film is stated with clarity and force. The electricity generated by the killing of Roderigo in the famous Turkish bath scene (a forerunner of the shower murder in *Psycho*) is remarkable: Iago's sword flashes in the steam, Cassio falls holding his leg, Roderigo's distorted face appears through the steam as he tries to pull open a barred door, he peers up through the floor at Iago, mandolins accelerate insanely as Iago sadistically looks down at his victim, a spinning shot of the underside of the floor reveals Iago's sword slashing through it, an unexpected rush of water blanks out the frame, and thudding low chords from a harpsichord punctuate the sequence as we stare at the tower with a light in Othello's bedroom window and the suspended cage awaiting Iago.

The acting in *Othello* is never as obtrusively bad as in *Macbeth*, but still it lacks force and variety. The roles are not only underplayed, they are seldom detailed or personal. As in Eisenstein's films, the actors are most eloquent when used well as compositional elements. What subjectivity they possess comes from their environment or from point-of-view shots, for faces are seldom emphasized and do not express much when they are. Memorable moments come not on but between the lines (what lines are left them in the case of the minor characters, for their parts are cut heavily). Brabantio, for instance, is best when, having lost his daughter, he pitifully looks back, then exits in solitude—ignored by the others who busy themselves with state affairs. Bianca is most effective when leaning drunkenly on Cassio's shoulder while wearing his helmet and fiddling amorously with his ear, or when bustling indignantly along the beach to confront Cassio with the handkerchief. Flabby-faced Roderigo is good when ridiculously paralleled with his curly-haired little white dog, or cutting a silly figure in a turban and ragged towel in the steam bath where he has been scratching hearts with "D" in them on the wall. But he is best (perhaps because of the preceding humor) when, terror-stricken, he is cornered and murdered by Iago. Bitter, cynical, middle-aged Emilia is a good foil for Desdemona—scratching her chin with her thumb and chuckling that women too have appetites—but her shrill, ludicrous death scene detracts from the film. Compared to these, the cold, arrogant unlikeable Cassio is sketchily drawn.

Suzanne Cloutier's Desdemona is a fairy princess, rescued from her wicked father's tower by an adventurous Moor. She wears pearls in her hair in Venice ("like the base Indian, threw a pearl away . . ."). Her wide-eyed innocence and softly lit angelic beauty, her playfulness when first urging Othello to forgive Cassio, and her stunned incomprehension at Othello's anger and accusations make her seem out of place among the soldiers and whores of Cyprus. She is a saint, an emblem of love and devotion. Except for her feigning sleep and convincing panic before being strangled, she is robbed of her inner life (Welles cut the scene with the willow song). It is her simplicity, her pearl-like opaque whiteness that becomes a horror to Othello and enrages him because it contrasts so vividly with the ugly labyrinths Iago has revealed in himself.

Ultimately he kills her not out of a sense of justice, but out of twisted desire (he kisses her as he strangles her), self-hatred, and envy at her inhuman perfection.

Micheál MacLiammóir plays a flat, business-like Iago—a relentless bureaucrat, a pedestrian mechanic who is clinical and disinterested to the point of boredom. Welles instructed his actor to eradicate all the playfulness, the flirting with giving himself away, the self-consciousness and ironic wit of Shakespeare's creature who takes immense delight in his own demonic powers. "No single trace of the Mephistophelean Iago is to be used: no conscious villainy." [6] Except for the sadistic killing of Roderigo (more important in the film than in the play),[7] the savagery is drained out of the character. His look as he peers down from the cage is wide-eyed, blank. His characteristic gestures are small ones: tugging at his dark stringy hair, glancing down to avoid revealing his cynicism, poking at Roderigo with a stick. The disease is hidden and surfaces only in his looks of disgust at Emilia, revealing "the underlying sickness of mind, the immemorial hatred of life, the secret isolation of impotence under the soldier's muscles, the flabby solitude gnawing at the groins, the eye's untiring calculation." [8] The soliloquies in which Iago draws us into his diabolical plots have been cut, placing him on the same plane of reality as the others, robbing him of his ability to step out of the fiction. From his first words "I hate the Moor," spoken in a context that stresses sacrilege and impotent envy[9] (the organ plays and the priest recites the ceremony while the parodic couple Iago and Roderigo look on), he is an altogether mortal Iago. Said Welles, "I have taken from him the diabolic quality and made him more human." [10] Oddly, in a film of the myth of the Fall, the mythical quality of Iago, the enormity not just of his acts but his way of thinking and being, is lacking. Here evil follows the definition of the medieval theologians—it is merely the negation of good with no form or positive qualities of its own.

[6] Micheál MacLiammóir, *Put Money in Thy Purse* (London: Methuen, 1952); reprinted in Eckert, pp. 81–82.

[7] Stressed by Alain Marie, "L'Esthetique Tragique D'Othello," *Etudes Cinematiques*, Nos. 24–25 (1963), p. 93.

[8] MacLiammóir, *Put Money in Thy Purse*, p. 82.

[9] Joseph McBride, *Orson Welles* (New York: Viking, 1972), p. 120.

[10] "Francis Koval Interviews Welles," *Film Makers on Film Making*, ed. Harry M. Geduld (Bloomington, Indiana: Indiana University Press, 1969), p. 262.

This underplayed Iago throws even more emphasis upon Welles' Othello, but this performance too is damaged by its subdued quality. To put it cruelly, "he never acts, he is photographed." [11] To put it sympathetically, Welles expresses Othello's character not through acting, but through sound effects, movement, and setting. Unlike Olivier, Welles cuts the scenes of bravado, avoids the big gestures and continual use of his magnificent voice. Othello does not face the "bright swords" of Brabantio and his followers, but warns that the "dew will rust them" from a balcony. It is Othello's officers who break up the fight of Cassio and Roderigo—he appears at the top of a staircase and pronounces judgement from an Olympian height. Welles holds himself to a narrow vocal range, delivering Othello's lines in low tones. Visually, his power is expressed by elongated low-angle silhouettes against the sky, harshly side-lit shots of his face framed by arches or set against large architectural forms. His passion takes the shape of sudden move-ments among grates and pillars, slamming shut huge gates and doors, sudden appearances of his shadow, swirls of marble behind him or a gargoyle beside his head (a contrast with the Madonna and Child). The subterranean world of the fortress becomes a metaphor for what Iago uncovers in the Moor. The whole frame "acts" as Othello is trapped inside himself. The Moor is the only character for whom sound is consistently subjective. The sound of the curtain rings as he flings them open to look at his bed is positively shattering. Cassio's laughter takes on a cosmic dimension as Othello hears it echo through the opening in the wall and blend with the screams of the gulls and a softly trilling flute. This flute sounds again as he regains consciousness on the rocky shore and looks up to see a gull slowly sail toward an upside down fortress wall; the cries of the gulls blend with the laughter of the soldiers and whores looking down at him from the wall. The ocean roars fiercely as his passions rise on the battlements, and sudden bursts of music and the echoing electronic clanking of the alarm bell give the film a nightmarish quality.

Welles plays Othello as the truly noble man, great even in defeat—a conception worlds away from F. R. Leavis' deflating "modern" view. There are a few moments of great pathos in the performance: imagining Desdemona, his "fountain," as a "cistern"

---

[11] Eric Bentley, *What Is Theatre?* (New York: Atheneum, 1968), p. 236.

for toads, he runs his hand slowly down the front of her white dress with a look of profound sorrow. But the usual effect is of stoically contained passion. Othello's flaw is also his greatness. He is "the only character capable of action in a world of impotent observers." [12] But the man of action is trapped in a labyrinth, doomed to destroy goodness inside and outside himself, become aware of it, and execute justice on himself. It is so much his story that Iago does not even appear at the end of the film, the last images being an overhead long shot of the tragic couple on the bed, and of their funeral processions against the horizon. It is not until the final credits that the dialectic of the Iago and Othello styles is reasserted.

It has been said that Welles' most notable achievement as a filmmaker is "his attempt to invest each shot with an impact and surprise which are greater than any relationship the shot bears to the dramatic content of the film." [13] People who dislike Welles' *Othello* do so for this very reason. One reviewer says Welles has destroyed the tale in order to concentrate on "half a hundred cinematic tricks." [14] Another asserts that Welles "apparently has no sense of narrative, that is, of the procession of incidents, but only an interest in the incidents themselves—no, not even that, but only an interest in separate moments within the incidents, and this just for the opportunity they offer for arbitrary effects, visual and auditory." [15] Roger Manvell finds that "the large number of strikingly lit architectural shots coming in quick succession on the screen makes the film restless, and to this extent more difficult to enter into. Satiety sets in; so much photographic beauty becomes a drug." [16] On the other hand, those who find Welles' *Othello* a great film respond to it as poetry of the screen, a film whose style is much closer to the essence of Shakespeare than the most literal and "respectful" adaptations.

[12] McBride, *Orson Welles*, p. 119.

[13] Donald Phelps, *"Othello," Film Culture*, 1 (Winter 1955), p. 32.

[14] *The New Yorker*, September 17, 1955.

[15] Bentley, *What Is Theatre?* p. 236.

[16] *Shakespeare and the Film* (New York: Praeger, 1971), p. 63.

Touch of Evil

by TERRY COMITO

One of the crucial changes Welles makes in adapting Whit Masterson's novel to his own uses is shifting the action from San Diego to the Mexican border.[1] But *Touch of Evil*'s "Mexico" is not the place liberal critics think it is. Such critics should have been warned by Janet Leigh's mistake: she pleads with her husband to "get me out of here" (this is not the "real Mexico," Vargas tries to tell her), and thinks she'll be safe in an American motel. Welles' Mexico is not a scene for acting out platitudes about bigotry and social justice; it is a place of the soul, the "foreign" place, the

[1] Vargas, a drug investigator for the Mexican government, and his bride Susan, witness the explosion of a car as it passes over the border. The American sheriff, Quinlan, fastens upon the Mexican boy friend of the wealthy victim's daughter as his chief suspect; meanwhile Susan is being terrorized by "Uncle Joe" Grandi, whose brother Vargas had convicted on a drug charge. Vargas discovers that Quinlan has planted evidence in order to frame his suspect; alarmed by these accusations, Quinlan makes common cause with Grandi in order to discredit Vargas. Susan is held captive in an American motel owned by Grandi and (apparently) drugged, so that Quinlan can claim that both she and Vargas are addicts. But when Grandi, with the still unconscious Susan, meets Quinlan in a hotel on the Mexican side of the border, Quinlan strangles Grandi and leaves the corpse behind to be discovered, along with Vargas' half-naked bride, by the police. Meanwhile, Vargas discovers that Quinlan, obsessed by the unsolved murder of his wife, has made a career of falsifying evidence. When Quinlan's best friend, Pete Menzies, discovers Quinlan's cane at the murder scene, he reluctantly agrees to work with Vargas. Equipped with a "bug," Menzies seeks Quinlan out at a brothel where he has taken refuge with Tanya and engages him in a long conversation, which Vargas, tracking the two, gets down on his tape recorder. After he has confessed, Quinlan discovers the deception, shoots Menzies, and is about to kill Vargas, too, when he is himself shot by the expiring Menzies. Vargas learns that the young Mexican Quinlan framed was in fact guilty and has confessed to dynamiting the car.

nightmare from which a lost Hollywood sweater girl—Mrs. Tony Curtis and the antithesis of all Dietrich's weary experience—begs to be awakened.

To put it differently: Mexico is not geographical but visual space, a way of experiencing the world. Welles' habitually deep focus means that any place a character may for an instant inhabit is only the edge of the depth that opens dizzily behind him, receding along the arcades of Venice, California, like some baroque hallucination. The violence of the motion Welles sets plunging through these depths means that "foreground" and "background" no longer serve as static games for a comfortable middle distance (a "middle" both optically and ethically). Instead, all three are points on a single system, through which, just beyond the circle closed about any given moment's awareness, the assassin pursues his prey, and through whose sinuous passages the investigator must seek out an unknown evil. Menace lurches suddenly forward, and chases disappear down long perspectives; or we may be confronted with more interior searches: a single figure, dwarfed by the geometry of empty streets and arcades, wandering through a landscape of memory, littered with blown papers and the ruins of an abandoned carnival.

We may best understand the perceptual world of *Touch of Evil* by thinking of it as a labyrinth, in which the viewer too is invited to lose himself: the network of odd angles; the brutally discontinuous montage; the chiaroscuro and intermittent glare of neon; the pervasive, only half-heard, Latin drums and sudden blasts of fortyish jazz; the overlapping voices and, particularly in scenes in which the depth of field is most in evidence (e.g., Grandi pursuing his "boys" and losing his hairpiece), the dislocation of sound in space, as if the seen and the heard could no longer be held together in a single coherent world. At a time when this film is still praised for its "love of the film medium," as if Welles were only an avatar of Norman Jewison, it is important to insist on the rigor with which all the cinematic means converge toward a single end: menace, disequilibrium. The middle shot, as André Bazin has written, appeals to the "natural point of balance of [the viewer's] mental adjustment." [2] The intention of Welles' style is precisely to subvert

[2] André Bazin, *What is Cinema?* trans. Hugh Gray (Berkeley: University of California Press, 1967), p. 32.

this balance: by opening upon the vertiginous ambiguities of space to deny us the safety of the frame of reference through which we habitually contemplate the world—the *plan-Américain* of our waking life. Consider, for example, Quinlan's first appearance. No establishing shot allows us to orient ourselves before his massive intrusion: first, a low-angled shot of the car door opening, then, looming above it, a close-up of the great puffy face and huge cigar—not so much seen as felt, like the disquieting presences of nightmare.

At those points when the action becomes most conclusive (the murder of Grandi, for example, or the earlier acid-throwing episode), Welles sets camera and actors moving in opposite directions so that, deprived of any fixed point of reference, we are pulled into a vortex of irrational motion, of violent gestures no longer commensurable. The vertigo of such moments is the exact optical equivalent of the moral hysteria whose precipitate (as Welles has observed) is the idiotic motel keeper, hopping and giggling away over a windswept, featureless landscape, a vast emptiness marked by a single ghostly tree and by the shabby buildings where Vargas' wife sought refuge in what he now learns to have been the very bosom of her tormentors—"Who do you think this place belongs to anyway?" Welles speaks of this night man as a "Shakespearean fool," [3] but his own sensibility has always seemed less attuned to tragedy or comedy than to melodrama or farce, modes whose dreamlike and incommensurate gestures create their own space. The night man's scenes—or many of those with Akim Tamiroff's superb Grandi—suggest that the special landscape of *Touch of Evil* is the unstable place where farce and melodrama converge; or, more exactly, the place where farce is born from the convulsions of melodrama: the "estranged world" of the grotesque. It is here, I think, that we find the most exact and comprehensive term for Welles' dizzying theatrics. The grotesque—"a play with the absurd," a sinister game that may "carry the player away, deprive him of his freedom" ever to return to the familiar daylight.[4]

"I believe, thinking about my films, that they are based not so much on pursuit as on a search," Welles has said. "If we are looking

[3] Jean-Claude Allais, "Orson Welles," *Premier Plan*, 16 (March 1961), p. 68.

[4] See Wolfgang Kayser, *The Grotesque in Art and Literature*, trans. Ulrich Weisstein (Bloomington, Indiana: Indiana University Press, 1963), pp. 184–189.

for something a labyrinth is the most favorable location for the search." [5] An odd enough remark, if we care to press it closely. The labyrinth is the "most favorable" place for a search only to an investigator preoccupied with the tortuousness of his own seeking: only if what the searcher really wants is to lose himself, if his real goal is the hall of mirrors where at last he comes upon his own image shivered into a thousand fragments. (For one hallucinatory moment, as Kane passes between two mirrors, the camera hovers as if to plunge down the corridor of images, as if to lose itself—and us—in reflected depths more real than the hallway along which the hunched manikin Kane has become disappears off the side of the screen.) The reporter of *Citizen Kane* does not, to be sure, run any such risks; faceless himself, a fabricator of public images, he uncovers the labyrinth without entering into its mystery. But as Van Stratten learns in *Mr. Arkadin*, such labyrinths are places of pursuit as well as of search, places in which the search inexorably becomes a pursuit when the mystery closes down about the hapless inquisitor—as it does about Vargas, smashing with impotent fury through the narrow barroom where his enemies celebrate their inexplicable triumph, then, without transition, winding through the corridors of Quinlan's jail to find his bride delirious in her cell. The peril that must be confronted is finally the nature of the search itself; the puzzle of the labyrinth and its menace are one: the bomb moving slowly through narrow streets.

Welles' preoccupation with such images may suggest why the energies of his art are most fully liberated by the thriller, the *roman noir:* stories that violate the autonomy of space and time and reassemble their fragments in order to satisfy the investigator's taste for conspiracy—or hallucination. Such an enterprise presupposes the breakdown of conventional categories of understanding—moral, social, even psychological; things are not what they seem, there is more than meets the eye. Deprived of their familiar aspect, things portend (like the debris Kane leaves behind him in Xanadu) a significance *not yet* made manifest: the blind woman presiding over Vargas' telephoned declarations of love and assurance; the strangely elongated bed in an empty room of an empty motel in an empty landscape; Quinlan's very face, like a mask or an icon. A

[5] Andrew Sarris, ed., *Interviews with Film Directors* (New York: Avon, 1967), p. 532.

world of clues, as the etymology of the word suggests, assumes a labyrinth. If Welles' style seems rhetorical, it is because his characters, like medieval mystics, inhabit a universe whose least component is an exhortation, a summons, to hidden mystery—for one who knows how to listen. In Welles, however, the abyss to which one is called by all things is not the abyss of God, but Quinlan's vision of inexplicable violence and universal guilt: "guilty, guilty, every last one of them guilty."

I have so far been speaking rather melodramatically and obliquely, because this seems to me the appropriate way to deal with Welles, and in particular with the peculiarly parabolic manner in which *Touch of Evil* communicates its intuitions. What the film is "about" is not distinct from what we might call the phenomenology of its cinematic style. It is, quite simply, about being lost in the labyrinth whose dimensions I have been trying to adumbrate. "What's that got to do with me?" Janet Leigh asks the whispered menace through the walls of the Mirador Motel. But when she wakes, her conventionally pretty blond face illuminated by blinking neon, it is to open her eyes on the inverted farcically leering mask of the strangled Grandi, to plunge half naked into a cacophony of street sounds, jazz, and strident jeering, to watch from her fire escape while her husband, oblivious to her cries for help, passes slowly away through the maze of indifferent or threatening strangers.

As the film's center of gravity shifts from the trials of Susan Vargas to the figure of Quinlan himself, we begin gradually to see not only the terror and perplexity of the labyrinth, but also its moral and psychological dimensions. There is a shift, in other words, from the lyric to the dramatic, from passion to action—from a mode of understanding that seeks to come to grips with the "foreign place" by submitting wholly to its darkness, to another mode whose aim is to humanize the void by placing it in the sequence of choice and striving that constitutes the history of a man's life. To put the matter crudely: in *Touch of Evil* we gradually see that the labyrinth in which innocence loses its way is simply *time,* simply the life a man lives—any man, "some kind of man," everyone being hooked on something, as Tanya says—and which he builds up around himself, fragment by fragment, until finally there is no escape. The gradual enrichment or specification of its central image constitutes the film's visual structure; for the sake of exposition, we may distinguish three stages in Quinlan's career.

The first sequence enacts Quinlan's absorption into the labyrinthine world of Uncle Joe Grandi (or we should say, "reenacts," for obviously Quinlan is in fact no stranger to its deviousness). "We're both after the same thing." Quinlan and Grandi confer in the street, while Menzies looks on sadly through a window reflecting their figures, and a church bell rings in the distance. Later, in the cafe, Quinlan protests "that 'we' stuff," hunched rigidly behind a table as Grandi cringes and scurries behind him; but as Quinlan capitulates and begins to drink, the camera rises to see the two men as a single unit.

Confronted with Vargas' evidence, Quinlan offers to turn in his badge and is followed out into the hotel's deserted lobby. Having been questioned, a career, a life, loses its solidity—the camera constantly circling and probing—and what is left is a dance of silhouettes through empty space: disembodied voices and shadows cast by the dim institutional lighting. And then, two scenes later, rhetoric and nostalgia are gone. Time freezes into a labyrinth of steel filing cabinets, a tangle of lies and falsification seen with the hard edge of public record, under a glare without mystery or reprieve. Even here, however, Menzies interposes matters that suggest the persistence of shadows, of a more human chiaroscuro, beyond the range of the prosecutor's vision: the story of Quinlan's murdered wife, and of his peculiar intimacy with Tanya (with whom, in his concern, Menzies has just been speaking).

In the final sequence, Quinlan's life is recapitulated as a kind of night journey, a labyrinth threaded over stagnant waters. All the film's stylistic preoccupations are here in their purest form: the space of nightmare, at once claustrophobic and fragmented, wholly shaped by the network of derricks and aborted construction, slashed through by inexplicable lighting; voices echoing over the canal or metallically disembodied on Vargas' tape recorder. And now it becomes clear that the dark tangle in which Quinlan is lost—which turns into a trap where his mind drifts and wanders without control—is nothing else than the long obsession of which he speaks to Menzies. "Drunk or sober, I always think of her," he says. "Or of my job, my dirty job."

The Mexico of *Touch of Evil* is, finally, Quinlan's world: he embraces the film as the dreamer does his own nightmare. I have spoken of Dietrich and Janet Leigh as antitheses, but this is itself to imply some basic correspondence. What the pianola summons Quinlan to, across the vacant windy plaza, is simply the dream of all he has lost, the negation of the world he has built up around himself along with the layers of fat: the nostalgic melody in a world of raucous sounds, the embrace of the brothel's tacky *décor* in a world of bare rooms and empty arcades. No wonder, then, that Tanya's ageless face, wreathed in cigarette smoke, hovers in the doorway like a figure of memory, a dream within a dream, a myth. Not, however, the brittle falsehood represented by Janet Leigh or the abandoned pasteboard showgirl momentarily glimpsed in the plaza's debris. Dietrich's special magic has always been to suggest the human face behind cinema's masks of glamour and romance, the dream saddened by a knowledge of its own evanescence. Her first words are "We're closed." What this face knows is that the work of time is as irrevocable as the work of candybars. And when, just before the end, Quinlan asks Tanya to read his future in her cards, it appears that this too is deprived him: "You don't have any, your future's all used up." Time has become a single moment, a labyrinth open only to the junk heap on which (like Kane) Quinlan finally dies, his rotting face still cunning, as used up and inscrutable as the debris around him. He was "some kind of a man," Tanya says. Janet Leigh continues to suppose that Vargas can "take me away from here," but Welles reserves the last words for Dietrich's stylized epitaph, and the last shot for her melancholy walk away into the night.

The Study of Persecution: *The Trial*

by PETER COWIE

> *"Prague does not let you out of its grip; it has claws, and whoever wanted to shake himself free of this town would have to set fire to it!"*
>
> FRANZ KAFKA
> *in a letter[1]*

. . . *The Trial* was the first film since *Citizen Kane* to be released in the form that Welles intended. It was hailed as a masterpiece by a majority of continental critics. With few exceptions, it was dismissed as a boring failure by the British and American press. To my mind, *The Trial* remains Welles' finest film since *Kane* and, far from being a travesty of Kafka's work, achieves an effect through cinematic means that conveys perfectly the terrifying vision of the modern world that marks every page of the original book (first published, incidentally, in 1925, two years after Kafka's death).

During the winter of 1959–60 Welles was playing the role of Fulton in Abel Gance's *Austerlitz*. The producer was the astute Alexander Salkind and he offered Welles 650 million francs with which to make a film of *The Trial*. The script took Welles about six weeks to write. The film was eventually shot in 1962 and, though rumour had it that it would appear at Venice that year, it did not open in Paris until just after Christmas. "I don't know why there was any fuss about the film's not being shown at Venice," says Welles. "There were still some scenes that had to be shot. Perkins

Reprinted by courtesy of the author and The Tantivy Press, London/A. S. Barnes and Company Inc. Cranbury, New Jersey.

[1] Petr Nowák, "Kafka's Prague," *The Observer*, (November 17, 1963).

had to do a film with Cayatte [*Le Couteau dans la plaie/Five Miles to Midnight*] and he had arranged to shoot these scenes for *The Trial* afterwards." * In any case, the soundtrack was incomplete and unsatisfactory.

Most of the film was photographed in Zagreb (but locations in Dubrava, Rome, and the Gare d'Orsay were also used). The Gare d'Orsay, scheduled for demolition these past ten years and more, has sprawled on the Left Bank of the Seine since the turn of the century. As William Chappell (Titorelli in the film) has recalled: "Welles is a poor sleeper, and standing sleepless at five in the morning at the window of his hotel in Paris he became half-hypnotised by the twin moons of the two great clocks that decorate the deserted and crumbling Gare d'Orsay, that triumphantly florid example of the Belle Epoque that looms so splendidly across the trees of the Tuileries gardens. He remembered he had once been offered the empty station . . . as a location, and his curiosity was aroused." [2] His choice was a stroke of genius. The monstrous perspectives, dwarfing the characters, the vistas of imprisoned glass, the iron stairways, and myriad corridors combine to form a symbolic background to the film that is an equivalent to the labyrinthine ways and mournful buildings of Prague. "For the shy Kafka the periphery of Prague was an unexplored, obscure world of proletarians, even though it began only a few hundred yards from the Café Arco, where he was a regular. This district, called Zizkov, probably inspired the eerie setting of the 'interrogation' in [the novel] *The Trial*." [3]

The Trial is so rich and complex a Wellesian creation that only a detailed analysis can begin to do justice to it. Initially it should be stressed that Welles has adapted the novel fairly freely, while at the same time he has adhered to Kafka's basic views and situations. After all, Max Brod acted just as arbitrarily when, after Kafka's death, he arranged the chapters in the order he thought fit. For the record, Claude Miller[4] maintains that Welles has changed the order of the chapters to: 1,4,2,5,6,3,8,7,9,10.

The film opens with a remarkable sequence composed of designs

* From interview between Cowie and Welles, 1963.
[2] William Chappell, "Orson Welles Films Kafka," *The Sunday Times*, London (May 27, 1962).
[3] Nowák, "Kafka's Prague."
[4] Claude Miller, fiche on *The Trial*, *Téléciné*, No. 10 (April–May, 1963).

by Alexandre Alexeïeff and his wife on their patent "pin screen." The figures are not animated, a wise precaution to prevent their assuming a dramatic, as opposed to an illustrative, effect. Over these "prints," as it were, Welles narrates the fable that Kafka puts into the mouth of the priest in the latter part of the book. It contains the theme of the film in a nutshell and Welles felt that his audience would understand the film better if they grasped the idea behind it at the outset. "Before the Law there stands a Guard. A man comes from the country, begging admittance to the Law. But the Guard cannot admit him . . . for years he waits. Everything he has he gives away. . . ." Eventually, on the threshold of death, he asks the Guard one final question: "How is it then, that in all these years, no one else has ever come here seeking admittance?" The Guard then tells him: "This door was intended only for you—and now I am going to close it." Welles pauses, then comments in a heavy, monitory voice, "This tale is told during the story called 'The Trial.' It has been said that the logic of this story is the logic of a dream—of a nightmare," and as the last word fades on the soundtrack, the screen becomes black and gradually fades in on the head of Joseph K, seen from above as he is disturbed by the police entering his room. One has the feeling that K awakes (or is *born*) guilty. Guilt is a disease.

In an unusually long take, K argues with the officers who come to arrest him. The use of reflected light through the window gives the scene a grey, sombre effect. The bedroom "has trick perspectives as though the scene had been painted by a medieval painter; the floor seems to be raked, the ceiling almost presses on his head and people's trunks are too big for their limbs." [5] Immediately, Welles's dialogue has an ambivalent, disconcerting logic that introduces a sinister note into what otherwise might be merely a routine check-up. Every time K trips over his words the officers toss them back at him, pinning him to an offence. The air is heavy with intimidation, and K's anguished query, "The real question is—who accuses me?" hangs unanswered as the officers and the three clerks who have betrayed him surround K blackly. "It's not for me to talk about your case," says the inspector (everyone in society shirks responsibility and the Advocate is the only one who may state the charge).

[5] Penelope Gilliatt, review of *The Trial, The Observer,* (November 17, 1963).

As the scope of the action expands, one notes that Welles has located K's room in an ultra-modern apartment block, and while he watches the arrival of Miss Burstner from a taxi far below, the buildings seem already to encroach on the human beings in their midst (as in Antonioni's *La Notte*). K's landlady, Mrs. Grubach, is introduced briefly. "With your arrest I get the feeling of something abstract," she muses, thereby stressing a point that is to be reiterated visually throughout the film. K behaves perfectly normally as in the novel, fulfilling Kafka's memorable description: "He had always been inclined to take things easily, to believe in the worst only when the worst happened, to take no care for the morrow even when the outlook was threatening." [6] His encounter with Miss Burstner (not his typist, as in the book, but a cabaret entertainer) emphasises his shyness and vulnerability. He confides to her that when his father accused him as a child, and he was innocent, "I'd still feel guilty." Thus the notion of a preordained guilt, or of original sin, creeps insidiously into the film (as it does into *Macbeth*). K, in Welles's eyes, stands for a society that is to blame for the ghastly knots into which it has tied itself. "In my opinion, for Kafka, Joseph K was guilty. For me also . . . he is guilty because he is part of the human condition." [7] At the same time he molds into the pattern Welles usually imposes on his films; he approximates to Leland, to O'Hara, to Van Stratten in his gullibility. As he says bitterly when he glances at the books in the courtroom later, "Of course I must remain ignorant of any law."

Now one comes to one of the most staggering scenes in Welles' cinema. The camera follows Joseph K into the office—in the novel, a bank—where he works; and then tracks—almost hovers—beside him to reveal a vast exposition hall filled with typists seated at hundreds of desks in all directions. The noise of the thousands of keys tapping away is magnified together with long musical chords on the soundtrack so that K seems virtually to drown in the cacophony. The image, such a *frisson* in itself, is a masterly reminder of a bureaucracy gone mad. K lives in a bureaucratic society, where everything has a reference, and everything is referred to someone else. Welles rented between 700–850 typewriters from the Olivetti

---

[6] Franz Kafka, *The Trial*, with an introduction by Max Brod, trans. Willa and Edwin Muir (London, n.d.).

[7] Jean Clay, interview in *Réalités*, No. 201 (1962).

company and found the gigantic building just outside Zagreb. By contrast to this frenzied, futuristic activity, the storeroom where K leaves a cake he has bought for Miss Burstner's birthday is dusty and oppressive. He is surprised there by his deputy manager who, when he sees a girl trying to attract K's attention through the glass walls of the building, thinks she is his mistress. She is in fact K's cousin, Irmie. But this misunderstanding, which contributes to K's sense of shame and isolation, is only one of a number of incidents hinting at eroticism that Welles has scattered throughout *The Trial.* To a certain extent, the women in the film are all temptresses in the tradition of Elsa Bannister. They weaken K's resistance and draw him inexorably toward his doom with their blandishments or accusations.

The scene now moves to a stretch of wasteland near K's office. It is dusk, and K carries on a Pinterish conversation about free will with Miss Pittl (a friend of Miss Burstner's), who is dragging a trunk from one building to another. The camera accompanies the couple as they move slowly over this eerie landscape, K trying desperately to ingratiate himself with this woman and she—like nearly everyone else in the film—rejecting him suspiciously. He ends by admitting responsibility for Miss Burstner's being turned out of her lodgings. Welles' talent lies of course in making K a sympathetic character while at the same time giving credence to his detractors' viewpoint. This dismal scene, with the mournful howling of dogs in the background, foreshadows the end when Joseph K is led away to his death, also in the gathering dusk. It is in this sequence (consisting of one long take) also that one can distinguish the difference between the style of Kafka and the style of Welles. In the words of Elliott Stein, "Kafka's novels presents a rather realistically described world—but it is inhabited by dream people. . . . In Welles's film real people inhabit a nightmare world." [8] Every image holds a portent, every conversation a veiled threat. Thus in the next sequence, after K has been called from the opera, there is a clear clue to his fate. The inspector leads him from the opera house (and, by implication, from the normal surroundings that might prevent him from losing his reason), and pauses in a derelict hall. Welles' script describes these buildings as "monumental in aspect but dilapidated, sinister and cold. They exude the

[8] Elliott Stein, "The Trial," *The Financial Times*, London (February 18, 1963).

melancholy atmosphere of all public institutions." [9] Two men stand in the shadows. They are wearing raincoats and squat, baleful hats. One has glasses like pebbles. The inspector tells K the way to the court, now in session, and, when K asks sarcastically why the two silent men should not follow him, watching his every move, he is blandly assured, "That isn't their job." Their "job," as one finds out later, is to kill Joseph K.

Like a man lost in a maze, K pursues the twists and turns of the route. Suddenly he comes upon a girl, Hilda, who is washing clothes. She nods in the direction of the door to the tribunal. K opens it and the camera swoops in behind him. This moment is one of the most terrifying in the film, for precisely as K enters one hears the roar of hundreds of feet as everyone in the packed courtroom stands up and stares at him. And now the long takes used hitherto give way to staccato cutting; Welles shows the court and its occupants from many different angles, rather like the election speech scene in *Citizen Kane*. It is interesting to recall Kafka's description of the event: "K felt as though he were entering a meeting-hall. A crowd of the most variegated people—nobody troubled about the newcomer—filled a medium sized, two-windowed room, which just below the roof was surrounded by a gallery, also quite packed, where the people were able to stand only in a bent posture with their heads and backs knocking against the ceiling." [10] The film differs only in that everyone *does* trouble about the arrival of Joseph K and this, visually speaking, underlines the hostility shown toward him. He is guilty in advance and human society, represented in the court, regards him as a scapegoat. He belongs, like all else, to the court. His apologia on the platform beside the magistrate is worthless. He is doomed in advance and the violent manner in which Hilda is suddenly carried out by the law student seems to carry a foretaste of K's own destruction. The monstrous door of the courtroom dwarfs him as he leaves.

The fast cutting between shots continues until the end of the film. The storm, as it were, has broken about K's head. In the early part he had still not been engulfed. But from now on his sole

[9] *The Trial/Le Procès*, (complete with details of camera movements and positions, and of the soundtrack), No. 23 in the series *L'Avant-Scène du Cinéma* (Paris, February 1963). In French. Also in English, (London: Lorrimer Publications; New York: Simon & Schuster, 1970).

[10] Kafka, *The Trial*.

preoccupation is with his case. Back at his office he finds that the two officers who had arrested him the previous morning are about to be flogged in a lumber room because K had complained of their stealing his shirts. In this nightmarish scene, with everyone talking at once and the whipper snarling like a predatory animal eager to consume his victims, still more guilt seems to transfer itself to K and to weigh on his conscience. One should never forget that one clear implication of both the book and the film is that K is made aware of his guilt by suggestion. Welles, having lived through an epoch where the torture chamber and the concentration camp became law, has, not unnaturally, a more bitter viewpoint than Kafka's. Joseph K is all the more responsible because he does not and cannot stop the whipping. The music of Albinoni, detached from the action and opposed to the flurried montage (some shots last only a few frames) lends an air of inevitability to the sequence.

Welles himself plays the crucial role of Hastler, the Advocate, to whom his Uncle Max leads K after hearing about the case. Once again, the *décor* has an importance of its own. Hastler's long, lofty chambers are illuminated by hundreds of candles, as if signifying the eternal vigilance of the law. The Advocate himself is ill, sprawled on a gilt bed. Leni, his secretary and mistress, places a hot flannel over his face as Uncle Max and Joseph K approach him. When he hears *who* is accused, however, Hastler starts up and peels off the flannel. For a second the steam drifts about his chin and imparts a diabolical look to his face. He represents Lucifer; he is evil incarnate, like Harry Lime or Arthur Bannister. K escapes his gaze and follows the nubile Leni behind a glass partition, to another room. Then she wraps K in one of the Advocate's black coats, metaphorically stifling him in the folds of authority. She shows him how her hand is deformed with a web of skin between the fingers. One remembers Miss Pittl's club foot, and later Irmie is seen dragging her leg down the steps of the court building. The physical warp is an outward and visible sign of the psychological deformity. The prominence given to hands by Welles in this film is fascinating, and recurs in the later scene when Block kisses the Advocate's hand. It is as if the hand were a symbol of tyranny, from whose clutches no one may escape.

Leni talks with K in a huge room filled with aging files and newspapers, and points out a picture of one of the judges. "He's little, almost a dwarf," she whispered, "but look at the way he had himself painted." This is the nearest K ever comes to encountering those responsible for his fate; he is always fobbed off with the *accessories* to the law. A call from Hastler interrupts the love-play, and K stumbles down the mountain of newspapers with his coat fluttering around him like a Mephistophelian cloak, as though some of the rancid evil of the place had attached itself to him. Then, with a storm raging outside, the immense silhouette of the Advocate moves behind the glass partition of the junk room, demonstrating his impalpability and shadowy power.

Suddenly, quite by chance, Joseph K catches his first glimpse of Block. He peers into a cell-like room and sees the old man seated on a bed. The flash of apprehension vanishes as Leni interrupts, but in that moment when Block's eyes meet his, K has foreseen his fate. Block might as well be a prefiguration of K in twenty years' time, downtrodden by the law, bereft of all will to escape, resigned to perpetual imprisonment—the man come from the country to seek admittance to the law, no less.

The erotic element introduced by Welles appears again in the next scene, when K returns to the empty law courts. Hilda meets him there and as they talk together ("even though it's forbidden") about the tribunal, K glances at one of the judge's textbooks. Immediately he finds a "dirty" picture, a reflection of his own jaundiced imagination (one could argue at length that the entire film is seen through K's eyes and that perfectly normal people and events are distorted by his mind). The accent is again on eroticism as Hilda strokes K's ankles and tries to seduce him. Their conversation is interrupted when a student guard comes and carries Hilda off on his shoulders. As he clambers toward them through the supports of the platform in the courtroom, there is an echo of Kafka's *Metamorphoses:* spars and struts seem to merge with the snarling man and give him the look of a beast of prey. Then, as if pursued by this vivid image (and bars are as important in *The Trial* as they are in *Othello*), K shortly afterwards sees another man approaching him along a catwalk below the roof of the Gare d'Orsay like a spider leaving his web. He vents his anger on K. Talking of the student who has abducted his wife, Hilda, he says slowly and with infinite sadism: "I would have squashed him flat against the wall long ago . . . all twisted out and writhing—like a smashed cockroach." The last word is savoured carefully and floats menacingly in the air. Here one can again prove that Welles is faithful to the spirit of Kafka's dialogue. In the book the guard says, "I see him squashed flat there, just a little above the floor, his arms wide, his fingers spread, his bandy legs writhing in a circle, and splashes of blood all around." [11] At the same time one discerns the persistent undercurrent of *jealousy* that runs through the book and still more strongly through the film. It is as if everyone is possessive in the extreme, Hastler of Leni, the guard of his wife, K of Leni with Block, and Irmie of K.

Joseph K now has his first encounter with the other fugitives from the law like himself. "The accused," says the guard, as he points out to K an entire hall filled with silent men. K talks with one of them and is frustrated by his naïve, trusting attitude. "You think I'm a—judge?" asks K fearfully. One sees in this particular old man an exact personification of the supplicant in the prologue. "Yes, I handed in several affidavits," he tells K. "That was some time ago. I'm waiting here for the result." The words could also belong to Block.

When even those in the same predicament as himself begin to doubt him, K realises that his case is hopeless. Like the destitute figures who surround the shrouded statue of Christ on K's way to the tribunal earlier in the film, these mute captives hint at a lost harmony in the world, over and above their immediate significance *vis-à-vis* the Nazi concentration camps. K flees this hideous waiting room and it is now that one can appreciate Welles' brilliant dovetailing of locations. K walks out of the Gare d'Orsay to discover that outside, on the steps of the Palazzo di Giustizia in Rome, his cousin Irmie is waiting for him. They walk together to the entrance of a Milan factory, he says goodbye to her, and a few seconds later approaches the council house in Zagreb where he lives.[12] Irmie's presence is valid, for she is the only "normal" person (excepting Mrs. Grubach) in the entire film—thus the simple replies she gives to K when she wants to marry him. "But I'm your cousin," he says, aghast. Irmie: "Cousins get married." K: "You wouldn't want to marry a criminal?" Irmie: "Crooks get married too." Her interventions are like those of Shakespeare's clowns. They anchor the drama in normality and also serve to heighten the bizarre feeling of ensuing scenes.

[11] Ibid.
[12] Elliott Stein, "The Trial," *The Financial Times*, London (February 18, 1963).

The next sequence, involving Katina Paxinou as a scientist, was cut from the final version of the film; not surprisingly, because the final lines of the script here hint that the crime K is most likely to commit is suicide. Instead the scene switches to the Advocate's rooms once more. The theme of the film is growing noticeably more serious, and there is a brief interlude while K and Block writhe in uncontrollable laughter about the old man's having five other Advocates of whom he never tells Hastler. Then, as K is about to be interviewed by the Advocate, Block says, chillingly, that he is only being received because his case is still at "the hopeful stage." Block, then, is a symbol of a man crushed by the law and its intolerable burden. K dies because he openly rejects the Advocate. Block survives because he acquiesces in the situation—he hires his five other Advocates secretly, but he survives—nourished, presumably, by his furtive liaison with Leni. As Kakfa wrote: "So the Advocate's methods, to which K fortunately had not been long enough exposed, amounted to this: that the client finally forgot the whole world and lived only in hope of toiling along this false path until the end of his case should come in sight." [13] Block, like everyone else, shies away from mentioning the nature of the charges—"They even say that he's [Hastler] a better Advocate for business . . . than for *the other kind*" (my italics), rather as "cancer" is a word to be avoided at all costs in contemporary conversation.

When K enters the Advocate's presence (significantly, he and Block do not wear their coats on entry), the pace of the film begins to accelerate—and never slows again. This time Hastler's attitude has hardened; there is a threat behind the velvet voice: "You can pick out an accused man in the largest crowd," and that final remark of Welles' own invention: "To be in chains is sometimes safer than to be free." K, repulsed by the sight of Block, kissing Hastler's hands and crying "Master!" to him, rushes out, with the braying, demoniac laughter of the Advocate pursuing him. It is a decisive moment. Block has described the Advocate as "a very revengeful man," and K's rejection of his services marks him as a man to be eliminated. He, K, can no longer be identified with the man in the prologue. Leni advises him to see Titorelli, the court painter, and in desperation K seeks him out. He is followed up ladders and a narrow spiral staircase by a flock of screaming

[13] Kafka, *The Trial*.

children. Some critics have said that Welles' touch is too heavy here, but a glance at Kafka's text shows that although the scene has been altered visually, its overall impact has not been exaggerated. "In the tenement where the painter lived only one wing of the great double door stood open, and beneath the other wing, in the masonry near the ground, there was a gaping hole out of which, just as K approached, issued a disgusting yellow fluid, steaming hot, from which a rat fled into the adjoining canal. At the foot of the stairs an infant lay bellydown on the ground bawling, but one could scarcely hear its shrieks because of the deafening din that came from a tinsmith's workshop at the other side of the entry." [14]

When K eventually reaches Titorelli's studio, he finds himself in a kind of wooden cage, the bars of which encroach on him. The children peep through the cracks, and Titorelli shoos them away, tossing off a disturbing "Remember my ice pick?" to one of them, and then rounds unexpectedly on K with a glib "What can I do for you, chum?" (the camera dollies back suddenly to emphasise K's shock). The terrifying atmosphere of the studio weighs on K. The children rustling outside like impatient birds, the sinister hum in the background, and the almost stifling heat, prevent him from assimilating Titorelli's elaborate disquisition on "ostensible acquittal." He puts on a pair of spectacles to look closely at the artist's work, and again one is reminded of *Metamorphoses*—K's face is for an instant seemingly transmogrified into that of a beetle.

Titorelli shows him some paintings; one, of Justice and Victory reunited, prompts K to think of "the goddess of the Hunt . . . in full cry." Everyone in the film is divided, in fact, into hunters and the hunted. One feels that Titorelli, too, is a hunter beneath his gleaming charm. K bursts out of the studio and finds himself in the law courts office. It is a point of betrayal, like the Knight's discovery that he has been "confessing" to Death in the church in *The Seventh Seal*. K brushes past a group of men awaiting trial in the archive room and then rushes down a subterranean passage. As he runs, the children pursue him, their screams filling the soundtrack. Stripes of light flood through the slatted corridor and make a dancing, abstract pattern on K's body as he dashes toward the camera (which was being pushed by a Yugoslav runner!). "We built it out of wood, and put the camera on a wheelchair—it was the only way we could move it along the wooden planks." * The effect is astonishing. K is literally absorbed into his surroundings; he is completely disorientated, like O'Hara as he is swept down the "Crazy House" at the end of *The Lady from Shanghai*. Reverse tracking shots sweep back alternatively in front of K and in front of the children as they plunge through the passage after another, their shadows writhing on the walls in a manner reminiscent of that final chase in the sewers of Vienna (*The Third Man*). The sequence runs less than half a minute, but contains some twenty-five closely knit shots.

K no longer knows where he is going; he is caught in the net of the law. His flight leads him into a huge cathedral (though even here Welles strikes a frightening note by covering the pillars of the building with tactile rivets), where a priest in a pulpit warns him how badly his case is going. The Advocate also makes an unexpected appearance, and projects on a screen the allegory of the law with which the film began. There is a memorable moment here as K, caught in the light from the projector, is superimposed before the gates of the law like the man in the story. And when Hastler repeats the words of the guard, "And now I'm going to close it [the door]," the audience, though not K, senses that Hastler himself *is* the guard. Once more, and for the last time, K breaks away. As he passes the priest on his way out of the cathedral, the latter asks him, "Can't you see anything at all?" "Of course," replies K, "I'm responsible." "My son—" begins the priest. "I'm not your son," snarls K fiercely. In these two answers lies the key to *The Trial:* on the one hand, the cry of an entire world in the knowledge that it is guilty of allowing such an evil administration to gain power (Hastler: "A victim of society?" K in response: "I'm a *member* of society"); and on the other the defiant gesture of a Wellesian hero, refusing to surrender meekly in the style of Block.

So to the *dénouement*. K emerges into the dusk and is confronted by the two police officers he had so innocently thought to be his escorts on his first visit to the tribunal. They take his arms and then lead him away brusquely. So carefully has Welles followed the novel at this juncture that Kafka's own words are the best description of the scene: "K walked rigidly between them, the three of them were interlocked in a unity which would have brought all three down

* From interview between Cowie and Welles, 1963.

together had one of them been knocked over. It was a unity such as can be formed by lifeless elements alone." [15] The noble chords of Albinoni's Adagio swell above the scene as the trio pass through the streets and across some wasteland to a quarry. "K's route to the execution can be traced from the old town, across Karls Bridge, 'through steeply rising streets'—Neruda Street and Uvoz—to the old Strahover Quarry (which no longer exists)." [16] There is a strange visual dignity in this last journey that is, perhaps appropriately, lacking in other sequences of the film.

Welles' end is radically different from Kafka's. The final sentence of the book: " 'Like a dog!' he said: it was as if he meant the shame of it to outlive him," [17] implies a defeatism that Welles cannot accept, and that would be contradicted had Welles retained the scientist's earlier forecast that the crime K is most likely to commit is . . . suicide. In the film K shouts defiantly, "You'll have to do it!" when the killers scramble out of the quarry. He refuses to take the knife from them because he is too aware of the injustice of the sentence. Rightly, the last shot of K is of his laughing with an almost insane glee as he reaches for the dynamite that has been flung down beside him. There is a mighty explosion, and over the grim wasteland rises a cloud of smoke that assumes the shape of a mushroom. It dissolves into nothingness as Welles reads the cast list. This final image has been another butt for the critics' attacks. Yet the cloud is no more irrelevant or fatalistic than the closing shot of the street lamp in Antonioni's *The Eclipse*. Both images can assume whatever meaning the spectator ascribes to them. The main impression is one of complete finality, catastrophe, waste, physical death.

Apart from *Citizen Kane* and *Chimes at Midnight*, no other film of Welles' bears so clearly the stamp of his personality. One perceives his presence in every frame, in every shadow, in every angled shot. He dubbed no fewer than eleven of the speaking parts, the main one (apart from Hastler) being Titorelli, and others including the magistrate, K's deputy manager, and the man with the whip. The key to the style of the film lies in the subjective track and dolly, repeated in endless permutations. Welles is not a *reflective* director

[15] Ibid.
[16] Nowák, "Kafka's Prague."
[17] Kafka, *The Trial*.

here, and the richness of his imagery in *The Trial* precludes any attempt to ponder on the deeper implications of the *décor* or various incidents. It is the immediate and then the cumulative effect that counts. *The Trial* is an expressionist film if expressionism can be described according to Carl Hauptmann's dictum: "The phenomena on the screen are the phenomena of the soul." But whereas most expressionist films ignore the importance of the soundtrack, *The Trial* gains largely from the imaginative blend of music and natural noises that Welles has arranged. Jazz seems suddenly suitable when juxtaposed with classical music, just as the modern buildings of Zagreb merge successfully with the baroque of the Gare d'Orsay. Anthony Perkins as Joseph K gives one of the best performances of his career. Resembling Kafka himself, he suggests with every movement and facial contortion the perplexity that undermines Joseph K in the book. "The human mind isn't that complex," complained Albert Schweitzer to the author when he returned to him a copy of *The Trial*. But human society *is* as complex as Kafka maintained, and the inability of the human mind to understand that complexity is the tragic moral of the novel and of this extraordinary, hallucinatory film.

Chimes at Midnight

by JOSEPH McBRIDE

Chimes at Midnight is Welles' masterpiece, the fullest, most completely realized expression of everything he had been working toward since *Citizen Kane*, which itself was more an end than a beginning. The younger Welles was obsessed with the problem of construction, and solved it perfectly with a style which locked the apparently powerful hero into an ironic vise of which he was almost totally unaware. We could not be farther from the characters, and perhaps this distancing, however suited to the telling of a story of futile omnipotence, was an acknowledgement of artistic immaturity on Welles' part: faced with the problem of defining himself, he contrived a style to prove that definition is illusory. In *Chimes at Midnight*, Welles has fused his own viewpoint and that of his hero into a direct communication of emotion. His style, though it is every bit as deliberate and controlled as in *Kane*, no longer demands our attention for itself. There is nothing here to correspond with *Kane's* mirror trickery; there *is* a battle sequence which is one of the greatest achievements in action direction in the history of the cinema, and which moreover is constructed in a highly rhetorical pattern, almost as tightly as a fugue, but it presents itself to the audience not as an artistic demonstration but as an overwhelming physical experience.

I think that here Welles finds himself where Beethoven found himself when he replaced musical instruments with voices in the Ninth Symphony: he has broken the bounds of his tools (the camera and the cutting bench) and has given everything over to human instruments (his actors). When told that no one could possibly sing some of the notes he had written, Beethoven replied that it was no concern of his. Welles is more pragmatic—since he himself must make the actors correspond to his purposes—but there is the same rhapsodic exhilaration in his submersion into faces and voices. As Pierre Duboeuf has put it, "He broods with a disquiet like Rembrandt's over his own face, and it is not inconsequential that he finds there other attunements, accents less brilliant but more human, which he substitutes for the dazzling flashes of the past." We feel, as we do in *The Magnificent Ambersons*, that Welles is rejecting the mask of self-conscious stylization in order to find himself in a relaxed, sensual spontaneity. A crucial difference, however, is that Welles hid himself behind the camera in *The Ambersons*, revealing himself through his attitude toward other people, and here he looms before us buoyantly fat, literally and figuratively much more himself than he has ever been before.

And, appropriately, the story he is telling is the story of a man who is completely candid, a man whose complete lack of pretense, when confronted with the world's demands of responsibility and self-denial, becomes the very cause of his destruction. During production, Welles explained his intentions: "*Chimes* should be very plain on the visual level because above all it is a very real human story. . . . The Falstaff story is the best in Shakespeare—not the best play, but the best story . . . Everything of importance in the film should be found on the faces; on these faces that whole universe I was speaking of should be found. I imagine that it will be the film of my life in terms of close-ups. . . . A story like *Chimes* demands them, because the moment we step back and separate ourselves from the faces, we see the people in period costumes and many actors in the foreground. The closer we are to the face, the more universal it becomes. *Chimes* is a sombre comedy, the story of the betrayal of friendship." And after the film was completed, he observed, "*The Ambersons* and *Chimes at Midnight* represent more than anything else what I would like to do in films . . . what I am trying to discover now in films is not technical surprises or shocks, but a more complete unity of forms, of shapes. That's what I'm reaching for, what I hope is true. If it is, then I'm reaching maturity as an artist. If it isn't true, then I'm in decadence, you know?"

The reader of these descriptions should not suppose that *Chimes* is as fluid and deceptively nonchalant as a Renoir film; far from it.

When we talk about a "plain" style, we mean that the camera is at the service of the actors, and not vice versa (as in *The Trial*, for instance). When a director matures, his work becomes more lucid, more direct, allowing room for deeper audience response; as Truffaut has put it, what is in front of the camera becomes more important. And "direct," in the complex rhetorical world of Welles' films, means not that the issues are simplified, but that their presentation is—we feel them with more intensity and passion. Compare the climax of *Kane*, in which Kane slaps Susan, to the muted climax of *Chimes at Midnight*, in which Hal banishes Falstaff and the old man murmurs, "Master Shallow, I owe you a thousand pound." The scene in *Kane* is exciting and moving, but its theatricality tends to widen the gulf between Kane's emotions and our comprehension of them. If *Citizen Kane* has a flaw, it is in its relative dispassion—a scheme in which we are so far removed from the hero that we may easily watch his struggle with mere fascination. *Kane* is perhaps too mathematical in conception; the true hero, it is not unfitting to say, is not Kane but Welles himself. But in *Chimes* there is finally no distance between Welles and Falstaff; a simple exchange of close-ups between Hal and Falstaff conveys emotions infinitely deeper than does Kane's explosive action. It is the difference between the expression of an emotion and the sharing of an emotion.

Welles' liberties with the text generally escape our notice, extreme as they are, not only because he has so smoothly transformed Shakespeare's concerns into his own but because his concentration on Falstaff enables him to achieve a dramatic focus which Shakespeare's historical concerns tend at times to dilute. The story is taken from *1 Henry IV* and *2 Henry IV*, with bits from *Henry V*, *The Merry Wives of Windsor*, and *Richard II*, and a narration from Holinshed's *Chronicles*. Shakespeare seems to have intended Falstaff as a relatively simple comic counterpoint to the King-Prince-Hotspur story in the first part of *Henry IV* (as the rather awkward alternation of historical and comic scenes would suggest) and only gradually discovered that Falstaff was so profound a character that he all but overshadowed the drama of kingship. Not only the greater length given to Falstaff's scenes but the immeasurably more fluid structure of the second part—in which the imbalance threatened by Falstaff's pre-eminence becomes qualified by the crisis in his relationship with the Prince—attest to Shakespeare's fully ripened understanding of Falstaff's meaning. We have of course been prepared for the rejection of Falstaff by the great tavern scene in the first part, but in the second, Falstaff takes on a graver aspect, not only in Hal's eyes as a threat to his princely dignity but in his own as well. Images of age, disease, and death suddenly proliferate, and the gay denunciations of honour give way to sober, more closely reasoned (and more witty) inward reflection. Shakespeare also creates four new companions for Falstaff—Pistol, Doll Tearsheet, Shallow, and Silence—as if to compensate for Hal's growing absorption into himself. "In the first part of the play," Welles comments, "the Hotspur subplot keeps the business of the triangle between the King, his son, and Falstaff (who is a sort of foster father) from dominating. But in my film, which is made to tell, essentially, the story of that triangle, there are bound to be values which can't exist as it is played in the original. It's really quite a different drama."

We can see in Welles' decision to make Hal a subordinate figure to Falstaff not only an extremely ironic attitude toward the idea of the "Christian king" (a concept as alien to Welles as it is central to Shakespeare and, in a modern guise, to John Ford, from whom Welles borrows greatly in this film) but also a more definite emphasis on the essential *goodness* of Falstaff's character, the tragic nobility of even those attributes—his disregard of health and social discretion—which will inevitably destroy him. The act of banishment by Shakespeare's Hal is not a tragic decision; it is the seal of moral maturity, the "noble change" he proclaims to the "incredulous world." The war he will wage on France as Henry V, which Shakespeare is at pains to present in that play as the God-given and ancestrally determined right of empire, becomes in *Chimes at Midnight* a totally unmotivated, madly wilful action. On our first sight of Hal after the ceremony of coronation, he proclaims the war with no reason given but for a sentry's cry of 'No king of England, if not king of France!' In other words, Hal, on accepting responsibility, immediately puts it to blindly destructive ends, just as K did in *The Trial*. Welles does not invoke, as Shakespeare does, a higher imperative for Hal's action, presenting it solely as a function of his will.* Welles' Hal is as truly a tragic figure as is his father, who had

---

* *Author's Note*: After my book was published, Mr. Welles suggested that my analysis of Hal's conduct here was mistaken. A re-examination of the film makes it

wrested his kingdom illegitimately from Richard and was then doomed to face unceasing rebellion.

Hal comes into his crown legitimately, by right of birth, and in Shakespeare's terms is thus rightfully able to purpose the building of an empire. But for Welles (for Shakespeare too, but to a lesser degree of emphasis), Hal has lost the better part of himself in his rejection of Falstaff and all he stands for. The banishment is inevitable if he is to acquiesce to his position of power, but the price of the world dominion he will thus achieve is the subjection of his own moral nature, as Welles makes clear in the arbitrariness of his first action after the banishment. Hal's final words to Falstaff have a meaning entirely opposite to their meaning in the play: "Being awaked, I do despise my dream. . . . Presume not that I am the thing I was. . . . I have turned away my former self." And his last words in the film show how much he has deluded himself: "We consider it was excess of wine that set him on." Welles holds on the new king's pose of bemused reflection for several long seconds, and in the next shot shows us Poins eating an apple (the end of innocence) and Falstaff's coffin.

For Shakespeare, Falstaff is essentially a comic figure because, while completely innocent, he is destructive of kingly power, and must be sacrificed without question to the demands of a greater order. For Welles, the greater order is *Falstaff*, and Hal sacrifices both Falstaff and himself in the submission to his own will. Hal is as destructive of innocence as Falstaff is of kingship. And Welles gives us a strong sense of a curious moral trait of Falstaff's which several Shakespearean commentators have pointed out: though innocent, he seeks out the very force which will destroy him. In this we can see a quality in Falstaff which precludes calling him a merely comic figure. If we can call *Chimes at Midnight* the tragedy of Falstaff (and we can, even though he makes moral decisions only by instinct), it is tragedy perhaps more in the Aristotelian than in the Shakespearean sense of the term. Welles's description of Falstaff is profound: "What is difficult about Falstaff, I believe, is that he is the greatest conception of a good man, the most completely good man, in all drama. His faults are so small and he makes tremendous jokes out

---

clear that Hal's motivation is not blind egotism but rather a shrewd, if callous, political opportunism. The waging of war on France is a direct result of his father's dying advice to "busy giddy minds with foreign quarrels."—J.M.

of little faults. But his goodness is like bread, like wine. . . . And that was why I lost the comedy. The more I played it, the more I felt that I was playing Shakespeare's good, pure man."

We do not see in Falstaff an essentially noble man of extraordinary gifts who destroys himself through a grave flaw in his nature which is also the source of his nobility; we see in him something rather more subtle and less absolute—a man of extraordinary gifts which destroy him because he fails to acknowledge their irreconcilable conflict with the nature of the world. His moral blindness (which is to say his childlike candour, an attribute he is sometimes apt to use as a ploy) is his only flaw. Much as Othello was blind to the existence of the kind of power Iago possessed, Falstaff is blind to the possibility that Hal could reject his gift of absolute love. A. C. Bradley remarks of Othello that we share his "triumphant scorn for the fetters of the flesh and the littleness of all the lives that must survive him." Falstaff we can say has a triumphant acceptance of the absoluteness of the flesh and a spontaneous respect for all the lives around him.

The likeness of Hal to Iago is more than casual. Just as his father has been careful to cover the illegitimacy of his kingship with actions which assert his legitimacy—the vanquishing of internal rebellion—Hal schools himself in hypocrisy. From the first, Welles makes clear that Hal's merry-making with Falstaff is fraudulent, both a distraction from his impending moral crisis and a testing of his ability to withstand the temptations of instinct. Iago's "I am not what I am" finds many echoes in Hal, from his first soliloquy (". . . herein will I imitate the sun, / Who doth permit the base contagious clouds / To smother up his beauty from the world"), delivered with Falstaff musing vaguely in the background, to his final "Presume not that I am the thing I was," which leave Falstaff destitute and uncomprehending. A great deal of the film's pathos and irony comes from the reversal of old and young men's roles. Falstaff's innocence is a sublimely defiant gesture on Welles' part. As a young man he played both Falstaff and Richard III in *Five Kings*, as if to impart a Jekyll-and-Hyde duplicity to the character. Now, as an old man, he makes Falstaff's constant protestations of youth an accusation not only of Hal's unnatural suppression of youth but of death itself. Much more than in Shakespeare, the spectacle of an old man shepherding the revels of a saturnine young man strikes us as a bitter defiance of age and the logic of destiny.

Falstaff seeks out Hal because Hal is the least capable, due to his princehood, of casting off responsibilities and the promise of power, and when this ultimate test of his goodness fails, Falstaff fails with it. The heroism lies in the disparity between the greatness of the purpose and the inadequacy of the means.

When a tragic hero is destroyed, Bradley remarks, the primary impression is of *waste*. Waste is our feeling when Welles, at the end, shows Falstaff's huge coffin being wheeled slowly across a barren landscape with only a quiescent castle breaking the line of the horizon, the narrator telling us of Hal, "a majesty was he that both lived and died a pattern in princehood, a lodestar in honour, and famous to the world alway." We know that what the narrator is saying is literally true (it was written of the historical Henry V, who had Sir John Oldcastle, Falstaff's prototype, executed for treason), but we cannot help sense the tragic irony as we see the remnants of Hal's humanity being carted away. His expressions and carriage during the banishment speech convey that mingled grandeur and grief-stricken horror that came so naturally to his father after a lifetime of scheming, and when he turns away from Falstaff into a tableau of banners and shields, he becomes a smaller and smaller figure vanishing into the endlessly repetitive corridors of history. If we never sympathize fully with Hal, if we feel, as Welles does, that there is something "beady-eyed and self-regarding" about him even after he becomes king, we never cease to admire him, even in his tragic folly.

Thanks to Keith Baxter's marvelous performance—next to John Gielgud's incomparable Henry IV the finest in a near-perfect supporting cast—Hal is dignified and comprehensible even at his cruellest and most vain. Welles' instincts are acute here, for the unpleasantness of Joseph K is almost fatal to *The Trial*, and Hal, who quite resembles K in his self-righteousness, needs a sense of human dignity and compassion to make him a suitable subject of Falstaff's attention and to make him fully aware of what he is rejecting when he banishes Falstaff. Hal fills us with awe in that chilling moment when he turns from Falstaff and whispers to himself, 'At the end, try the man,' as if reciting a prayer; in his sudden childlike humility when his father appears, wraith-like, and demands his crown; and most of all in his powerful, serene silence after the battle, when he drops his pot of ale and walks mutely off to follow his destiny. Welles creates a mythic finality about Hal when, cutting away from Hotspur resolving to duel him to the death, he shows us a cloud of dust, which rises to reveal Hal standing helmet and shield in hand on the battlefield (a copy of Ford's introduction of John Wayne in *Stagecoach*, dust rising to show him with rifle in one arm and saddle in the other).

Death hangs over the entire film, and the gaiety seems desperate. Both Hal's foster-father and his real father are dying, and he is too preoccupied with his own legendary future to be of solace to either. His fun takes odd and vicious forms, as if he were reproaching both himself, for wasting time, and the butts of his humour, for encouraging him. He wants to see Falstaff "sweat to death" running from the Gad's Hill robbery, wants to expose him as a monstrous liar, wants to "beat him before his whore." One critic has suggested that in the first part of *Henry IV*, Hal is killing his patricidal tendencies (by killing Hotspur, his father's rival), and in the second part is killing his libido, his narcissistic self-adoration (Falstaff, of course), in order to prepare himself for the assumption of kingship. Welles replaces this sense of "penance" with a sense of vertiginous self-destruction. Like his father, like Hotspur, like, indeed, Falstaff, Hal has sought precisely the course which will destroy him. Hal is frightening because he is so young and yet seems so old. Welles draws a striking parallel in the feelings of Hal and both his "fathers" when he follows the king's speech on sleep with Hal telling Poins, "Before God, I am exceeding weary," and Falstaff murmuring, "S'blood, I'm as melancholy as a gibbed cat or a lugged bear."

Bells ringing in the distance give funereal punctuation to the very first scenes in the film, and motives of rejection and farewell are dominant throughout. The battle sequence, the cataclysm of destruction at the centre of the film, begins in splendid romantic exuberance and ends with agonizingly slow, ponderous clouts from soldiers writhing dully in the mud. Welles edits the battle on the principle of "a blow given, a blow received," and the predominant feeling is of a monumental impasse, of incredible exertion without effect. Falstaff's flesh finally gets the better of him, and he lies helplessly sprawled in bed as Hal and Poins taunt him before Doll Tearsheet, his wit his only reprieve. The king seems chilled and mummified in his huge tomb-like castle. Hal and Hotspur seem almost inert when they duel in their armour shells. But Falstaff! Falstaff runs with a breathtakingly funny agility through the charging troops (a stroke of genius), and weaves his way through an unheeding, mindless tavern full of dancers. But he does not disappear into the aimless masses; he seems doomed to stand out awkwardly from the landscape, like a castle. Everything in the film is on the verge of slowing to a standstill.

But for the battle sequence, *Chimes at Midnight* has none of the violent movements from exhilaration to dejection of Welles's earlier films; its equipoise reflects an achieved serenity. Throughout the film, most bitterly in the strained play-acting between Hal and Falstaff in the tavern scene which foreshadows the climax, the awareness of destruction is present even in moments of 'respite'. Falstaff battles this awareness throughout; his attempts to ignore it provide the comedy. He has none of Kane's guile and worldly ability, and his greatness presents itself as a monstrous jest impossible to ignore but easy to dismiss. He demands nothing but attention, and offers all of himself in return. His egocentricity, like his body, is carried past the ridiculous into the sublime, to the point of melancholia. He fears nothing but death, and reproaches Doll Tearsheet with, "Thou'lt forget me when I am gone." It is unlikely that Welles as director or actor will achieve again so moving a scene as that of Falstaff's expulsion. With the author's consent we may feel superior to Kane, but we are never superior to Falstaff. He is naked before us. *Chimes at Midnight* is Welles's testament.

The Immortal Story

by CHARLES SILVER

Behold the Child among his new-born blisses,
A six-years' Darling of a pygmy size!
See, where 'mid work of his own hand he lies,
Fretted by sallies of his mother's kisses,
With light upon him from his father's eyes!
See, at his feet, some little plan or chart,
Some fragment from his dream of human life,
Shaped by himself with newly-learned art;
    A wedding or a festival,
    A mourning or a funeral;
      And this hath now his heart,
    And unto this he frames his song:
      Then will he fit his tongue
To dialogues of business, love, or strife;
    But it will not be long
    Ere this be thrown aside,
    And with new joy and pride
The little Actor dons another part;
Filling from time to time his "humorous stage"
With all the Persons, down to palsied Age,
That Life brings with her in her equipage;
    As if his whole vocation
    Were endless imitation.

WILLIAM WORDSWORTH
from *Intimations of Immortality*

Orson Welles' most recent film has predictably been cited by his detractors as clear evidence of further decline. Even from his admirers, *The Immortal Story* has evoked only a minimal defense. One senses that Welles' friends are asking, with Wordsworth, "Whither is fled the visionary gleam?/ Where is it now, the glory and the dream?" What follows is offered as a reply to these questions.

Film Comment, *Summer 1971. Vol. 7, No. 2.* © *1971 Film Comment Publishing Corporation, reprinted by permission.*

It's not very hard to find things wrong with *The Immortal Story* if, as the estimable Mr. Bernstein might say, all you want to do is find things wrong with it. The sound, at least in the English-language version, is rather bad. The lighting, sets, props and make-up have a decided air of cheapness and haste, reflecting the fact that this was, after all, only a television production. The continuity and editing tend toward a certain sloppiness, and the acting and mise-en-scène appear stolid, completely antithetical to the wild Welles we have known. Even more damning, perhaps, is the virtually total subservience to the narrative structure and dialogue of Baroness Blixen's fable. Unlike *Citizen Kane, The Magnificent Ambersons, The Lady from Shanghai, Touch of Evil,* and even *Falstaff,* the points here seem to be made verbally rather than visually and, superficially at least, they appear to be those of Miss Dinesen, not those of Mr. Welles.

But most of what is important about *The Immortal Story*—or, for that matter, about the vast majority of other films—is the extent to which the director makes the film an expression of self. In this endeavor, despite all the aforementioned obstacles, Orson Welles succeeds in quite a lovely manner. Careful analysis of the mise-en-scène of *The Immortal Story* reveals it to be one of the most poignantly personal works in all cinema.

As in so many earlier Welles movies, the filmmaker assumes the role of narrator. In no previous film, however, has Welles' conception of himself been so crucial to the essence of the work. He is no mere interlocutor here, for he is telling a story about the telling of a story—a story about a fat old man who tells a story—a story, in fact, about Orson Welles.

The director immediately asserts his independence by arbitrarily switching the locale from Miss Dinesen's Canton to Macao. We are introduced to nabob Clay and to Elishama Levinsky—the latter a servile and sexless insect whose relationship to the former parallels that of Bernstein to Kane, or (even better) that of Pete Menzies to Hank Quinlan. Just as Menzies is to be stage manager for the drama in which Quinlan—Pete's only reason for living—will die, so Levinsky performs the same function for his master; both Menzies and Levinsky know that, in doing so, they are setting in motion the machinery of their own destruction.

We learn from Isak Dinesen that, when Clay took possession of the house formerly belonging to his bankrupt and deceased partner (M. Dupont, Virginie's father), he found that everything had been removed except the mirrors. When we see the mirrors, we are immediately reminded of the mirrors from that other palatial prison, Xanadu; and we are not surprised, therefore, to find that the house also contains an Amberson staircase. By comparison with Xanadu, however, Clay's house is as austere as its owner, and there is every reason to believe that Clay lacks Kane's flamboyant past, that he has never really been a participant in any of the games of life other than those related to "making money." He feels powerful because he is a recluse. He maintains his feeling of omnipotence, we are told, "by ignoring that part of the world which [lies] outside the sphere of his power." And the world, on the whole, seems to ignore Mr. Clay, except for an occasional gaggle of gossips we see chatting about him on the street, as though they were wagging their tongues over the latest exploit of Georgie Minafer.

When Levinsky reads Clay the prophecy of Isaiah, it sparks in the old man the desire to render into fact the fictional story of The Sailor and The Girl. Welles' execution of this sequence carries with it clear connotations of making a film from the story. Clay's response to the prophecy is: "Who put that thing together?" The old man's concern focuses on his budget: "It will involve expenses." The fable indicates that Clay's intent is "to manifest his omnipotence, and to do the thing that could not be done." Miss Dinesen almost seems to echo Welles' assertion that he makes films like *Touch of Evil* "because of the greedy need to exercise, in some way, the function of my choice." The world of *The Immortal Story* is one in which, as Levinsky says, "we go where we are told" by merchants like Mr. Clay. This is, indeed, the world in which Welles has had to struggle for thirty years.

The key to *The Immortal Story* lies in the relationship between Mr. Clay and the sailor. The interchange between them—visual, verbal, and intensely symbolic—reveals to us as inspired and confessional an apologia as that of Chaplin in *Limelight* or Kazan in *The Arrangement*. When Clay first enters the dining room the sailor is already seated at the table. As he crosses to his seat, the massive shadow of Orson Welles falls upon the boy, blocking out the chandelier's garish golden light. This is paralleled by the shadow of the sailor falling upon Clay as he returns to his place at the table after threatening to leave, succumbing to Clay's bargain, offering up his innocence in exchange for the price of a boat that will return him to that corrupt and impure world we designate as civilization.

At the beginning of this sequence, Clay treats his sailor/actor as though he were a Hitchcockian bull; he speaks of the youth to Levinsky as if the subject of their conversation were not present. Eventually turning his attention to the boy, Clay talks about his consuming love for his gold, and of his desire to pass it on to someone whom he has "caused to exist." In return the sailor tells Clay of his shipwreck on a desert island where he was completely alone. This tale of solitude intrigues the old man because it so closely resembles his own condition, and he remarks on what a pleasant thing it must have been to be "where nobody can possibly intrude upon you." The sailor agrees and expresses regret at having been picked up by a ship, thus losing his sanctuary, his niche in an almost pure state of nature. The boy and the man are irrefutably linked, and it follows logically that we are later told by Welles that sailors (like artists?) are lonely liars whose stories are dreams of things they do not have.

Clay then "directs" his story according to his own rules—in effect, exercising the right of final cut. "You move at my bidding," he informs his actors from behind a lace curtain, hidden like the Wizard of Oz, but with the authority of Kane telling Susan Alexander that she'll be a great opera star whether she wants to be or not. Levinsky has suggested to Virginie, whom he as casting director has chosen as the co-star of Clay's production, that the prophecy of Isaiah has transformed Clay into a child whose fantasies are establishing the myth of The Sailor and The Girl, thus playing with the legend of transforming it into a "fragment from his dream of human life." Clay/Welles, now seated in his (director's?) chair on the porch, says: "It's all nothing but a story . . . my story."

Until the last sequence in the film, Welles has followed Miss Dinesen's narrative plan with only the slightest variations. (Levinsky's proposal to Virginie, for example, is broken up into several different scenes with several different locations in an apparent attempt to be more cinematic.) But in the fable, the sailor leaves a shell, which is intended as a memento for Virginie, with Levinsky. In the film, he presents it to Clay, soldering the link between them. We next see the shell, fallen from the dead man's hand, rolling on the porch like Kane's snow-scene paperweight following his dying utterance, "Rosebud." Like Kane's sled, the shell, salvaged from the sailor's idyllic island isolation, is a symbol of lost innocence. The sailor has surrendered his virginity to Clay's drama, and he is now to return to Europe. For the boy, just as irrevocably as for Clay/Kane/Welles, and for Wordsworth, "there hath passed away a glory from the earth."

The Wellesian hero, from Kane to Falstaff, is almost inevitably vanquished by his illusions. Mr. Clay, who has spent his whole life avoiding them, is finally killed in the attempt to transform illusion into reality. Clay does not succeed, for the sailor tells Levinsky that he will not repeat the story, thus frustrating the old man's design. In this, Welles suggests an admission of failure on his own part, a sense of defeat about his lifelong struggle to transcend his mortality through his skill at lying. Welles' lies—those cinematic "ribbons of dreams," as he calls them—are to him what Clay's million dollars are to the old merchant: "my brain and my heart; it is my life." Whereas Charles Foster Kane three decades ago could make choices, Mr. Clay moved ineluctably toward defeat and death. His very name implies mortality. Thus, it is all too appropriate that the mise-en-scène of *The Immortal Story* should be somber, static, and humorless.

Like Mr. Clay, Welles in 1941 had achieved everything, and, in its own way, "the cup of his triumph had been too strong for him." As Levinsky reflects, "it was very hard on people who wanted things so badly that they could not do without them. If they could not get these things it was hard; and when they did get them, surely it was very hard." Surely no one has had to struggle more against his own premature deification than Orson Welles.

> *Thou, over whom thy Immortality*
> *Broods like the day, a Master o'er a Slave,*
> *A Presence which is not to be put by . . .*

And there must be a part of this tragic being which genuinely feels that his whole vocation has been an endless imitation. Levinsky listens to the sound of the shell and says, "I have heard it before . . . long, long ago. But where?" The film ends with a slow fade to white.

Tell Me Lies

by JOHN RUSSELL TAYLOR

The first and most impenetrable mystery about Orson Welles'
latest film is what, exactly, it is called. The place in the film which
might be expected to provide the answer is strangely ambiguous.
First we see the screen filled with the word "Fake" over and over
again, small, running diagonally, as though to form a background.
Then imposed on this, a question-mark. This seems to leave open
three possibilities: that it is called *Fake*, that it is called *Fake?*, or
that it is called *?*. Sources close to Welles incline to the third
solution, and generally refer to it as "Question Mark." But it does
seem characteristic of the old illusionist that he should help a
sabotage an already unclassifiable and perhaps not very commercial feature by presenting right off this area of puzzlement. How,
after all, do you start to sell a film you cannot even certainly refer
to, except as what's-its-name, you know, that film?

If the spectral presence of the word 'fake' in or around the title
rings any bells, it is meant to. Anyone with an interest in the
eccentricities of the art market and its shady fringes will probably
recall this as the title of a book by Clifford Irving about Elmyr de
Hory, often called the greatest art forger of them all, the virtuoso
inventor of hundreds of Picassos, Matisses, Dufys, Modiglianis,
etc.—more, he gives us to believe, than anyone dare suspect, many
of them hanging in respected places in the best galleries of the
world. Some five years ago François Reichenbach made a short
documentary about de Hory, showing us his seemingly idyllic,
heavily name-dropping life in retirement on Ibiza and talking, as
well as to de Hory himself, to a lot of friends, associates, and
observant bystanders. Among the latter, Clifford Irving, who had at

Sight and Sound *(Autumn 1973)*. Reprinted by permission.

that point been researching *Fake*, and was quite expansive on the subject of de Hory in particular and forgery, its means and motives, in general.

The film was shown around on television, then filed away. But that, of course, was before Irving himself hit the headlines as the forger of the supposedly official autobiography of Howard Hughes. Which is where Welles comes in. Obviously he has, presumably some time around the middle of last year, while the subject was inescapable, seen the Reichenbach film and realised the ironic sub-text it contains: here we have Clifford Irving talking about forgery possibly at the very moment that he was conceiving his own great enterprise in that line. Hence "Question Mark." In the course of some seventy-two minutes the material filmed by Reichenbach is taken apart, rearranged, gone over again backwards and forwards, as Welles speculates on Irving's situation at the time, finds curious parallels between de Hory's career and Irving's, applies Irving's words about de Hory to Irving himself, and manages here and there to turn the tables by putting de Hory, filmically speaking, in the position of commenting on Irving just as Irving has been commenting on him.

All of this, you will gather, is done with material actually shot (much of it rather prettily) by Reichenbach, who gets some sort of credit as the producer or presenter of the Welles film. Welles' contribution is the angle of vision, some very fancy effects of montage, and the framework into which the material is put. This includes a discourse on magic and deception by Welles himself, who pervades the film, performing a few offhand effects of prestidigitation, massively cloaked, or posing the way filmmakers are meant to in the labs, intensely scrutinising a foot or so of film held picturesquely up against the light. Also, in evidence is a spectacular-looking Yugoslavian girl who strides glamorously around Paris while Welles mutters darkly about strange coincidences connected with her and promises that all will eventually be made clear. And then there is a certain amount about the impossible search for Howard Hughes himself, represented mostly by zoom shots of the outside of his Las Vegas eyrie, evidencing no signs of habitation.

Clearly this is Welles harking back to something like his original radio format of programmes which he prepared and presented and pervaded, commenting and acting roles and nudging his audience toward the right attitudes. This particular film is enjoyable and holding, if somewhat over-extended (one is very conscious of a little material being made to go a very long way, with the quickness of the hand not always managing to deceive the eye). And it is disappointing that there is not more actually shot by Welles. But the old master has a couple of tricks up his sleeve for the conclusion. Everything, he assures us at the outset, that he will show us in the next sixty minutes is true, however incredible it may seem.

As the film progresses, in wider and wider circles, the Yugoslav girl keeps recurring, until finally we get her story. She was, it appears, holidaying in the south of France when she attracted the attention of Picasso, who was painting in the same village. (This is all very funnily done, with an ingenious use of still photographs of Picasso edited in such a way as to establish, jokily, his physical presence.) He begs to paint her; she agrees, on condition that she will own all the paintings so produced; he agrees, provided that they remain her property alone. At the end of her holiday she goes off with two dozen superlative late Picassos. A few months later, Picasso reads a review of a revelatory exhibition of his latest work in an obscure Left Bank gallery. Furious, he rushes up to Paris, charges into the gallery concerned, and finds—two dozen superlative late Picassos he has never laid eyes on before. The girl explains: her grandfather, now dying, is the greatest art forger of them all, and this tribute to his genius constitutes, as it were, her going-away present to him. And is it true, asks Welles? Look at your watches, ladies and gentlemen. Seventy-two minutes ago I promised you that everything you would see in the next sixty minutes was true. . . .

Falstaff in King Hollywood's Court: An Interview Concerning "The Other Side of the Wind"*

by CHARLES CHAMPLIN

The restaurant in Century City, Orson Welles said, had high ceilings, good food, attentive waiters and, surpassing all its other virtues, no Hollywood types. Why didn't we meet there?

Welles is no present stranger in Hollywood; he is almost an annual visitor in fact. But he has no press agent and no agent, making his own deals in consultation with his lawyer-friend for more than 40 years, Arnold Weissberger of New York; and he so steadfastly avoids the standard watering holes and social circuitries that he seems more than ever a figure of myth and mystery, the surviving American director who could fairly be called a legend in his time.

I am early for our meeting, but he is earlier, almost treasonable behavior in Hollywood. He is nursing a glass of iced tea and does not even take wine with the meal. He smokes a slender and splendid cigar and has a box of them on the table as other men would have a pack of cigarets.

He is very large, Falstaffian, wearing a dark blue sports shirt and matching slacks, and blue and white sneakers. The hair is silver, long, neat, brushed straight back. That unforgettable rich voice, melodious and commanding, fills the room, and the explosive, sibilant laughter, resonant and delighted, reminds you of Charles

* *Los Angeles Times*, May 12, 1973. Reprinted by permission.

Foster Kane and somehow also of Harry Lime of "The Third Man."

Just now Welles is waiting to resume shooting on what sounds like an extraordinarily interesting movie he has been working on for more than two years. He recently finished one stretch of shooting on location at a ranch near Phoenix with his star John Huston and costar Peter Bogdanovich. Welles is scheduled to resume here when Huston returns from scouting locations for his own next film. Meanwhile Welles, who did much of the early shooting with his own money, is hoping to set up an American distribution deal to finance the final push. Huston's agent and Welles' friend Fred Kohner is handling the negotiations.

The movie, which Welles wrote, is called "The Other Side of the Wind."

"It centers on a birthday party for an old Hollywood director," Welles says. "He's meant to be older than Huston, more like Hawks. But he isn't Hawks, isn't John, isn't me, although the buffs all seek keys. I suppose you can say he wouldn't exist a character if Hemingway hadn't existed. The director's unmasking as a man's man is part of the story."

The party is given by an old friend of the director's, a Dietrich-like figure played by Lilli Palmer, and the idea is to introduce the great man to some of the New Wave washing over Hollywood and elsewhere, with the cool young director played by Bogdanovich chief among them.

The Bogdanovich character has been a protege of Hanniford, the old man, and the movie watches the deterioration of their friendship.

"There's a film within the film, which I made two years ago with my own money. It's the old man's attempt to do a kind of counterculture film, in a surrealist, dreamlike style. We see some of it in the director's projection room, some of it at a drive-in when that breaks down. It's about 50% of the whole movie. Not the kind of film I'd want to make; I've invented a style for him.

"Had to invent two styles, in fact. I've assumed that the party is being covered by a documentary crew from the BBC and another from West Germany and by a whole lot of amateurs with cameras. You'll see only what they've recorded of this evening. It's a device that would only work once, I suppose, but, God, it's fun, using three and four cameras at once."

Having commenced the film two years ago [actually in 1970] Welles had to abandon it temporarily when the government decided his European operation was a holding company, not a production company, and presented him with a whopping tax bill. "Once again I was working like hell to pay taxes and looking for other money to get on with the film." He got back in production earlier this year.

The film is partly a reunion of Mercury Theater players. Paul Stewart, the crafty butler of "Citizen Kane," is in the cast, along with Mercedes McCambridge and Norman Foster. Others in the cast include director Claude Chabrol, Susan Strasberg (as a critic-historian in the tradition of Pauline Kael), Edmund O'Brien and Cameron Mitchell. Dennis Hopper, Paul Mazursky and Henry Jaglom will play themselves. "I would love to have Bobby Evans play the part of a studio boss," Welles says. "He would be perfect, but I fear it might inhibit the sale."

The film obviously will give Welles a chance to say a great many things about movies, movie makers, film buffs, critics, producers, stars, executives, styles and the lifespan of a Hollywood now seen at twilight. "Of course, I thought I was getting in just under the wire when I came out here in 1939," says Welles, "so you know what I think now."

"The Other Side of the Wind" will end amid the crumbling remains of a deserted back lot.

"I've always pretended I love Hollywood," Welles says, "in spite of everything. I never feel sour grapes; it's not an emotion I have time for or one that does you any good. But last year my daughter bought a stack of books about the movies and on nights when I couldn't sleep I began to read them, read what the executives had done to the directors, the writers. And I'm afraid the balance of evidence is against this town, not for it. I say this fearlessly, not forgetting all the smarmy statements I've made about Hollywood before this.

"I'm tired of hearing what a great man Irving Thalberg was. The whole thing gets pretty sickening. The ones who succeed are the lucky ones. On balance, the system has been against the individual artist. It's not even directly related to money. I suppose it goes back to the beginning of time, when an animal instinctively had to put a foot atop its prey. The brass had to put their feet on the director if they could.

"Yet there is no pleasure in the world as great as directing a movie on a stage here with a Hollywood crew. The atmosphere then is great and truly professional. If you could have that by day and get in a capsule and go to London at night, that would be paradise."

Identifying Miss Strasberg as a Kael-like figure (Welles has not actually ever met Ms. Kael) raised the question of Ms. Kael's long essay, "Raising Kane," which, while in no way diminishing the achievement of "Citizen Kane," concluded that the importance of Herman Mankiewicz as author had been minimized by and in favor of Welles.

"I'm a fan of Pauline," Welles says. "She's readable, even if you disagree with her. But she took off on a theory which she didn't check out as a responsible journalist should have. She never tried to talk to me. Peter's book on me, which he's been working on for years, has all the documentation and will lay all of that to rest. But her piece caused me pain when it came out.

The dispute between Herman and me was not whether he should be off the credits but whether I should be on. I didn't really care; credits are the last thing I care about. She accepted John Houseman's version of things. Houseman went up to the desert with Herman and he assumed that the whole script was flowing out of Herman's head. But Mankiewicz and I had developed the story alone before he went up there. It gets to be very ugly.

She found an obscure movie with Peter Lorre which she thought resembled 'Kane' in some ways. I'd never seen it until Peter found a print of it a while ago. Gregg Toland said I could learn as much as I needed of the technical side of movies in two days. He said it; I didn't. She thought it arrogant of me; I quoted it to mean only that I shouldn't have credit I didn't deserve.

"The irony is that I had been refusing for years to publish the script of 'Kane.' I finally gave in and she was asked to do the introduction. I get royalties from the book. But she never sought me out. She knew it would spoil her copy. 'Orson Welles on the other hand insists that . . . Welles maintains, however . . .' It would have been boring for her rhetoric."

Except for its ending, which was redone by someone else, Welles still prefers "The Magnificent Ambersons" to "Citizen Kane."

"I had always dreamed of getting Joe Cotten and Agnes Moorehead together and doing another ending for 'Ambersons,' 25 years later, and rereleasing the film. But I waited too long. I'm so sorry about Agnes (who died April 30). I hadn't known she was ill."

Welles, having got through an ample but far from outlandish meal, lit a fresh cigar. "Damn," he said, "I've had enormous fun here, great friends here. People have trouble distinguishing the community and the system. What's against us is the semitropical climate. The South is mischievous anywhere. There's a south of Sweden, you know, where the people are lazier and more charming. It's true here as well: horrendous and curiously beguiling. You can be so turned off and yet it's so wonderful."

Welles had moved to Europe originally after he lost nearly $400,000 of his own money on a stage production of "Around the World in 80 Days" and incurred a huge tax bill. He worked it off in low-tax Europe, bought a house near Madrid when most of his work seemed to be in Spain. He goes to Spain briefly to film a sherry commercial for British television, then returns to Malibu to commence editing what he has already shot on "The Other Side of the Wind." He and his family now live principally in London, where it is charming but anything but semitropical.

"People say I should be making American films. One answer is that Hollywood hasn't made that many American films lately. Nostalgia and dreams, not that much about what's been happening in the last 10 years. Bogdanovich is pro-Hollywood in the best sense, of course: Movies *have* to be popular, and all that.

"I'd like to think I wouldn't have made all bad films if I could have stayed in Hollywood. But of course you don't know."

Filmography

Most of the information reproduced below is drawn from Joseph McBride's *Orson Welles* (1972), to which the reader is also referred for an account of Welles' "unrealized film projects."

The Hearts of Age (1934)

Producer	William Vance
Directors	Orson Welles, William Vance

With Orson Welles, Virginia Nicholson, William Vance.

Filmed (in 16mm) in Woodstock, Illinois, during the summer of 1934. Running time, approximately 4 min.

Too Much Johnson (1938)

Production Company	Mercury Productions
Producers	Orson Welles, John Houseman
Director	Orson Welles
Assistant Director	John Berry
Script	Orson Welles. Based on the play by William Gillette
Director of Photography	Paul Dunbar

Joseph Cotten *(Johnson)*, Virginia Nicholson, Edgar Barrier, Arlene Francis, Ruth Ford, Mary Wickes, Eustace Wyatt, Guy Kingsley, George Duthie, John Berry, Herbert Drake, Marc Blitzstein, Howard Smith.

Filmed (in 16mm) in New York City and elsewhere in New York during the spring of 1938. Made for a Mercury Theatre stage production of *Too Much Johnson* (Stony Creek Summer Theatre, New York), but never edited or shown publicly. Running time, approximately 40 min. The only copy of this film was destroyed in a fire at Welles's villa in Madrid in August 1970.

In 1939 Welles made a film for use in his vaudeville show *The Green Goddess*, and shot test scenes in Hollywood for *Heart of Darkness*.

Citizen Kane (1941)

Production Company	Mercury Productions
Executive Producer	George J. Schaefer
Producer	Orson Welles
Associate Producer	Richard Barr
Director	Orson Welles
Assistant Director	Richard Wilson

Script	Herman J. Mankiewicz, Orson Welles
Director of Photography	Gregg Toland
Camera Operator	Bert Shipman
Editors	Mark Robson, Robert Wise
Art Director	Van Nest Polglase
Associate Art Director	Perry Ferguson
Set Decorator	Darrell Silvera
Special Effects	Vernon L. Walker
Music/Musical Director	Bernard Herrmann
Costumes	Edward Stevenson
Sound Recordists	Bailey Fesler, James G. Stewart

Orson Welles *(Charles Foster Kane)*, Joseph Cotten *(Jedediah Leland;* also *Newsreel Reporter)*, Everett Sloane *(Bernstein)*, Dorothy Comingore *(Susan Alexander Kane)*, Ray Collins *(James W. Gettys)*, William Alland *(Jerry Thompson;* also *Newsreel Narrator)*, Agnes Moorehead *(Mary Kane)*, Ruth Warrick *(Emily Norton Kane)*, George Coulouris *(Walter Parks Thatcher)*, Erskine Sanford *(Herbert Carter;* also *Newsreel Reporter)*, Harry Shannon *(Jim Kane)*, Philip Van Zandt *(Rawlston)*, Paul Stewart *(Raymond)*, Fortunio Bonanova *(Matisti)*, Georgia Backus *Miss Anderson, Curator of Thatcher Library)*, Buddy Swan *(Charles Foster Kane, aged 8)*, Sonny Bupp *(Kane, Jr)*, Gus Schilling *(Head Waiter)*, Richard Barr *(Hillman)*, Joan Blair *(Georgia)*, Al Eben *(Mike)*, Charles Bennett *(Entertainer)*, Milt Kibbee *(Reporter)*, Tom Curran *(Teddy Roosevelt)*, Irving Mitchell *(Dr Corey)*, Edith Evanson *(Nurse)*, Arthur Kay *(Orchestra Leader)*, Tudor Williams *(Chorus Master)*, Herbert Corthell *(City Editor)*, Benny Rubin *(Smather)*, Edmund Cobb *(Reporter)*, Frances Neal *(Ethel)*, Robert Dudley *(Photographer)*, Ellen Lowe *(Miss Townsend)*, Gino Corrado *(Gino, the waiter)*, Alan Ladd, Louise Currie, Eddie Coke, Walter Sande, Arthur O'Connell, Katherine Trosper, and Richard Wilson *(Reporters)*.

Filmed at the RKO studios in Hollywood, 29 June–23 October 1940. US premiere in New York, 1 May 1941; GB, October 1941. Running time, 119 min. Distributors: RKO Radio (USA and GB).

The Magnificent Ambersons (1942)

Production Company	Mercury Productions
Executive Producer	George J. Schaefer
Producer	Orson Welles
Director	Orson Welles (additional scenes directed by Freddie Fleck and Robert Wise)
Assistant Director	Freddie Fleck
Script	Orson Welles. Based on the novel by Booth Tarkington
Director of Photography	Stanley Cortez
Additional Photography	Russell Metty, Harry J. Wild
Editors	Robert Wise, Jack Moss, Mark Robson
Art Director	Mark-Lee Kirk
Set Decorator	Al Fields
Special Effects	Vernon L. Walker
Music	Bernard Herrmann
Additional Music	Roy Webb

Costumes	Edward Stevenson
Sound Recordists	Bailey Fesler, James G. Stewart
Narrator	Orson Welles

Tim Holt *(George Amberson Minafer)*, Joseph Cotten *(Eugene Morgan)*, Dolores Costello *(Isabel Amberson Minafer)*, Agnes Moorehead *(Fanny Minafer)*, Anne Baxter *(Lucy Morgan)*, Ray Collins *(Jack Amberson)*, Richard Bennett *(Major Amberson)*, Don Dillaway *(Wilbur Minafer)*, Erskine Sanford *(Roger Bronson)*, J. Louis Johnson *(Sam)*, Gus Schilling *(Drugstore Clerk)*, Charles Phipps *(Uncle John)*, Dorothy Vaughan and Elmer Jerome *(Spectators at funeral)*, Olive Ball *(Mary)*, Nina Guilbert and John Elliot *(Guests)*, Anne O'Neal *(Mrs Foster)*, Kathryn Sheldon and Georgia Backus *(Matrons)*, Henry Roquemore *(Hardware Man)*, Hilda Plowright *(Nurse)*, Mel Ford *(Fred Kinney)*, Bob Pittard *(Charlie Johnson)*, Lillian Nicholson *(Landlady)*, Billy Elmer *(House Servant)*, Maynard Holmes and Lew Kelly *(Citizens)*, Bobby Cooper *(George as a boy)*, Drew Roddy *(Elijah)*, Jack Baxley *(Reverend Smith)*, Heenan Elliott *(Labourer)*, Nancy Gates *(Girl)*, John Maguire *(Young Man)*, Ed Howard *(Chauffeur/Citizen)*, William Blees *(Youth at accident)*, James Westerfield *(Cop at accident)*, Philip Morris *(Cop)*, Jack Santoro *(Barber)*, Louis Hayward *(Ballroom extra)*.

Filmed at the RKO studios in Hollywood, 28 October 1941–22 January 1942. US premiere, 13 August 1942; GB, March 1943. Running time, 88 min. (originally 131 min.).
Distributors: RKO Radio (USA and GB).

It's All True (1942)

Production Company	Mercury Productions, for the Office of the Coordinator of Inter-American Affairs and RKO Radio
Executive Producers	Nelson Rockefeller, George J. Schaefer
Producer	Orson Welles
Associate Producer	Richard Wilson
Director	Orson Welles (and Norman Foster as co-director of the *Bonito* episode)
Script	Orson Welles, Norman Foster, John Fante
Director of Photography	W. Howard Greene
Second Cameraman	Harry J. Wild
Colour Process	
(*Carnival* episode)	Technicolor
Editor	Joe Noriega

José Olimpio Meira or Jacaré, Tata, Mané, Jeronymo, Sebastião Prata or Grande Otelo, Domingo Soler, Jesús Vasquez.

Filmed on location in Brazil from January to August, 1942. Uncompleted and never shown.

Journey Into Fear (1943)

Production Company	Mercury Productions
Executive Producer	George J. Schaefer
Producer	Orson Welles

Director	Norman Foster (and Orson Welles, uncredited)
Script	Joseph Cotten, Orson Welles. Based on the novel by Eric Ambler
Director of Photography	Karl Struss
Editor	Mark Robson
Art Directors	Albert S. D'Agostino, Mark-Lee Kirk
Set Decorators	Darrell Silvera, Ross Dowd
Special Effects	Vernon L. Walker
Music	Roy Webb
Costumes	Edward Stevenson

Joseph Cotten *(Howard Graham)*, Dolores Del Rio *(Josette Martel)*, Orson Welles *(Colonel Haki)*, Ruth Warrick *(Stephanie Graham)*, Agnes Moorehead *(Mrs Mathews)*, Everett Sloane *(Kopeikin)*, Jack Moss *(Banat)*, Jack Durant *(Gogo)*, Eustace Wyatt *(Dr Haller)*, Frank Readick *(Mathews)*, Edgar Barrier *(Kuvetli)*, Stefan Schnabel *(Purser)*, Hans Conried *(Oo Lang Sang, the magician)*, Robert Meltzer *(Steward)*, Richard Bennett *(Ship's Captain)*, Shifra Haran *(Mrs Haklet)*, Herbert Drake, Bill Roberts.

Filmed at the RKO studios in Hollywood, 1942–3. First shown in USA, 12 February 1943; GB, October 1943. Running time, 71 min.
Distributors: RKO Radio (USA and GB).

The Stranger (1946)

Production Company	International Pictures
Producer	S. P. Eagle [Sam Spiegel]
Director	Orson Welles
Assistant Director	Jack Voglin
Script	Anthony Veiller (and John Huston, Orson Welles, uncredited)
Story	Victor Trivas, Decla Dunning
Director of Photography	Russell Metty
Editor	Ernest Nims
Art Director	Perry Ferguson
Music	Bronislaw Kaper
Orchestrations	Harold Byrns, Sidney Cutner
Costumes	Michael Woulfe
Sound	Carson F. Jowett, Arthur Johns

Orson Welles *(Franz Kindler alias Professor Charles Rankin)*, Loretta Young *(Mary Longstreet)*, Edward G. Robinson *(Inspector Wilson)*, Philip Merivale *(Judge Longstreet)*, Richard Long *(Noah Longstreet)*, Byron Keith *(Dr Lawrence)*, Billy House *(Mr Potter)*, Martha Wentworth *(Sarah)*, Konstantin Shayne *(Konrad Meinike)*, Theodore Gottlieb *(Farbright)*, Pietro Sosso *(Mr Peabody)*, Isabel O'Madigan.

Filmed in Hollywood, 1945. First shown in USA, 25 May 1946; GB, 25 August 1946. Running time, 95 min. (85 min. in USA; originally 115 min.).
Distributors: RKO Radio (USA and GB).

In 1946, Welles filmed sequences for use in his play *Around the World*.

The Lady from Shanghai (1946)

Production Company	Columbia
Executive Producer	Harry Cohn
Associate Producers	Richard Wilson, William Castle
Director	Orson Welles
Assistant Director	Sam Nelson
Script	Orson Welles. Freely adapted from the novel *If I Die Before I Wake* by Sherwood King
Director of Photography	Charles Lawton, Jr
Camera Operator	Irving Klein
Editor	Viola Lawrence
Art Directors	Stephen Goosson, Sturges Carne
Set Decorators	Wilbur Menefee, Herman Schoenbrun
Special Effects	Lawrence Butler
Music	Heinz Roemheld
Musical Director	M. W. Stoloff
Orchestrations	Herschel Burke Gilbert
Song 'Please Don't Kiss Me'	Allan Roberts, Doris Fisher
Costumes (gowns)	Jean Louis
Sound	Lodge Cunningham

Orson Welles *(Michael O'Hara)*, Rita Hayworth *(Elsa Bannister)*, Everett Sloane *(Arthur Bannister)*, Glenn Anders *(George Grisby)*, Ted de Corsia *(Sidney Broom)*, Gus Schilling *(Goldie)*, Louis Merrill *(Jake)*, Erskine Sanford *(Judge)*, Carl Frank *(District Attorney Galloway)*, Evelyn Ellis *(Bessie)*, Wong Show Chong *(Li)*, Harry Shannon *(Horse cab driver)*, Sam Nelson *(Captain)*, Richard Wilson *(District Attorney's Assistant)*, and players of the Mandarin Theatre of San Francisco.

Filmed at Columbia Studios in Hollywood, and on location in Mexico and San Francisco, 1946. First shown in GB, 7 March 1948; USA, May 1948. Running time, 86 min.
Distributors: Columbia (USA and GB).

Macbeth (1948)

Production Company	Mercury Productions. For Republic Pictures.
Executive Producer	Charles K. Feldman
Producer	Orson Welles
Associate Producer	Richard Wilson
Director	Orson Welles
Assistant Director	Jack Lacey
Script	Orson Welles. Adapted from the play by Shakespeare
Dialogue Director	William Alland
Director of Photography	John L. Russell
Second Unit Photographer	William Bradford
Editor	Louis Lindsay
Art Director	Fred Ritter
Set Decorators	John McCarthy, Jr., James Redd
Special Effects	Howard Lydecker, Theodore Lydecker

Music	Jacques Ibert
Musical Director	Efrem Kurtz
Costumes	Orson Welles, Fred Ritter (men's), Adele Palmer (women's)
Make-up	Bob Mark
Sound	John Stransky, Jr., Garry Harris

Orson Welles *(Macbeth)*, Jeanette Nolan *(Lady Macbeth)*, Dan O'Herlihy *(Macduff)*, Edgar Barrier *(Banquo)*, Roddy McDowall *(Malcolm)*, Erskine Sanford *(Duncan)*, Alan Napier *(A Holy Father)*, John Dierkes *(Ross)*, Keene Curtis *(Lennox)*, Peggy Webber *(Lady Macduff/Witch)*, Lionel Braham *(Siward)*, Archie Heugly *(Young Siward)*, Christopher Welles *Macduff child)*, Brainerd Duffield *(1st Murderer/Witch)*, William Alland *(2nd Murderer)*, George Chirello *(Seyton)*, Gus Schilling *(Porter)*, Jerry Farber *(Fleance)*, Lurene Tuttle *(Gentlewoman/Witch)*, Charles Lederer *(Witch)*, Robert Alan *(3rd Murderer)*, Morgan Farley *(Doctor)*.

Filmed at Republic Studios in Hollywood in twenty-three days during the summer of 1947. First shown in USA, 1 October 1948; GB, 31 May 1951. Running time, 107 min. (later cut to 86 min.).
Distributors: Republic (USA and GB).

In 1950, Welles made a short film, *La Miracle de Saint Anne*, for use in his play *The Unthinking Lobster*.

Othello (1952)

Production Company	Mercury Productions
Producer	Orson Welles
Associate Producers	Giorgio Patti, Julien Derode, with Walter Bedone, Patrice Dali, Rocco Facchini
Director	Orson Welles
Assistant Director	Michael Washinsky
Script	Orson Welles. Based on the play by Shakespeare
Directors of Photography	Anchise Brizzi, G. R. Aldo, George Fanto, with Obadan Troiani, Alberto Fusi
Editors	Jean Sacha, John Shepridge, Renzo Lucidi, William Morton
Art Director	Alexandre Trauner
Music	Francesco Lavagnino, Alberto Barberis
Musical Director	Willy Ferrero
Costumes	Maria de Matteis
Sound Recordist	Piscitrelli
Narrator	Orson Welles

Orson Welles *(Othello)*, Micheál MacLiammóir *(Iago)*, Suzanne Cloutier *(Desdemona)*, Robert Coote *(Roderigo)*, Michael Lawrence *(Cassio)*, Hilton Edwards *(Brabantio)*, Fay Compton *(Emilia)*, Nicholas Bruce *(Lodovico)*, Jean Davis *(Montano)*, Doris Dowling *(Bianca)*, Joseph Cotten *(Senator)*, Joan Fontaine *(Page)*.

Filmed at the Scalera studios in Rome, and on locations in Morocco (Mogador, Safi, and Mazagan) and Italy (Venice, Tuscany, Rome, Viterbo, Perugia, and the island of Torcello), from 1949 to 1952. First shown at the Cannes Film Festival, 10 May 1952; USA, June 1955; GB, 24 February 1956. Running time, 91 min. Distributors: United Artists (USA and GB).

Don Quixote (begun in 1955)

Producers	Oscar Dancigers, Orson Welles
Director	Orson Welles
Assistant Director	Paola Mori
Script	Orson Welles. Based on the novel by Miguel de Cervantes
Director of Photography	Jack Draper
Assistant Cameraman	Orson Welles
Narrator	Orson Welles

Francisco Reiguera *(Don Quixote)*, Akim Tamiroff *(Sancho Panza)*, Patty McCormack *(A girl; Dulcinea)*, Orson Welles *(Himself)*.

Filmed in Mexico (Puebla, Tepozlan, Texcoco, Rio Frio, Mexico City) and in Paris.
Running time, approximately 90 min. Uncompleted.

Mr Arkadin [British title: *Confidential Report*] (1955)

Production Company	Cervantes Film Organisation, Sevilla Studios (Spain)/Film Organisation (France). A Mercury Production
Executive Producer	Louis Dolivet
Production Manager	Michel J. Boisrond
Director	Orson Welles
Assistant Directors	José Maria Ochoa, José Luis De la Serna, Isidoro Martínez Ferri
Script	Orson Welles. Based on his own novel
Director of Photography	Jean Bourgoin
Editor	Renzo Lucidi
Art Director	Orson Welles
Music	Paul Misraki
Costumes	Orson Welles
Sound	Jacques Lebreton
Sound Recordist	Jacques Carrère
Narrator	Orson Welles

Orson Welles *(Gregory Arkadin)*, Paola Mori *(Raina Arkadin)*, Robert Arden *(Guy Van Stratten)*, Akim Tamiroff *(Jacob Zouk)*, Michael Redgrave *(Burgomil Trebitsch)*, Patricia Medina *(Mily)*, Mischa Auer *(The Professor)*, Katina Paxinou *(Sophie)*, Jack Watling *(Marquis of Rutleigh)*, Grégoire Aslan *(Bracco)*, Peter Van Eyck *(Thaddeus)*, Suzanne Flon *(Baroness Nagel)*, Tamara Shane *(Woman in apartment)*, Frédéric O'Brady *(Oskar)*.

Filmed in France, Spain, Germany, and Italy during eight months of 1954. First shown in GB, 11 August 1955; USA, 11 October 1962. Running time, 100 min. Distributors: Warner Bros. (GB), Dan Talbot (USA).

Touch of Evil (1958)

Production Company	Universal
Producer	Albert Zugsmith
Production Manager	F. D. Thompson
Director	Orson Welles (additional scenes directed by Harry Keller)
Assistant Directors	Phil Bowles, Terry Nelson
Script	Orson Welles. Freely adapted from the novel *Badge of Evil* by Whit Masterson
Director of Photography	Russell Metty
Editors	Virgil W. Vogel, Aaron Stell
Art Directors	Alexander Golitzen, Robert Clatworthy
Set Decorators	Russell A. Gausman, John P. Austin
Music	Henry Mancini
Musical Supervisor	Joseph Gershenson
Costumes	Bill Thomas
Sound	Leslie I. Carey, Frank Wilkinson

Orson Welles *(Hank Quinlan)*, Charlton Heston *(Ramon Miguel 'Mike' Vargas)*, Janet Leigh *(Susan Vargas)*, Joseph Calleia *(Pete Menzies)*, Akim Tamiroff *('Uncle Joe' Grande)*, Valentin De Vargas *(Pancho)*, Ray Collins *(District Attorney Adair)*, Dennis Weaver *(Motel Clerk)*, Joanna Moore *(Marcia Linnekar)*, Mort Mills *(Schwartz)*, Marlene Dietrich *(Tanya)*, Victor Millan *(Manolo Sanchez)*, Lalo Rios *(Risto)*, Michael Sargent *(Pretty Boy)*, Mercedes McCambridge *(Gang Leader)*, Joseph Cotten *(Detective)*, Zsa Zsa Gabor *(Owner of strip joint)*, Phil Harvey *(Blaine)*, Joi Lansing *(Blonde)*, Harry Shannon *(Gould)*, Rusty Wescoatt *(Casey)*, Wayne Taylor, Ken Miller, and Raymond Rodriguez *(Gang Members)*, Arlene McQuade *(Ginnie)*, Domenick Delgarde *(Lackey)*, Joe Basulto *(Young Delinquent)*, Jennie Dias *(Jackie)*, Yolanda Bojorquez *(Bobbie)*, Eleanor Dorado *(Lia)*.

Filmed at Universal Studios in Hollywood and on location at Venice, California during the winter of 1957–8. First shown in USA, February 1958; GB, 1 May 1958. Running time, 93 min.
Distributors: Universal (USA), Rank (GB).

The Trial (1962)

Production Company	Paris Europa Productions (Paris)/FI-C-IT (Rome)/ Hisa-Films (Munich)
Producers	Alexander Salkind, Michael Salkind
Production Manager	Robert Florat
Director	Orson Welles
Assistant Directors	Marc Maurette, Paul Seban, Sophie Becker
Script	Orson Welles. Based on the novel *Der Prozess* by Franz Kafka
Director of Photography	Edmond Richard
Camera Operator	Adolphe Charlet
Editors	Yvonne Martin, Denise Baby, Fritz Mueller
Art Director	Jean Mandaroux
Music	Jean Ledrut, and the Adagio for Organ and Strings by Tomaso Albinoni

Costumes	Hélène Thibault
Sound	Jacques Lebreton
Sound Recordists	Julien Coutellier, Guy Villette
Pin-screen prologue	Alexandre Alexeieff, Claire Parker
Narrator	Orson Welles

Anthony Perkins *(Joseph K.)*, Orson Welles *(Hastler)*, Jeanne Moreau *(Miss Burstner)*, Romy Schneider *(Leni)*, Elsa Martinelli *(Hilda)*, Suzanne Flon *(Miss Pittl)*, Madeleine Robinson *(Mrs Grubach)*, Akim Tamiroff *(Block)*, Arnoldo Foà *(Inspector)*, Fernand Ledoux *(Clerk of the Court)*, Maurice Teynac *(Director of K.'s office)*, Billy Kearns *(1st Police Officer)*, Jess Hahn *(2nd Police Officer)*, William Chappell *(Titorelli)*, Raoul Delfosse, Karl Studer, and Jean-Claude Remoleux *(Executioners)*, Wolfgang Reichmann *(Usher)*, Thomas Holtzmann *(Student)*, Maydra Shore *(Irmie)*, Max Haufler *(Uncle Max)*, Michel Lonsdale *(Priest)*, Max Buchsbaum *(Judge)*, Van Doude *(Archivist in cut scenes)*, Katina Paxinou *(Scientist in cut scenes)*.

Filmed at Studio de Boulogne, Paris, at the Gare d'Orsay, and in Zagreb, 26 March–2 June 1962. First shown in Paris, 21 December 1962; GB, 14 November 1963; USA, 20 February 1963. Running time, 120 min. (118 min. in English version).
Distributors: UFA-Comacico (France), BLC/British Lion (GB), Astor (USA).
French title: LE PROCÈS

Chimes at Midnight (1966)

Production Company	Internacional Films Española (Madrid)/Alpine (Basle)
Executive Producer	Alessandro Tasca
Producers	Emiliano Piedra, Angel Escolano
Production Manager	Gustavo Quintana
Director	Orson Welles
Second Unit Director	Jesús Franco
Assistant Directors	Tony Fuentes, Juan Cobos
Script	Orson Welles. Adapted from the plays *Richard II, Henry IV Parts I and II, Henry V*, and *The Merry Wives of Windsor* by William Shakespeare, and (for the commentary) *The Chronicles of England* by Raphael Holinshed
Director of Photography	Edmond Richard
Camera Operator	Adolphe Charlet
Second Unit Photographer	Alejandro Ulloa
Editor	Fritz Mueller
Art Directors	José Antonio de la Guerra, Mariano Erdorza
Music	Angelo Francesco Lavagnino
Musical Director	Carlo Franci
Costumes	Orson Welles
Sound Recordist	Peter Parasheles
Narrator	Ralph Richardson

Orson Welles *(Sir John Falstaff)*, Keith Baxter *(Prince Hal, later King Henry V)*, John Gielgud *(King Henry IV)*, Jeanne Moreau *(Doll Tearsheet)*, Margaret Rutherford *(Mistress Quickly)*, Norman Rodway *(Henry Percy, called Hotspur)*, Marina Vlady *(Kate Percy)*, Alan Webb *(Justice Shallow)*, Walter Chiari *(Silence)*, Michael Aldridge *(Pistol)*, Tony Beckley *(Poins)*, Fernando Rey *(Worcester)*, Andrew Faulds *(Westmoreland)*, José Nieto *(Northumberland)*, Jeremy Rowe *(Prince John)*, Beatrice Welles *(Falstaff's Page)*, Paddy Bedford *(Bardolph)*, Julio Peña, Fernando Hilbert, Andrés Mejuto, Keith Pyott, Charles Farrell.

Filmed in Barcelona, Madrid, and other Spanish locations, Winter 1964–Spring 1965. First shown at Cannes Film Festival, 8 May 1966; USA, 19 March 1967; GB, 23 March 1967. Running time, 119 min. (115 min. in GB).
Distributors: Planet (GB), Peppercorn-Wormser (USA).
Spanish title: CAMPANADAS A MEDIANOCHE; US title: FALSTAFF

The Immortal Story (1968)

Production Company	ORTF/Albina Films
Producer	Micheline Rozan
Production Manager	Marc Maurette
Director	Orson Welles
Assistant Directors	Olivier Gérard, Tony Fuentes, Patrice Torok
Script	Orson Welles. Based on the novella by Isak Dinesen [Karen Blixen]
Director of Photography	Willy Kurant
Colour Process	Eastman Colour
Assistant Cameramen	Jean Orjollet, Jacques Assuerds
Editors	Yolande Maurette, Marcelle Pluet, Françoise Garnault, Claude Farny
Art Director	André Piltant
Music	piano pieces by Erik Satie, played by Aldo Ciccolini and Jean-Joel Barbier
Costumes	
(for Jeanne Moreau)	Pierre Cardin
Sound	Jean Neny
Narrator	Orson Welles

Orson Welles *(Mr Clay)*, Jeanne Moreau *(Virginie Ducrot)*, Roger Coggio *(Elishama Levinsky)*, Norman Eshley *(Paul)*, Fernando Rey *(Merchant)*.

Filmed in Paris and Madrid, September–November 1966. First shown on French television simultaneously with its theatrical premiere in France, 24 May 1968; USA, New York Film Festival, 18 September 1968; GB, 3 April 1969 (previously at London Film Festival, 29 November 1968). Running time, 58 min.
Distributors: Hunter Films (GB), Altura Films (USA).
French title: HISTOIRE IMMORTELLE

The Deep (1970)

Director	Orson Welles
Script	Orson Welles. Based on the novel *Dead Calm* by Charles Williams

Director of Photography	Willy Kurant
Colour Process	Eastman Colour

Orson Welles *(Russ Brewer)*, Jeanne Moreau *(Ruth Warriner)*, Laurence Harvey *(Hughie Warriner)*, Olga Palinkas *(Rae Ingram)*, Michael Bryant *(John Ingram)*.

Filmed off the Dalmatian coast at Hvar, Yugoslavia, 1967–9.

The Other Side of the Wind (1972)

Director	Orson Welles
Script	Orson Welles
Director of Photography	Gary Graver
Colour Process	Eastman Colour

Filming began 23 August 1970 in Los Angeles.

Selected Bibliography

The most complete listing (152 items) of writings by and about Orson Welles may be found in Peter Cowie's *A Ribbon of Dreams: The Cinema of Orson Welles*, pp. 249 and ff. I have listed only books or journal issues exclusively on Welles, a few items of special interest published since 1973, and items that do not appear in Cowie's list.

BAZIN, ANDRÉ. *Orson Welles*, Preface by Jean Cocteau (Paris: Editions Chavane, 1950). In praise of Welles' cinematographic realism and democratic humanism. Translated excerpt in *Focus On Citizen Kane*.

BESSY, MAURICE. *Orson Welles. Cinema d'Aujourd'hui*. Series No. 6 (Paris: Editions Seghers. 1963 and 1970). Includes writing by Welles himself and extracts from the scripts of *Citizen Kane, The Magnificent Ambersons, The Trial*, and *Salome* (never filmed). Revised edition trans. into English by Ciba Vaughan and published by Crown Publishers, New York, 1971. Available in paperback.

BOGDANOVICH, PETER. "Is It True What They Say About Orson?" *New York Times*, August 30, 1970, Section II, pp. 1, 3. An attack on Higham's book, which Bogdanovich claims is inadvertently hurting Welles' chances to attract financial backing by repeating false stories about Welles' inability to complete films on time and within budget.

————. *The Cinema of Orson Welles* (New York: Film Library of the Museum of Modern Art, 1961). More useful for summaries than as a source of criticism.

————, and WELLES, ORSON. *This Is Orson Welles* (New York: 197?). Often promised, eagerly awaited, long overdue.

CARRINGER, ROBERT. *"Citizen Kane." Journal of Aesthetics Education*

211

(April 1975), pp. 32–49. A graceful introductory essay on Welles and a study guide to the film.

————. *"Citizen Kane, the Great Gatsby,* and Some Conventions of American Narrative." *Critical Inquiry* (Winter 1975) Vol. 2, No. 2. On Jay Gatsby and Charles Foster Kane as American characters.

————. "Rosebud, Dead or Alive: Narrative and Symbolic Structure in Citizen Kane." *PMLA* (March 1976) Vol. 91, No. 2. On Rosebud as an ironic narrative device.

Cowie, Peter. *A Ribbon of Dreams: The Cinema of Orson Welles* (New York: A. S. Barnes and Company, 1973). A thorough, intelligent critical survey of Welles' directorial career. Several useful appendixes of material by and about Welles.

Farber, Manny. *Negative Space* (New York: Praeger, 1971). "The Gimp," pp. 71–83, written in 1952, blames Welles' *Citizen Kane* for a "revolution in Hollywood" that has led to "an absurdly controlled, highly mannered, overambitious creation that feeds on everything in modern art. . . ."

Fowler, Roy Alexander, *Orson Welles, A First Biography* (London: Pendulum Publications, 1946). A surprisingly good pioneering biography by a rather worshipful seventeen-year-old.

Gottesman, Ronald, editor. *Focus on "Citizen Kane."* (Englewood Cliffs, New Jersey: Prentice-Hall, 1971). A varied anthology of critical, biographical, and historical pieces that examine Welles' most famous film from many perspectives. Available in paperback.

Higham, Charles. "And Now—The War of the Welles." *New York Times*, September 13, 1969, Section II, p. 17. Higham's rejoinder and Bogdanovich's response. See Bogdanovich, above.

————. *The Films of Orson Welles* (Berkeley: University of California Press, 1970). Some very useful production background information, but tends to be florid and unreliable as criticism of the films and their director.

Houseman, John. *Run-Through: A Memoir* (New York: Simon and Schuster, 1972). Autobiography of man who worked intimately with Welles in the late thirties on many theater, radio, and film projects. Offers a complex if biased sense of Welles.

Entire issue of *Image et Son*, No. 139 (1961), is devoted to Welles.

KAEL, PAULINE. *The Citizen Kane Book* (Boston: Little, Brown; London: Secker and Warburg, 1971). Contains essay, "Raising Kane," first published in *The New Yorker*, 1971. Also contains shooting script and cutting continuity. The reproduction of stills is appallingly bad. Available in paperback.

MacLIAMMÓIR, MICHEÁL, *Put Money in Thy Purse*, Preface by Orson Welles (London: Methuen, 1952). An illuminating diary of the filming of *Othello* by the actor who played Iago.

McBRIDE, JOSEPH, *Orson Welles* (New York: Viking, 1972). The most satisfactory critical estimate of Welles. Available in paperback.

NOBLE, PETER, *The Fabulous Orson Welles* (London: Hutchinson, 1956). Adds some details, but the excessive adulation is tiresome.

"ORSON WELLES, l'éthique et l'esthétique," by various authors (Paris: *Etudes Cinematographiques*, Nos. 24–25, 1963).

PECHTER, WILHAM S. "Trials." *Sight and Sound*, 33 (Winter 1963–64), 4–9. A devastating review of *The Trial* followed by a tough-minded survey of Welles' career as director.

WOODWARD, IAN. "Could *You* Live With a Genius?" *Woman's Journal* (March 1974), pp. 44–47. An interview with Welles' wife, Paoula Mori, Countess di Girfalco.

YOUNG, VERNON, *On Film* (Chicago: Quadrangle Books, 1972). "The Brave American," pp. 405–413, written in 1969, is an intelligent, favorable assessment of Welles' career as a filmmaker.

Index